THE WOMEN CHANGING THE WORLD

EDITED BY PEACE MITCHELL & KATY GARNER

First published in Australia in 2021
by Women Changing the World Press
an imprint of KMD Books
Waikiki, WA 6169

Edited by Tracy Regan

Typeset in Adobe Garamond Pro 12/17pt by New Dawn Publishing Pty Ltd

A catalogue record for this work is available from the National Library of Australia

National Library of Australia Catalogue-in-Publication data:
The Women Changing the World/Peace Mitchell and Katy Garner

ISBN: 978-0-6451669-8-9
(Paperback)

ISBN: 978-0-6451669-9-6
(Ebook)

To the women who went before us, to our grandmothers and their grandmothers and the women around the world who have had the courage to speak up and speak out and take action on making the world a better place.

THIS BOOK GIVES BACK

We believe that investing in women is the most powerful way to change the world and these scholarships provide opportunities for deserving women to participate in Ignite – an online incubator program for early stage startups and businesses, and Accelerate – an online accelerator program for high potential and experienced entrepreneurs ready to scale their companies and expand globally.

Aligning with the United Nations' goals for sustainable development, The Women's Business School scholarships are awarded to marginalised women including those in remote and rural areas, Indigenous women, migrant women, survivors of domestic violence, women with disability and those facing financial hardship.

100% of royalties from the sale of this book goes towards providing scholarships for marginalised women.

FOREWORD DR TERERAI TRENT

I am deeply honored to write this foreword for Peace and Kate's book: *The Women Changing the World* anthology. After I read through this beautiful collection of stories, I felt a sense of belonging, an energy that empowers me to continue in the pursuit of my great hunger to create a fertile ground for women to thrive. I hope you will feel the same.

There is no doubt that this book and the stories from these incredible women lay a footprint whose impact invokes and awakens untapped potential in both young and old regardless of their gender, race and class. While each story inspires readers to take bold action to change their life, however, collectively, this anthology lays an architectural template of entrepreneurship, inspiration and a source of faith, enabling all of us to create a better world.

In this book, Peace and Katy show us that each of us is unique and each of us has a story to tell, but more importantly, these two sisters showcase how the world shifts in positive ways when women come together.

This collection of stories is powerful; how we choose to craft our life, choreograph our journey, chart our course and create our dreams is ours to own.

At the core of their work, Peace and Katy have a global vision to change the lives of women everywhere through celebration, acknowledgement, education, empowerment and entrepreneurialism. The power to rise by lifting others is in our grasp.

Indeed, women hold the power to change the world, and this collection of stories is a powerful source of lived evidence and why it's important to invest and support women if we want to achieve sustainable development goals (SDGS) that define the world we want. Therefore, Peace and Katy are calling us to pursue dreams that are tied to the greater good.

The UN states that achieving gender equality is of crucial importance in reaching the seventeen sustainable development goals by 2030 and explains that women are the key to changing the world:

'Achieving gender equality and women's empowerment is integral to each of the seventeen goals. Only by ensuring the rights of women and girls across all of the goals will we get to justice and inclusion, economies that work for all, and sustaining our shared environment now and for future generations.'

Now more than ever, the world is at a crossroad, and it's imperative to nurture creativity and culturally appropriate solutions that are driven by purpose, lived experiences and science. And this book shows us that women meet the criteria, and should be part of the solution to our global problems. Women have the capacity to inspire, to create, to transform and to change the world. This book has been designed to create and inspire this change. The world needs a cadre of visionary women – women in touch with the divine in them, women empowered by their femininity, women cultivating their sacred *why* and by doing so nurturing the sacred purpose in all. If you are seeking your *why* and are in need of an architectural template to change your life, then this book is for you. If you are driven by purpose and you want to take action to make a difference, this book is for you. If you truly support the notion that we can no longer afford to live our lives cut off from our sacred and collective purpose, then, this book is for you.

My sisters, we women are a massive, untapped, global resource, and this book is your spark plug to reignite that which is most sacred to you – the dream in your heart and the connection to your global sisters.

Thank you to all the women who make up this anthology. You have given us architectural template for resilience, conviction, power to create a platform for women and the world to thrive. After all, we owe our confidence to these phenomenal women who walked the path before us and help us believe in ourselves.

Peace and Katy, thank you for leading the way with this collection. We shall not be fearful to take on this journey, and together we will create a better world. Ubuntu!

Dr Tererai Trent
Author of *The Awakened Woman: Remembering & Igniting Our Sacred Dreams*

Contents

INTRODUCTION
PEACE & KATY

To become a woman changing the world is one of the most rewarding, generous and incredible things you can do with your life. You could leave a legacy for future generations and the ripple effect of your work may be felt around the world, far beyond where you live or where you started.

Although it is rewarding it's not always easy.

There are challenges and obstacles along the way testing your resolve and your might.

There are moments when it would be easier to quit, when you have given so much and wonder if it will ever be worthwhile.

But there will also be moments when you know in your heart that this is the work that you were born to do.

That your impact is wide reaching and profound.

And sometimes you'll experience firsthand the powerful ripple effect of your work in the world.

We hope this book inspires you to accept the call to change the world in your own unique and beautiful way.

KATHY RHODES

The starfish, the boy and the sea

I was nine years old when I first heard the story about the boy and the starfish.

For anyone who is unfamiliar with it, the story (adapted from *The Star Thrower* by Loren Eiseley), goes like this:

One day, a man was walking along the beach when he noticed a boy hurriedly picking up and gently throwing things into the sea.

Approaching the boy, he said, 'Young man, what are you doing?'

The boy replied, 'Throwing starfish back into the ocean. The surf is up and the tide is going out. If I don't throw them back, they'll die.'

The man laughed to himself. 'Don't you realise there are miles and miles of beach and hundreds of starfish? You can't make any difference!'

After listening politely, the boy bent down, picked up another starfish, and threw it into the sea. Then, smiling at the man, he said, 'I made a difference to that one.'

That story struck me, and it's stuck with me ever since.

I didn't realise it at the time, but the reason it resonated with me so profoundly, almost thirty years ago, is that it would become my life's purpose — to help one 'star' at a time.

Before I explain why and how, let me introduce you to three incredible women in my life. Noting, as you read their stories, I have changed their names to protect the innocent.

Stephanie

It was 1pm on a Friday. I just finished presenting a strategic marketing plan to a group of executives in an office tower that stood over twenty-five levels high in Sydney's CBD. I grabbed my pre-prepared pumpkin and couscous salad from the fridge and sat at the round table in the staff kitchen, fork in one hand and scrolling through my social media feed using the other.

When I eventually glanced up, I saw Stephanie. I waved her over and encouraged her to join me, preventing her from eating lunch at her desk like she, a classic workaholic, would normally do.

In the middle of our typical office did-you-get-my-email banter, Stephanie told me, in confidence, she was expecting to receive an internal promotion in the next few days.

After congratulating her and asking a few more questions about her new job, I asked: 'So, what's your new salary going to be?'

She looked at me. Shocked and confused.

Latoya

Latoya had never worked a day in a corporate office. Latoya was a personal trainer. And a damn good one. Always full of energy. Never shouty and highly reliable. Not like me.

Training me is *hard* work. I'm happy when I'm behind my laptop screen and a genuine pain in the you-know-what when I'm asked to do lunges, push-ups and burpees. Imagine you've just asked your four-year-old to turn off their iPad and sit at the table for lunch, and you'll start to have an idea of exactly how much I enjoy my PT sessions.

Thankfully, Latoya likes me in spite of my grumbles and protests. And I like her because she really knows her stuff.

Like most personal trainers, psychologists and beauticians, Latoya and I have an agreement. If I cancel on her at the last minute, I forfeit my fees for the session.

Pretty standard and super fair, right?

Well, one Monday morning at approximately 8am, I decided it was more important to move my eye muscles (aka reply to emails) than move the rest of the muscles in my body.

So with an hour or so to go, I messaged Latoya to let her know I was bailing on her and the session. No excuses. I was straight up with a text that said, 'I just want to hide behind my laptop today.'

Because Latoya is a fitness goddess, she rearranged my session for the following day.

I fronted up, knowing how hard she was going to push me. And boy did she push me!

At the end of the session, I handed over the business card thingy Latoya punches to keep track of how many sessions I had used in my 'tummies, butts and thighs fitness' package.

She punched a single star-shaped hole in the card and gave it back to me.

I gave it straight back to her.

She stared at me. Confused.

Padma

Padma is one of the most intelligent people I have ever met. She's razor sharp, incredibly well-read and commands every room she enters. It makes sense because she's an expert in her field and has a PhD to prove it.

I met Padma more than five years after I'd swapped my corporate job for the consulting life and more than eight years after I'd boldly asked Stephanie what her new salary was going to be.

There we were on a Thursday, about two hours into a strategy session when the conversation turned to an international conference she was running in a few months. This was back before COVID-19 and conferences could happen in real life. Remember those times?

As we were going through the agenda, I noticed it wasn't her name next to the opening keynote. Instead, it was her number one competitor. And when I say her competitor, I mean the guy who was similarly qualified but no less impressive or knowledgable.

'Tell me about this decision,' I probed.

'He's the best in the business, will draw a big crowd, and will make the conference sponsors happy,' she immediately fired back.

'You're wrong,' I said.

Padma is rarely wrong.

Her eyes narrowed with confusion.

* * *

At this point, dear reader, you might be confused. What do these women have to do with the boy and the starfish? What have they taught me? And most importantly, what in turn, am I offering you as a result?

Let me explain.

Each of these women couldn't see their value.

They didn't understand their worth.

And as the clever Marian Wright Edelman once said, 'You can't be what you don't see.'

In each case, incredible things happened when they saw it.

Let's return to what happened next.

Stephanie

More than ninety seconds passed. Stephanie wasn't sure if she should tell me or not. Something we, as women, have been conditioned not to talk about much, like religion and politics.

'I guess, given it's a promotion, I asked for a slight increase,' she replied sheepishly.

'Nonsense. How much are you earning now?'

This time her jaw actually dropped. In all fairness, it was an intrusive question.

Eventually, she told me. This time, I was the one who was shocked. It was far less than I was expecting.

'Oh Stephanie! That simply won't do. It's a significant promotion, a job grade increase, a huge team, and it's going to require more from you than you've ever given before — and you, my darling friend, and workaholic, already give so much!'

I went on. 'Have you ever asked anyone else performing at that level how much they earn?'

'No …'

'Well, I have! And THIS is what you should be asking for when you negotiate your salary.'

Stephanie didn't believe me.

At this point, I'd long forgotten about my salad or my socials. I was now passionately waving my hands around like a woman possessed, determined to convince her.

After ten minutes, she promised me she'd ask for something 'close' to my suggestion. I could see her anxiety spiking at the thought.

I washed my bowl, put it in the dishwasher and returned to my desk.

Latoya

'You were supposed to punch two holes,' I told Latoya.

'One for today. And one for the session I skipped yesterday. That's our agreement.'

She resisted. I insisted.

Eventually, she punched a second star-shaped hole.

I gladly accepted the card, returned it to my wallet and walked off.

Padma

'You are wrong,' I repeated.

'If I had a mirror in my bag, I'd hold it up right now. You're the one who should be delivering the opening keynote. Not your competitor. Why would you go and spend $15K employing someone else to do the job that YOU are best placed to do?'

'Let me call my conference co-chair to see what he thinks.'

'Sure thing,' I said. 'Put him on speaker phone.'

* * *

Long before I met Stephanie, Latoya and Padma, I had the opportunity to work in a HR department. It was a short-term admin role I secured as part of my Australian Working Holiday Visa in the UK.

Working in HR was never part of my plan, but the opportunity presented itself, so I took it.

This is what I discovered.

One day, when I was folding payslips ready to stuff them into corresponding envelopes, I noticed something. Even in teams where two or more people performed the same role, delivering similar outcomes, for a similar length of time, rarely do they get paid the same. Sometimes the difference was minor. And in some cases, it was stark.

What packing payslips taught me, early in my career, was that it's up to me to know my worth. And to *know* with confidence means researching and asking taboo questions.

Just like I'd research and reach out to people for help for other aspects of my life and my career, I started asking about salaries and charge-out rates. I'd ask about profit margins and how financial decisions were made. And you know what, when I explained my 'why' to people, I rarely got push-back.

That's how I knew Stephanie was being underpaid and could confidently ask for more.

Ever since I was a girl in tencel denim overalls and hyper-colour T-shirts my favourite word has been *yes*.

'Yes, I'll help you.'

'Yes, I'll make that happen.'

'Yes, I'll do that right away.'

The problem with saying yes — aka being a people-pleaser — is that the desire to give often takes over from the right to earn.

That's what happened to Latoya, my personal trainer, that day.

'That's okay, don't worry about yesterday,' she said. 'You don't normally cancel, so let's let it slide.'

'Latoya, if I do that,' I argued, 'we'll both be out of integrity. To me, it's important you punch the second hole because I knew that when I sent you the cancellation text. To me, it's a one-off payment of $65. But for you, it's about knowing your worth and sticking to the agreement in place to protect your income. It's about $65 today and over your career much much more than that.'

That's why I insisted Latoya punch that second hole.

Recently, a high-profile female thought leader was invited to attend a corporate luncheon as a guest. She arrived, took her seat among hundreds of other women, eagerly waiting for the event to start.

Imagine her surprise-turned-anger when the MC, as part of her opening remarks, turned to her and said (to the whole room), 'We're delighted to have you in the room today. I know I'm putting you on the spot, but would you mind taking the stage and sharing your story with us today? I know everyone will benefit from hearing how you overcame that personal struggle.' The crowd applauded.

Talk about an OMG moment if ever there was one.

Unfortunately, although this is an extreme example, it's all too common for thought leaders, especially my female clients, to be asked to provide advice, often in the form of speaking, for free.

Dear reader, I see you nodding. I hear you asking, 'How do I say no?'

and wondering whether saying no in these cases will come back to haunt you because you miss out on the lucrative exposure you've been promised the opportunity provides.

What if you answered like this: 'Sure, I'll consider speaking for free. So long as the venue is waiving their room hire fees, the catering has been donated, nobody else is charging you for their time and expertise to make the event possible, and if you're not profiting from the event itself.'

When reframed that way, it's easy to see why I coach my clients never to speak for free.

And more importantly, I coach them never to ask someone else to do the same.

* * *

So whatever happened to Stephanie, Latoya, and Padma?

Stephanie was incredibly nervous but asked for the raise she deserved. And she got it. In the eighteen months that followed, she was able to save enough money for a deposit to buy her first house. Stephanie has never doubted her financial worth again. These days, she commands a six-figure salary, works part-time and loves every minute of it. She even takes lunch breaks every now and then.

Latoya punched the second hole on my card, thereby charging me for the session I missed. She's never been 'nice' to anyone since. In fact, she estimates that on any given week, she reclaims up to $200 in income she'd otherwise had let go, had she not chosen to stand by the agreements she has in place. Over the rest of her career, that will add up to $144,000.

Padma saved herself $15K that day. She went on to be the keynote speaker at the international conference and received a standing ovation. It led to additional speaking engagements and several consulting contracts. She's promised she'll always put herself forward, as option A, and audiences all over the world will be better for it.

And herein lies my world-changing idea: what if we, as women, make sure we know our worth, charge appropriately for it, and relentlessly encourage others to do the same?

Sure, I do it as a vocation. Helping thought leaders change the world, be well-paid for it, and be ridiculously fulfilled doing it, is my jam. I have lots of other stories I could tell.

We all have Padmas, Stephanies and Latoyas in our lives. So like the boy in the story, let's help one star at a time:

Insist she finds out what's possible through research and boldly asking questions

Pay her what she deserves, even if she doesn't ask for it

Boost her confidence and remind her she's worthy, oh so worthy.

If we do that, we'll be well on our way to helping women change the world.

ABOUT KATHY

I am a bookish ambivert from Sydney who lives in Terrigal, NSW, with two fur babies, Luna and Ranger Agent Doom.

A few years ago, I realised I was put on this earth to bring out the gold in people and their ideas.

I do that as the founder and chief alchemist at Thought Alchemists, a consultancy dedicated to helping Australia's established and emerging female thought leaders change the world, get paid well for it and feel *ridiculously* fulfilled doing it.

It's my can't-get-enough-of-it dream job. The type that lights me up and takes me to places I've never imagined. The type that allows me to meet people I've long admired and those I am instantly impressed with.

I devote my time to transforming ideas into dividends for incredible women like:

- Peace Mitchell and Katy Garner, founders of The Women's Business School, who invest in the power of women to change the world.

- Jeanette Cheah, founder of HEX, who is on a mission to connect next-generation leaders to global innovation cities.
- Dr Kristy Goodwin, who decodes neurobiology for peak performance in a digital age for schools and corporate audiences.

Before that, I held a number of senior marketing leadership positions in the financial services sector. I was responsible for the introduction of content-led marketing to ANZ's wealth division, making superannuation sexy and insurance interesting.

If we had met in 2017, you would have found me in the Step Change office as their strategy director, onstage at marketing strategy conferences, and delivering keynote presentations. From baby wipes to retirement savings, I've helped over thirty brands solve their trickiest business and marketing challenges.

In 2015, I was a member of the marketing and communications division at The Cancer Council NSW. I was responsible for raising awareness and funds, for their flagship campaigns. Much of my time was spent getting to know cancer patients, survivors and their families.

Dear reader (#JuliaQuinnSwoon), if we'd met in 2007 (when I had far less grey hair, fewer wrinkles and wore stiletto heels), it would have been in London. There, I worked for Alfred Dunhill, a men's luxury clothing brand, part of the Richemont Group. I was often surrounded by Chloe handbags, Cartier jewellery and IWC watches.

If we go right back to the start of my career, you'd have found me, fresh out of university, working in a boutique PR agency with the likes of AICD and CPA and running The Australasian Reporting Awards.

Fast forward to 2021. I returned to The Cancer Council — this time as an ambassador, sharing what it was like to be diagnosed with stage three cervical cancer during a global pandemic. If you want to read about my journey, look me up on *Medium* (kathy-rhodes.medium.com).

Or if it's TL;DR: cancer and COVID was hard. Crazy hard. And a wonderful reminder of what really matters.

Looking ahead, I'm signing up for a future that sees and supports women, especially those who earn their incomes through their life-changing ideas, in all the ways that befits their intellect, determination and contribution. That starts with sharing podiums and making profits equal to their male counterparts.

Want to join me?

Connect with me on LinkedIn (linkedin.com/in/kathy-rhodes) or send me an email: kathy@thoughtalchemists.com.

If I don't reply at speed, it's likely I have my head buried in a book or I'm spending time with my highly curious son, Theodore, who I think is one of the most interesting people alive today. He's decided his purpose in life is to cure ageing. So if anyone is friends with Aubrey de Gray, could you please send him my way?

www.thoughtalchemists.com

PEACE MITCHELL

'You can't change the world, you know, Peace,' she said in a patronising huff.

It was like a slap across the face.

Stopping me in my tracks. Quick, hot, unexpected. From out of nowhere.

Everything went still as I took in what had just happened. Had she really said that?

Time seemed to slow down. I stared at her in disbelief as she stood there with her blonde hair, looking down at me with her arms crossed. She'd been the prettiest girl in high school at a time when I'd felt awkward and ugly. We'd never spoken to each other in those days, but now we were adults and had worked together for years, I thought we were friends. I thought we understood each other. I thought we shared the same values. Nothing made sense here.

Then I remembered we weren't alone, and the rest of the women were staring at us, watching the drama unfold, waiting to see who would make the next move. Wanting to know who would win and who would cave first. It was a group project after all and they were as much invested in having their say as we were. But in that moment, it was just her and me.

I can't change the world? Really?

This was one of my deepest core beliefs. If you can do something good for someone else, you should. You always should.

VISION: Anyone who ever achieved anything incredible started out with a strong vision for where they were going and why they were going there. Get clear on your values and what you will and won't stand for, but more importantly get clear on your WHY, your reason for this quest. When you have clarity on your purpose you are better able to see your big picture and less distracted by bright shiny objects or opportunities that are not in alignment with your vision and your values.

Ever since I was a little girl, I've wanted to change the world. No, not just wanted to, I somehow believed it was what I was born to do.

That one sentence was the beginning of everything. I realised in that moment I actually believed I could change the world, and she was wrong. It was a shock to know not everyone thought the same way, and that we weren't all on the same page with wanting to help others.

After all, changing the world was why I'd become a teacher, believing I could make a difference in childrens' lives and prepare them for a brighter future through education. But it didn't take long for me to see that all the progress and hard work I put in could be quickly undone the following year, if a child had a different teacher who was just there for the pay cheque and not committed to encouraging them.

My disenchantment with seeing how quickly my work could be undone and this lack of lasting impact led me to leave teaching.

For a long time, I didn't know how to change the world, and I was overwhelmed at the size of the task, but then I realised that through investing in women and focusing on creating a movement for women in purpose-led businesses, I could create a powerful ripple effect that would continue to make a bigger impact at a global level.

***

ACTION: Don't waste time trying to ensure everything is perfect before you start, it's far better to begin and then make adjustments along the way.

***

I believed if I wanted to make a lasting difference with children, the key was working with mothers because I realised that one year with a child made little difference compared to their home environment. If real and permanent change were to happen in a child's life, it would be through supporting mothers to provide a stable environment and positive influence.

Not many people remember the day they found their calling, but I do. As a teacher I've always been passionate about education, but it wasn't until my sister, Katy, and I had been through a tragic natural disaster in 2006 I recognised just how important women were in holding the world together. In the aftermath of Cyclone Larry, it was the mothers who were the glue holding the community together: supporting their husbands emotionally, caring for the children, checking in on elderly neighbours, helping each other to keep the wheels turning.

When women are supported to be their best, they can do amazing things. And it's this philosophy that's been the driving force behind everything Katy and I do.

***

TEAMWORK: Ask for help. No-one who ever achieved anything remarkable ever did it on their own. Stop pretending you will be the exception and start asking and accepting. Invite people to collaborate, tell people about your ideas, share your challenges, open up and be honest about the areas where you're struggling and ask others how you can help them. Asking for help gives others permission to ask you for help too. We're all stronger together than we are alone, so start reaching out and finding the people who can assist you to grow and reach your goals. We stand on the shoulders of giants; there is no such thing as self-made success. Every person who has become successful has done so by surrounding themselves with, and listening to, wise people who have also had the courage to be successful and follow their path.

***

Can you imagine a world where everyone worked towards making the world a better place?

Where every business owner intentionally wrote their strategy for giving back and making a difference in their business plan.

A world where individuals encouraged and supported each other to make small changes in their daily lives, collectively creating a bigger impact.

A world where governments spend more on health and education than on military expenses.

Imagine a world where everyone played their part, shared their gifts and did what they could, where they were, with what they had, to make the world a better place.

The impact on the world would be profound.

The celebrated anthropologist, Margaret Mead, said, 'Never doubt that a small group of thoughtful, committed citizens can change the world: indeed, it's the only thing that ever has.'

If we all played our part, I believe we could:

- Reverse the effects of climate change on the environment.
- Cure the world's diseases.
- End poverty and hunger.
- Provide quality education for children everywhere.
- Create a harmonious way of life for people globally through conscious leadership at a government level.

Not to mention the many, many more benefits there would be if we worked collaboratively and with a united intention to each make a positive impact and give back generously in our own way.

And take note that giving back does not always have to be financial. It could start with small and simple gestures, minor changes to the way you live or the things you do, reaching out to help those around you with no expectation of repayment of the favour.

There is enough for everyone but for too long, our world has lived in a state of fear and scarcity. People fear there is not enough money, wealth and resources to go around; that only the most wealthy and powerful should have access to them and everyone beneath them should miss out, but it doesn't have to be this way.

We can begin today to give back, lift others up and work together to create change.

Our dream is to change the world collectively through the power of bringing women together to support each other, to celebrate each other and to lift each other higher.

When we invest in women, celebrate women and enable women to see the magnificence they already have within them, powerful things happen and women begin to step into their power and share their gifts with the world.

***

COURAGE: Don't let your fear, self-doubt and insecurity hold you back from shining your light! Fear is a constant companion for anyone doing something new. Fear of failure, fear of embarrassment, fear of criticism, fear of overwhelm. It appears in many forms and I've seen it hold women back and stop them from reaching their goals again and again. You have to step up, believe in what you're doing and just start. It doesn't have to be perfect, you just have to start.

***

We need to see and hear more women doing all kinds of things. We need to hear women's stories. We need to be inspired by other women. We need to see there are women just like us doing big things in the world, alongside having children and making all of that work.

We need a range of diverse role models from different ethnicities and different countries and geographic locations. We need to see women in the world doing things across all industries, everywhere.

We also need to see more women represented in the media. We need more films with stories about women, where women aren't just one-dimensional, stereotypical characters, but have depth, complexity and richness. In so many children's films, the mother dies or is absent, is one-dimensional, or doesn't work outside the home. Where's the role model of what a mother should look like, or what's possible for women after they have children? And where are the female friends? Disney characters are more likely to be friends with animals than other girls. We must make new role models across the spectrum and challenge the outdated narratives created in the past.

In terms of elevating women as role models, we should be given more opportunities to be seen in the media; women celebrating women, encouraging them to put themselves forward for opportunities to show up and be seen. Nominating themselves for awards and accolades; putting themselves forward to be on boards; speaking out on the issues that are important to them; sharing their ideas and having the courage to do new things.

Whenever a woman steps up and tells her story, it gives someone else permission to tell theirs too. It's so important for women to get over the idea of having to be humble and quiet, and to understand that it's not only okay to talk about your accomplishments and your achievements, but it's necessary. As women we should be able to talk about who we are, what we're doing and why we're doing it. We shouldn't have to hide or make ourselves small.

***

GRIT: Grit is the ability to keep going despite setback after setback. To hit rock bottom and feel you could lose everything this time and still find the courage to pick yourself up again and keep going. As an entrepreneur this is a requirement, because no matter who you are or what you do, there will always be challenges.

***

We need to create more opportunities for women to show up and speak up. We must make this happen so the new generation coming through can see women who look like them; women being recognised, breaking new ground, or making their mark on the world. They must be given more opportunities to talk about their work, because if they're working hard behind the scenes or doing incredible things but not talking about it, often no-one knows about it.

We need women who are changing the world to be more visible, telling their story so other women and girls can see what's possible and take action to play their part too.

If you have a platform, then use that platform to celebrate women, lift others up, give other women a voice, and enable them to share their stories, ideas and messages with the world.

When you invest in women the ripple effect is powerful. We have seen it, and we know firsthand the difference it makes.

In the last twelve years, Katy and I have provided over a million dollars in scholarships for women's education through The Women's Business School. This is our way of giving back; of investing in women, of making the world a better place. It's important, though, to highlight the fact that we didn't have $1 million when we made the decision to allocate scholarships to deserving women. We started small by doing what we could, even when we weren't making much money. By mentoring women and sharing our advice where we could, we were able to invest in women and talk about the importance of investing in women, even when we weren't financially able to be investors in the traditional sense of the word. And by doing this, we made 'giving back' a part of our strategy from the beginning.

***

ENDURANCE: You need to have the ability to keep going because this is a marathon not a sprint. Changing the world is one of the most rewarding things you will ever do, but there will be challenges, obstacles and problems to solve and overcome. You have to be prepared to keep going, even when it's hard, even when it's not glamorous, even when everyone is telling you to quit. One of my favourite phrases has always been, 'It's not a race.' Be patient with yourself and with your journey. Stop comparing yourself to others. Your journey and their journey are two completely different things. Good things take time. Just because it hasn't happened quickly for you doesn't mean it won't happen. Practise patience and allow the magic to unfold instead of trying to force it.

***

Our scholarships have resulted in phenomenal outcomes that we could not have predicted. One scholarship recipient has doubled her business; a business that makes a difference by employing marginalised and disadvantaged women who have escaped domestic violence and need both financial and emotional support to get back on their feet. Through education, guidance and support we were able to help this scholarship recipient, who has now gone on to employ almost fifty women. That's fifty families who are now able to pay their rent, afford quality education, live free from violence and get a fresh start for themselves and their children. And each year, as this recipient's business grows, that number continues to increase, helping more and more women and their children to live better lives and create a brighter future. The ripple effect continues on and on in powerful and positive ways that we will often never know about.

This is just one example of the impact our work has made in the world.

Research shows that when women make money, they spend that money in their local community. There are also health benefits for their entire family, the educational outcomes for their children are improved, and their future trajectory and ability to save for retirement and old age is enhanced. Their quality of life and their families' quality of life is better, and on an even larger scale, cultural and generational change can be achieved.

We all need to find ways to invest in women, raise women up and inspire them to take action and be accountable for their lives.

For those who are ready to change the world and begin taking action, these are some of the qualities required:

- Vision
- Action
- Teamwork
- Courage
- Grit
- Endurance

As you can see, we have drawn on these across our own journey. Start with your vision. Take action. Surround yourself with people who share your values to help you. Rely on your grit and endurance to take you from one chapter to the next and don't be afraid to face your fears.

Dr Tererai Trent said, 'We have the power within. It's not your past that's going to define who you are, but it's what you believe about yourself.'

Changing the world isn't always easy but it's always worth it. Each of us has the power to use our talents for the greater good, to change attitudes and inspire others. Don't wait for the perfect time, because it starts with you. Our world depends on it, and we have the power to make a difference today!

ABOUT PEACE

Peace Mitchell is an investor, author, an international keynote speaker, CEO and co-founder of The Women's Business School, AusMumpreneur and Women Changing The World Press and the Australian ambassador of Women in Tech.

Peace is passionate about supporting women to reach their full potential and create the life they want to live. She has helped thousands of women achieve their dream of running a successful and profitable business and believes that investing in women is the best way to change the world.

Peace Mitchell and her sister Katy Garner co-founded AusMumpreneur in 2009 creating Australia's number one community for mothers in business and co-founded The Women's Business School in 2016 to provide entrepreneurial education for women globally.

Today, her commitment is stronger than ever to invest in the power of women to change the world.

'Through providing education, inspiration, guidance, connection and support for women, we are committed to providing access to education for women from all walks of life, all over the world. Our programs have been designed to provide connection with experienced women in business from a range of industries and backgrounds.'

We are proud to be creating better opportunities for entrepreneurial education for women globally through:

ADVOCACY

Passionate about supporting women, Peace has worked in advocacy with all levels of government to create change. Peace has been instrumental in being a voice for women by changing local government legislation to create more inclusive town planning at a local level, calling for a national conversation on women entrepreneurs at a federal level and partnering with the Queensland State Government to provide $1 million in grants for small business owners at state level.

EDUCATION

Investing in women is the most powerful way to change the world and it's this philosophy which has driven Peace's vision to create a global business school for women. In just three years The Women's Business School has seen four hundred women graduate, created partnerships with global brands including World Pulse, Emerging Women and Tererai Trent International and school alumni have won awards, received investor funding, been invited to speak internationally and taken their brands to global markets.

ACTIVISM

In working with thousands of Australian women entrepreneurs over the past twelve years Peace has discovered a surprising trend. Women aren't starting businesses to make money – they're starting businesses to create change. Today, women-led businesses are far more likely to be focused on helping people, creating a more sustainable environment and generally making the world a better place in their own unique, beautiful and creative way. What if we could inspire people everywhere to change the world in a small way? This was the inspiration for *Women Will Change the World TV* – a weekly Facebook Live show focused on inspiring purpose, vision and everyday activism featuring women changing the world through entrepreneurialism, conscious living, advocacy and innovation.

AMPLIFYING

We believe that providing a platform for women's voices is so important, women have the power to change the world but we must work together to help bring these voices to the world and let their message be heard. We do this through our books, podcasts, website features and in person events.

INVESTING

We believe investing in women in the most powerful way to change the world and our future vision includes creating opportunities for women to invest financially in each others' businesses through becoming shareholders.

Women hold the key to unlock the solutions to all of the problems the world is facing and it's up to all of us to come together to lift women up!

www.thewomensbusinessschool.com
www.wcwpress.com
www.ausmumpreneur.com

ANNA TIM

Something greater than oneself

My vision is simple: to create an integrative health care system so humanity has hope and everyone can have a choice on how they heal their body.

*At forty-seven I'm glowing with an inner luminosity that shines from the inside out; I'm a testament to my family, friends and business. I'm a mother, wellness specialist and educator, pursuing an important health mission greater than myself. With over twenty-six years in the wellness space, my experience has shown that given the right environment, support and nutrition, the body can heal itself.

My story

I grew up in central Queensland on a fruit farm where we had our own cattle, chickens and other animals. As part of a large family, the youngest of seven children, we all contributed to running the farm. At different times, depending on the season, we would pick and pack the fruit, milk the cows or just be an extra set of hands for any odd jobs my grandparents, parents or the neighbouring farmers needed. Some of my fondest memories are tending to the baby calves who needed medicine every four hours, waking at 2am to help Dad is probably where my compassion for healing stemmed from.

Every Sunday, we would have a *banya* (Russian bath house), where Grandma would scrub us from head to toe with the loofahs grown on the farm, and then fan us with the *venik* (bundles of twigs and leafy branches bound together from oak trees). I always felt amazing afterwards and for some reason it made food taste so much better. I remember feeling very calm and having the best night's sleep.

Rural life in Queensland offered the perfect environment to raise seven children; on a farm in the sunshine with everything we needed sourced locally or from our own backyard. This provided us with most of the daily nutrients and vitamins we needed. Like most family units, we had our fair share of issues and challenges. Looking back at my childhood and comparing with my school friends, I always felt different as we were a large Russian family in a stereotypical small Aussie town. We only spoke Russian at home and upheld most of our Russian family traditions. We were a working-class family; I never wore a school uniform and we didn't have money for tuckshop. Starting school was daunting, especially when you don't speak a lot of English, and the kids always said my lunch smelled. That was the garlic Mum used in every meal we ate, and we always took leftovers to school. Mum used to say; 'You must have garlic every day to boost your immune system.'

Although she is no longer with us, my mother has always been an amazing strength in my life. She worked hard to raise us and always did the best she could, holding down three jobs while we were young to feed and support our family. I loved my father dearly, but he was absent in many ways due to his alcoholism, which was challenging for both my mother and his parents, whose farm we lived on.

At age fifteen, I set out on my journey to the big smoke; young, bright and ready to live my life. I certainly had some experiences that this young girl from the country could not undo or unsee! Within two days of moving to Sydney, I was held at knife point for all my personal belongings. I found myself living with more alcoholics. I got my first real job working for a tow truck company, responsible for sending the trucks out to jobs as people called in requesting assistance. Unbeknown to me, the owners of the company were running a business on the side with some less-than-inconspicuous deals happening in the lounge room at the depot. As I started to get the hang of city life, I found the church. I thought it would be an opportunity for me to be part of a community, but the bishop behaved in a highly inappropriate way with me, and a lot of females, as it turned out. Let's just say it was a very harrowing time for a young country girl. These experiences were the beginning of my chronic illness. I was soon experiencing panic attacks and then diagnosed with PTSD and depression. You can only imagine the shape I was in!

By thirty I was back in the country in Far North Queensland; a fit, relatively healthy person, running twice most weekdays at what's called 'The Red Arrow' (a forested track) which has many steps in steep sections. I loved the place, my new home and being back in touch with nature. Unfortunately, the tropics bear some risks, and with extreme humidity comes disease-ridden blood-sucking vampires, commonly known as mosquitoes. After about a week of fevers and overwhelming fatigue, I was diagnosed with a viral infection which later I discovered was dengue fever. Through all the tests conducted, I was also told I had fallen pregnant with my first child. Dengue affects blood vessels; they become damaged and leaky and the number of clot-forming cells (platelets) in your bloodstream drops. There was nothing I could do except keep fluids up and rest. Then the headaches started and the recurring tonsillitis, for which the doctor handed out constant antibiotics, upsetting my gut biome. This set in motion a whole raft of changes to my body I could never have predicted.

I started to get sugar cravings, heavy-clotting periods, and a constant ache in my joints and bones, as well as weight gain. I was also living in a mouldy home at the time, so my immune system was under extreme stress.

I have since learnt that antibiotics wipe out your microbiome. Those years were a challenge every single day, with constant migraines ranging in severity, nausea, and allergies to common foods. The list goes on. I was no longer the iron guts I always thought I was. I was getting worse, not better, and I felt that modern medicine had failed me. Doctors seemed more insistent on prescribing me another pill or dismissing my symptoms, than in finding a solution to my ailments. Without realising at the time, I was also living in a domestic violence relationship and those days were some of my darkest, with little light at the end of the tunnel.

Nothing is ever a rejection – it's only a redirection. I began to research and educate myself and found all sorts of weird and wonderful therapies. I remember drinking and pouring dimethyl sulfoxide (DMSO) and magnesium all over my body; the smell was terrible but at least I know now what a skunk feels like! I was desperate. I just wanted to be well again after spending thousands of dollars on different treatments, doctors and supplements. I even went to a crystal healer who hit me with feathers, banged on a drum and told me the migraines were from my dead mother who was still attached to me. I felt I had fallen through the cracks! My general practitioner, a lovely man, tried to help me but nothing he tried was working. After years, we had a tough conversation. 'I think you have depression,' he said. 'I want you to go on antidepressants for ten weeks minimum.' I agreed, as it was the worst time of the whole journey – I felt no happiness or sadness, I was just existing. When I weaned myself off the medication, it was harrowing and I swore I would never judge a drug addict. I felt I was living what I could only imagine as being in their nightmare. I thought I would need to take pain meds or antidepressants for the rest of my life and just get on with it. I was completely miserable due to the inflammation and pain I was living with day to day. At the time it felt I was let down by the very people who took the Hippocratic oath of 'first do no harm'. So, in a way, from their actions, I was redirected.

The turning point for me was when I discovered colonics (colon hydrotherapy) and infrared sauna. It was absolutely life-changing! Although they didn't cure me, the effect was profound, even from the first session. What I now know is that I was detoxing my two largest elimination organs; the colon and the skin. For the first time in a long time, I had hope.

Moving a few years down the track, I remain a solo mum to two children Isabella and Daniel. Having raised and educated them, continuing to leave my legacy while still on my own healing and learning path, I have been fortunate to have the support of my extended family when times have been tough.

Health hits close to home when you have experienced years of chronic illness. My two children have also experienced life-threatening health issues and my sister battled cancer for many years. Working in the wellness space started as a passion, but I recognise that sometimes it's life experiences close to home, impacting those we love the most, that are all we need to provide the motivation to step up; to learn, know and do more.

With my experience, not only in my business but also as an educator, I feel there is a real need to share this information and knowledge. It's important to approach things from a heart centre and with compassion. This helps me relate to my clients. In many cases, I have experienced their symptoms or cared for someone close to me who has had similar symptoms. I now have a wonderful and powerful network of professionals who I work closely with. Some of our clients are very sick. One client, a fifty-seven-year-old woman named Derrianne, has a long list of chronic illness, and has been told by her doctor that she needs to remove her whole bowel. She states, 'I want to shout it from the rooftops! When I met Anna, she cared and educated me. She not only changed my life, but she also saved my life.' Many of our clients have daunting diagnoses, and we support them by working alongside their general practitioner or specialists.

I truly believe I am a vessel for something greater than myself. I am on a personal journey to create a new, global, integrative health care system. We are in progressive and exciting times where people are experiencing wellness on new levels every day. My Healing Humanity Foundation has been set up to give every human access to lifesaving modalities; high vibrational medicine that is created synergistically with the highest standards in purity and bioavailability, to assist the body's pathways to a place where anyone can be supported through a healing crisis. The foundation will bring professional people together for a greater good, offering education and choices on how people can heal their bodies. We will offer progressive personalised advice on nutrition and give a holistic health plan to give you options, including detoxing at a cellular level with colon hydrotherapy, hyperthermia, photodynamic and stem-cell therapy, oxygen chamber, ozone therapy and cryotherapy, just to name a few. We will also have state of the art integrative and functional medicine testing, which could include thermography and low radiation 3D digital imaging.

True healing is multifaceted and requires a thorough program to address many layers of disease, firstly by finding the root cause and treating holistically to bring everything back into homeostasis.

You can choose how you want to heal your body

We all want to create a body we enjoy living in. For some it may just be leveling up as not everyone is chronically ill. After educating myself, and knowing and understanding the right environment for proper healing, I have set about healing myself and my family via the many modalities I offer in the clinic and through the support of my integrative health care network. My day consists of running the business Wellness@Wilston, which is driven by my desire to help everyone achieve better health outcomes and wellbeing. We empower others to live a long, full and healthy life. Wellness@Wilston offers a range of services to enhance wellbeing, including colon hydrotherapy, lymphatic compression, far infrared sauna and cryotherapy, as well as an extensive range of specifically sourced and created products to level up our health. My wellness clinic is where my next venture came about. My clients kept telling me, 'I'm feeling so great now, Anna, what's next?' It was if they were constantly wanting to level up. This is how Leveld up was born. It's a high vibrational supplement range which assists the body's healing pathways.

These treatment modalities and nutritional supplements are real options for people who are unwell, and they work. The team and I see great results every day.

In the right environment the body can heal itself and you are born with that innate belief!

Creating a positive environment for the body to heal is paramount by honouring yourself for your sovereignty, honouring your path and feeding your body what it needs. I can and really enjoy helping those who are on their personal healing journey. I see it as an honour to be there for my clients facing their unique challenges, supporting them to find their way back to health and wellbeing again. As a healer and someone who sees challenges as opportunities, I am a progressive thinker and utilise the latest research and integrative practices to assist others on their path.

Through my struggles, I always felt the universe had my back when I needed to step up. I knew I was supported. When I wanted to be well so badly and was educating myself in everything food and detoxing the body, I also knew I needed to connect; connect with myself, connect to all that is. When you have that belief in yourself, you create a positive inner space for your healing to take place.

I remember not wanting to share my vision with some of my family and friends. I knew I would get the same feedback: 'You'll never do that! You never finish anything! You won't have a wellness clinic, you're not a naturopath.'

Our consciousness is our best currency, so don't let anybody into it who is threatening. If you're not comfortable – stand up! For too many years I gave up my power to men in my relationships because who am I to make a change in the world? I realise that alone I can't change the world, but by educating others I can create a ripple effect.

At an event in 2020 I found my power to rise and honour my inner vision of wanting to create a space where humanity can have a choice on how to heal their body. Everything on my journey has brought me to this! I have settled into having faith, listening to my intuition and knowing I am a vessel for something greater than myself. It has truly been the most enlightening time of my life. I am so grateful to everyone who has been on my path. As the saying goes, 'When the student is ready, the teacher will appear.'

Keep your vessel clean, nourish it with good food, move your body like you love it, keep your vibration high by doing all the things that light you up and make you happy. Put on music, dance, lay naked outside and charge yourself with the sunshine. Ground your bare feet in the earth, turn the TV off, put down your mobile phone and connect with those you love.

Love the life you are creating; nothing is ever a rejection – it's always a redirection!

So, I want you to know that we all have trauma, I've had my fair share. What you do with it is what defines you.

And even if no-one believes in you, think back to this chapter and remember that I do – I believe in you! Go out and do it. Do what your heart desires and create the world you want from the inside. Not everyone needs to know what you are doing; keep it to yourself in some cases. Guard yourself if you need to but just do you, do what you need to do. It doesn't matter what other people think, however, when just one person believes in you, a ripple happens. You can feel it, then see it in yourself and everything you have planned just happens!

After telling you a little about my story you may relate. We are busy living our lives and then life happens! Taking a level of responsibility for our health is what we need to do for having bliss in life. We each make our own decisions, everything is our choice; what we are eating, what we are doing and what we are thinking.

If creating a new health care system resonates with you and sounds like something you would like to be involved in, or even if you know someone who would like to be involved, please get in touch. I am currently seeking business partners who want to build a better health care system. If you are an investor, developer, doctor, nurse, naturopath, or someone who just wants to help humanity – let's start the conversation.

ABOUT ANNA

Anna Tim is the founder of Wellness@Wilston.

With her experience and what she has witnessed within the health care system, Anna has developed an inherent belief that in the right environment with proper nutrition, the body can heal itself. Driven by her desire to help clients achieve better health and wellbeing, Anna set out to empower others to live a long, full and healthy life and so Wellness@ Wilston was born.

Health hits close to home for Anna. She has two children, both experiencing life-threatening health issues, and a sister who went through a cancer battle for many years. Her own chronic illness and health journey has led her to natural health and alternative modalities, which she offers at her clinic.

Anna enjoys helping clients who are facing unique challenges. It is an honour to be there when they are going through health challenges, and assisting them to find their way back to health. As a trainer, Anna feels there is a real need to share her knowledge and assist others on their healing journey. What sets her apart is her commitment to training and a passion for helping her clients achieve their health goals.

Anna's vision is simple: to create an integrative health care system so humanity has hope and everyone can have a choice on how they heal their body. Anna truly believes she is a vessel for something greater than herself.

anna@healinghumanityfundation.com
www.healinghumanityfoundation.com

CARRIE RHEINBERGER

Humble beginnings

I went from shooting photographs in the backyard to being published in *Vogue.*

I've always had an interest in photography. As a young girl, I watched my mother photograph family and friends as a hobby and I couldn't wait to get my hands on a camera of my own. The day came soon enough when I was presented with a special gift from Mum and Dad – my very own 35mm camera and two rolls of film. So what does an aspiring young photographer snap pictures of? Well let's just say my mother wasn't very impressed when she paid to have seventy-two 6x4s of my cat printed!

Fast forward to high school. When I completed year twelve I was accepted into a Bachelor of Photography and a Bachelor of Musical Theatre. It wasn't an easy decision as I was faced with choosing between my two biggest passions, but in the end I packed up and moved to Townsville to undertake my three-year Bachelor of Photography. I went through those years with a basic plan of graduating and becoming a wedding photographer. And that's exactly how the story unfolded, but what happened after graduation was completely unexpected. I wasn't happy. I felt unfulfilled by my work. I loved photographing the bride by herself but I didn't like working with large groups, and I found the whole wedding attitude a bit much for me. And yet I spent the better part of two decades going through the motions, hoping to wake up one day and somehow love what I was doing. TWO DECADES. And then I quit. I decided it was time to focus on having a family.

Giving up my job seemed like a great idea because it didn't bring me joy, just a humble income. However, there was one more hurdle to overcome before my new dream of becoming a mother could come true for me.

Beer bongs to babies

What's holding you back from living your best life?

If you met me five-plus years ago, chances are I was drunk. Back when I was a wedding photographer, I may have failed to mention my other hobby – drinking large amounts of alcohol.

I was a very shy child and young adult. When I discovered alcohol I was loud and felt confident for the first time. People seemed to like me and I thought it was the alcohol and the false confidence it delivered. I saw myself as an 'average' person at best. Nothing special.

I was a daily drinker since I started university. I drank in the afternoons until I fell asleep or passed out. On the weekends, I binged. I guess for all purposes and appearances, I was a functioning drunk, except at the expense of disappointing and distancing my family and friends. While I worked hard to present a professional exterior, I frequently didn't show up in the lives of people I cared about by my lack of either physical or emotional presence. I had no drive to reach my personal or professional goals.

I had grand ideas, especially when it came to photography, that mostly seemed to come to me when I was under the influence. Hence, I tied being intoxicated to being creative. However, there was one rather large problem with this. Whilst I was abusing alcohol and coming up with all these amazing creative ideas, I was also way too drunk to put any of them into action!

When I decided to remove alcohol from my life, I was terrified. My first step was to take the time to learn as much as I could about addiction in general. I'm a person who loves to read and take notes, so this was actually fun for me. The book that helped the most is Jason Vale's *Kick the Drink … Easily!* I loved the book so much that I not only bought a copy for several friends and family members, but also donated a copy to my local library and counselling centre.

I also did something a little weird; feel free to laugh because I sure do looking back at myself. I found my childhood Baby Born doll and started caring for it as if it was my real baby. I lived on a property by myself with my husband working away, so for the majority of time, it was just me and my doll. I would walk the doll around singing to her, rocking her to 'sleep' and changing her clothes and nappy. When I found myself pretending to breastfeed her one day I decided it had gone a bit far and popped her back in the cupboard – *lol!* But silly as it may sound, it's in my nature to care for others, and for me it was an integral part of reaching my goal of sobriety.

Bit by bit my mind changed about alcohol and as my quit-day approached, I realised I was no longer terrified. I was excited. Though I still thought I would never have another creative idea. I didn't know it at the time but removing alcohol from my life was an integral part of finding myself, reaching my true potential and *peaking* my creativity. On top of that, I had a notepad FULL of creative ideas that were now finally coming to life before my very eyes because I finally had the drive to see them through. That gave me the greatest feeling of achievement I had ever experienced. I started kicking goals, I started achieving and I started succeeding. I stepped into my authentic power and experienced a freedom and joy that I'm so grateful for.

Sober and ready to take on the world, I fell pregnant with my first child. Oh boy, I had *nooooo* IDEA what I was in for! As an only child and a bit of a loner, I really hadn't been around many pregnant women. Clearly no-one was willing to tell me the truth about it, anyway! What a massive shitstorm pregnancy is! One day I'm doing my forty-five-minute morning jog, next thing I know I'm practically bedridden with morning sickness for nine months! Now, morning sickness, in my opinion, is a woefully inaccurate term. Let's get real. It would be much better to call a spade a spade and go with all-day-throw-up-till-you-piss-your-pants-a-little-bit sickness. I felt I couldn't do anything except just be pregnant. All other aspects of my life were put on hold and I found myself wondering how women with other children possibly coped!

I searched for help online to see what other mothers in my situation were doing. Looking at the pregnancy websites and trying to decipher the lingo can also be a bit daunting. I mean who's going to figure out that BFP is big fat positive? In my opinion the whole thing is RFS. Really fucking stupid. I went old-school and grabbed the ever-informative book *What to Expect When You're Expecting* by Heidi Murkoff. That book felt like my best friend, and answered just about every question I had.

By the time I entered the labour ward, I could easily have been confused for the last woolly mammoth in existence. Fat, hairy and just completely over it, but finally, FINALLY I was going to meet my baby! I wanted a natural birth with no drugs and although I didn't really know what to expect, the birth went smoothly and according to plan. Before long I was holding my little girl. Just as suddenly, I was born into a whole new world where cutting your toenails is a luxury.

I remember visiting relatives in hospital to see their new babies and had no idea the poor woman was actually wearing a maxi pad, inside an adult diaper, sitting on a giant waterproof pad to protect the mattress from the ocean of blood pouring out of her, along with an icepack that looks exactly like an icy pole glued to her vagina.

So I finally had my little baby and it was time to settle into everyday life, which brings me to something I can only refer to as 'his thing vs.

my thing'. My husband would get up and do 'his thing' i.e. have a cup of coffee and toast on the verandah while I breastfed the baby. Then I would be invited to do 'my thing' while he watched the baby. 'My thing' had changed somewhat after having the baby and now included scoffing down breakfast, putting on the first of many loads of washing, putting away washing, washing up and changing the kitty litter. After 'my thing' the baby was handed back to me before hubby rushed off to work. It was then I would realise I was still in my pyjamas, hadn't brushed my teeth and had toast crumbs in the corner of my mouth … from the day before!

Knowing I would be a stay-at-home mum, I thought I knew pretty well what I was in for. But I never expected to feel, well … bored. Motherhood had always been my dream, surely this would be my calling! But the days were lonely on my isolated property, and the nights were long and sleepless while my husband worked away. I felt myself slipping into depression. I felt I was losing myself. How dare motherhood not be the beautiful, fulfilling, exciting journey of pure loveliness I had anticipated for so long! Of course, there were nice parts to it too, but I felt my life had become all about a tiny human constantly clamped to my breast and there was nothing left for me.

When bub was ten months old, we got up at 5am when she woke. I grabbed my camera and we went and shot a location I'd had my eye on for ages but thought I'd never have time for. I came home, sat her in her highchair with a rusk and edited for twenty-five minutes while she chewed happily. As soon as she started crying, I stopped. Even from such a small amount of time focused on myself, I found I had new energy. I felt on top of the world, like I'd really accomplished something and done something I really enjoyed. I thought to myself, *Maybe you don't have to give up everything and all of yourself for your baby.* So I endeavoured to find half an hour a day to do something just for me. I focused on my photography. I picked up my camera and turned it towards myself. I edited in a way I'd never tried before. From there I found my niche, my style and my calling.

Drag up your life

Finding your inner drag queen.

People often enquire as to where I find my inspiration and style. One of my earliest memories is watching *The Rocky Horror Picture Show*. I remember seeing the lead character, Frankenfurter, and thinking to myself *Who is this magnificent man-woman?!?* The confidence, the style, the music; I was home and a little bit in love.

As an adult I take a lot of inspiration from drag queens in styling my shoots and coaching my subjects in confidence and attitude. The definition of 'drag' is generally understood to be a person wearing clothing normally worn by the opposite gender. While that definition addresses an important logistical aspect of drag, it fails to address the true essence that is felt and shown during a performance. This is due, in part, to the fact that drag is *so many* things. Drag is an umbrella that covers drag queens, drag kings, and some other performers. Drag, at its core, is an exaggerated and/or unconventional performance of gender roles and presentation. It can be vibrant, edgy, cutting-edge, delicate or even dangerous.

If you're looking for a place to start, I suggest immediately sitting down to binge watch as many seasons of *RuPaul's Drag Race* as possible! These queens know how to work their bodies and give every kind of attitude. I draw the most inspiration from one queen in particular, Adore Delano.

Adore, in my opinion, is an insanely talented singer/songwriter whose music is a constant source of inspiration to me. Versatile, down-to-earth and beautiful, this queen makes every day of my life feel just a little bit more special. It is my dream to photograph Adore and when that dream comes true, suffice to say, I will be one happy little Vegemite! Notice that I say 'when' not 'if'.

Drag queens are now a part of mainstream culture and their influence on the entertainment industry is unquestionable. They mesmerise millions with their skills and dramatic transformations and taking tips from these amazing performers could be the key to unlocking your best self and finding the self-esteem and confidence you deserve to have!

Self-esteem and confidence

Building self-esteem and confidence takes time and practise. As mothers we are not only tasked with our own self-esteem and confidence, but also nurturing that of our offspring.

Kids with high self-esteem might see benefits like stronger values, a sense of purpose, increased resilience and better stress management. By engaging in practices that build self-esteem, over time we can effectively boost our confidence, but for many it's a lifelong journey.

'We cannot underestimate the power of photographs to keep us feeling linked to others and belonging. They cement us into our networks. For children, in particular, looking at photographs is part of the socialising process, learning who you are and where you fit into the family. By displaying photographs of our children at different stages of their lives, we are making a very public statement that we are proud of them,' says Professor Geoff Beattie, Head of School and Dean of Psychological Sciences at the University of Manchester. (www.dailymail.co.uk/health/article-1117243/Family-photographs-help-develop-childs-positive-self-image.html)

Creating a photograph with positive memories will remind us of good times, and in turn, provides motivation to keep moving through any trials and hardships.

As a portrait photographer I feel honoured to be able to create pieces that enable positive memories and feelings for years to come.

Often, regular 'non-model' people don't have the confidence to feel they can take a good photograph, which can lead to visible tension and awkwardness in a photo. They've seen so many unflattering photos of themselves they assume all photos are going to be that way. But, with the right instruction and posing tips from your photographer, this fear can be conquered. The right photographer can help anyone of any age to feel radiant and look natural.

As a photographer, I aim to help people through their session by leading by example. I am a strong believer in practising what you preach and you will often find me down on the floor showing poses and repeating my mantra of, 'Shoulders down, chin down, nice long neck!'

So what can you do to immediately improve your confidence in front of the camera? Just imagine it. That's right, the old 'fake it till you make it'! When we imagine things, the brain attempts to simulate the responses that would occur if these situations actually happened. In our minds, we can play out future scenarios to predict how we respond to them. By doing so, we can experience thoughts and emotions similar to those that would occur if the situations were actually happening right now. So while real confidence can take time to build and nurture, you can still experience the feeling of complete confidence right away just by believing you can!

The success of your photo shoot really rests on the shoulders of your photographer, so choosing the right one can be the difference between a family heirloom and just another average snapshot. A really good photographer can make your photo shoot a fun and exciting experience for everyone. They will inspire confidence, empowerment and leave you feeling excited about your session. I would love to take you on that journey. I would love to create art with you.

ABOUT CARRIE

Those who love fantasy, whimsy and vintage style would be great admirers of the works of Carrie Rheinberger. Carrie combines old-fashioned sophistication and charm with modern photography technology to produce the amazing pieces of art that her clients travel from all over Australia to create with her. Her classic vintage vibe is paired with a contemporary style that can only be described as magical. Photographing people, in particular women and children, is fundamental to Carrie's photography. Carrie seeks to capture her subject's stillness and natural beauty through a style that is somewhat less mainstream than the standard calling out of 'CHEESE!' heard from other photography studios. What Carrie loves most is the opportunity to capture something different: something with the feel of time gone by; something you may have once seen hanging in a castle. Think dukes and duchesses, queens and kings; Carrie can transform you into photographic royalty.

But Carrie is more than just a photographer, she's an artist and her vision extends beyond her one client to their next generation. For some families, an heirloom may be a ring that has been handed down through the generations. It may be a painting or journal. For others, the heirlooms may be something simple, or an object that doesn't have a lot of monetary value, but reminds us of a special time or person. Common among many heirlooms is the sentimental value we place on the item, and that is why for Carrie, her fine art prints are the perfect family heirloom. Carrie's studio is a full photographic lab, producing heirloom quality, fine art prints and museum quality canvas designed to be passed down through generations. Carrie takes pride in handprinting every piece herself and shipping to clients as far away as Germany. The beautiful fine art prints are kept safe in stunning archival folio boxes handmade in Australia.

Carrie is a university-trained photographer, having studied her three-year Bachelor Of Photography at James Cook University. She has mentored with some of the best photographers in the world and now mentors her own team of photographers and editors.

Starting off with one small home studio in Calliope, Queensland, Carrie has big plans for her business. Earlier this year she opened a studio in Brisbane and is planning a third studio to open in the new year.

Carrie's work has been featured in *Vogue Australia,* graced the cover of *International Kid Model Magazine* and featured in dozens of other publications worldwide.

Along with her passion for photography, Carrie is keen to offer opportunities to aspiring young models in the community by running yearly competitions for local talent. Building self-esteem and confidence begins at a very young age, and it is Carrie's mission to provide a safe and compassionate environment where women and children of all ages can celebrate their individuality and know they are worthy of feeling beautiful. Fresh Faces Competition was started by Carrie in 2019 and continues to be a huge success with over three hundred youngsters having participated so far. Positive feedback from the competition is what keeps Carrie motivated to run it every year, with parents commenting on how much confidence their child gains from the experience.

Carrie is the mother of two children; a three-year-old and a one-year-old. She lives on a property in Calliope, and spends her free time with her family, gardening, swimming, listening to music and creating art.

www.sixcrowsfineart.com

MADEEHA USMAN

Over many recent nights, I have been trying to consolidate what's the most 'impressionable' thing I can write which will actually help the readers for their future. At last, I realised that perhaps the best approach would be to share with you how I reached where I am at now and what lessons I learnt along the way.

I was born and bred in Pakistan to a close-knit family. In my house, there were only five people – me, Mum, Dad and my two siblings. I was the eldest. As a child, I was very introverted and quiet. I was an avid reader, top in my class and my life revolved around my family. I used to go to school, return home on the school bus and then mum would sit with us to finish our homework, just like every other family around us in our colony.

Unlike the common perception for Muslim women around the globe, education was considered very important in our family. I can still remember days when Mum did not cook any dinner during our exams. This was because she wanted to invest all her time and energy helping us to prepare the best we could. It was fun for us because food was delivered from the restaurant!

My dad was my support system. He was the epitome of selflessness and simplicity. Despite being a celebrated accountant, what made him larger than life was that he was not just well versed in his profession, but also held matters of the soul in high esteem. The commitment he showed to his family was reflected in his effectiveness as a father-friend and he instilled in us similar qualities that he possessed. He always told us we should follow what he did rather than what he told us to do.

He ensured we went to the best schools and had the best education, so we never felt less than anyone in our lives.

My mum, on the other hand, was the heart of the home, the spine of our family. Mum and Dad both loved and respected each other. Since she was a qualified professional herself, she ensured we always got good grades and were equally involved in extracurricular activities.

At the age of twenty, I finished my chartered accountancy and started my career as an auditor in one of the leading accounting firms in Pakistan. Life was beautiful. I was protected by my parents; if there was any problem, I shared my agony with Mum or Dad and the problem was resolved.

I loved teaching and while I was doing my accountancy training at Ernst and Young, I gave lectures to accounting students in my university. Initially it was daunting, because I, a twenty-two-year-old, was teaching a class of twenty to thirty men, who generally looked much older than me! But there is a certain fulfillment and a sense of achievement – hard to describe in words – from teaching. I was addicted to it, to transfer my skills and knowledge to my students. I still miss those times.

As I turned twenty-four, it was time to get married. My father began searching for the right groom for me. He asked me if I had found someone, but I gave the responsibility to him. I thought this was wise. I trusted he would find the best partner for me.

He was convinced I would be happiest if my husband was also an accountant. There and then, the search began for the perfect Mr Accountant for me. My father had strong hindsight. He told me the kind of life we lived was like heaven, so protected, so secure – but the world outside was not always like that. He said I was too simple, too vulnerable. Later I realised you only discover your biggest strengths when you reach the boundaries of your vulnerability.

At twenty-five, my dad asked me, 'Have you ever thought of living in Australia?' I was surprised, because for all those years I hadn't left my hometown in Pakistan, not even for a holiday. He convinced me I was too talented and my qualifications and skills would be embellished if I established a new life in Australia. I am still unsure how he reached this decision for me, but now when I think of it, I am so thankful to him, because he was the first person who identified the spark in me to rise high.

In October 2014, I got married to Kaleem. It was an arranged marriage, like most of the marriages in Pakistan. But unlike the common stories we hear about Pakistani marriages, my mum and dad left the decision for me to decide if Kaleem was the right life partner for me. Kaleem is a professional accountant, my friend and my confidant.

I said yes, after several interviews with Kaleem, ensuring he was the right person and wouldn't let me down.

My new home – Australia

We left for Australia on 23 October 2014, and within twenty days of arriving, I was working in my first job in one of the BIG4 in Adelaide. I can still remember the sparkle in my dad's eyes when he heard the news. As if all his sacrifices had worked out. Seeing him so happy made that day one of the best days of my life.

At one of my job interviews, I remember the interviewer asking me, 'You are from Pakistan … so how are you able to speak such good English?' He was surprised to know that English happens to be the official language of Pakistan.

This reflects how the world has made an impression of people from

Pakistan based on a single story. This makes me see how vulnerable we are in the face of a single story we hear about other nationalities and people.

These stories portray that only a certain kind of people live in Pakistan; that the women there are distressed, the victim. I don't think the image the interviewer had of me was his fault, it was because he had only heard and seen my homeland as a place where certain kind of people live, and he had formed a picture in his mind based on a story. It is due to this I feel we, as humans, need to assess people by exploring them individually without categorisation, not based on a single story we have heard about them.

Embracing motherhood

I was at the top of my career when my bundle of happiness, my son Musa was born. One evening, just a few days before Musa's birth, I was working in my office when I received a call from my husband. 'Can you come down, I have come to pick you up.' I was surprised at the odd time he had come to pick me up, until he said, 'Your dad is no more.' He was only sixty-three.

I still become teary whenever I recollect that moment. I wasn't able to bid him a final goodbye. I couldn't attend the funeral because it was too risky to travel at that stage of my pregnancy. My husband took me back to his office. He was an employee at a firm and had no other option but to finish the tasks assigned to him. We did not have any family in Australia. For hours, I waited in the small, dark kitchen in his office. Life changed after my dad left me.

Years have passed but I still feel the void whenever I need advice, or don't know what to do. I feel incomplete because I have achieved so much, but the man who made me who I am is not there to witness the fruit of the seeds he sowed.

God's miracle was that Musa, my son, was born on the same day my father was born. Musa and my father share the same birthday. In a way, it was God's gift to me after Dad was gone. I always remember him just by looking at Musa, who I want to be a reflection of him.

Processing the unthinkable

In 2017, we were pregnant again. This time we were expecting a baby girl, our little baby Ayra. But fate had different plans for us. We lost baby Ayra before she was born at twenty weeks; my husband and I buried her with our own trembling hands.

God wanted us to learn some life lessons. In February 2018, we were expecting our third child, Sa'ad. He was born premature and stayed in the NICU for several weeks. After a month-long stay at the hospital, we were elated to be taking him home. It was a Sunday afternoon and as I arrived at NICU to pick up my little prince, I saw that Sa'ad's incubator was not at his designated cubicle. The head of NICU greeted me.

He told me Sa'ad hadn't been well since last night; he had contracted a bacterial infection. All his words seemed muffled to me. He said the bacteria had somehow taken over the whole of my baby's brain and the MRI showed multiple cysts in his brain. I couldn't comprehend his words and inadvertently, I asked him, 'What does all of this mean, Doctor?'

His answer shattered me. 'It means, ermm, your son is going to die, Mrs Usman …' I had to process the unthinkable; the thought that my son was going to die. I was going to lose my child again. I felt God was being unfair, but I was helpless.

The next few weeks were the most difficult. The team at the hospital told us we had to decide if we should let our son live or take him home for palliative care. They told us the bacteria had done too much damage; his systems were shutting down and I could expect my son not to recognise me, talk, walk or speak … It was heartbreaking. The decision was in my hands, the ball was in my court. I had to decide if I wanted my son alive or not. At that time, I had to make a strong decision. I did not want my son to just survive. I wanted him to live, because if he did not live his life, there was no point of a life in a body run by machines.

We made the decision and brought him home. I cuddled him for as long as I could, dressed him up in all the fancy clothes I had purchased for him, and took as many photos as possible. He did smile at us, but he did not cry. Within days, his body temperature started to fall. I was holding him in my arms, shivering, as he slipped away. I remember the exact moment he took his last breath and turned pale. We were crying. We had lost our son. But suddenly he screamed and took another breath. He was back again. He was fighting, not letting go. He kept fighting. Two hours passed as we watched our son going away and coming back again. It was a strange feeling, a stabbing pain. I was helpless, because I couldn't do *anything* for him.

Sa'ad finally stopped fighting and passed away. And so began the long, excruciatingly difficult grief journey for me and my husband – a journey no parent can ever be prepared to take.

But God blessed us again with Mirha our little baby girl, on 23 July 2019. I could never love anyone the way I love her. She is my little treasure; she brings me joy and takes away all the pain I've been through.

Birth of the Kalculators

After I left PwC and became a mum, I started to think how I could balance both work and family life. I had worked all my life and couldn't forego my career, but also I couldn't leave Musa alone. I wanted to give him the same amount of time and attention my mother gave me.

I started doing tax returns from our garage. Every day I would turn on my baby monitor, put Musa in his cot in a room right next to my tiny office and attend to my clients. There were times when I prepared tax returns while Musa was in my lap. My clients were always so supportive and respectful of my priorities. They had faith I could multitask and still provide great service. This taught me that goodness is more common in the world than we imagine.

In April 2016, we decided to start our own accounting firm. Kaleem asked me what we should name our business. Every night we would sit in our garage office and brainstorm. Our Australian friends used to call Kaleem 'Kal'. One night I was scribbling different names on my notepad and suddenly I saw the calculator right in front of me. *Kalculators it is.* That was the day we gave birth to another child, our accounting firm, The Kalculators.

My most prized experiences come from helping a variety of entities – from factory workers to multimillion-dollar turnover businesses, such as pharmacies, construction businesses and retail stores.

As I came to Australia, I realised many people were not getting the support they needed, especially in the multicultural community. I wanted to support people like me – business mums and immigrants starting their new businesses – in my capacity as an accountant. I wanted to provide accounting and business solutions so my clients, and mums like me, could follow their dreams, but balance their work and life simultaneously.

Lessons learnt

I have realised that adversity doesn't discriminate. Look around you. If you are alive, you are going to have, or already have had, some tough times.

Because I've clawed my way from the depth of unimaginable pain, suffering and sorrow, again and again, today I feel that when the joy comes, however and whenever it does, it is a joy that reverberates through every pore of my skin and every bone in my body. I feel all of it, deeply: the love, the grief, the joy, the pain. I embrace and thank every part of it.

My life is richer now, more vibrant and full, not despite my loss, but *because* of it. In grief there are gifts, sometimes many. These gifts cannot make the pain 'worth it', however, I am grateful beyond words for every gift that comes my way. I bow my head to each one and say, *Thank you, thank you, thank you.* Because there is nothing, and I mean absolutely nothing, I take for granted.

Living life in this way gives me greater joy than I ever thought was possible.

I end with the ideology that If you fail, don't lose hope, because as the wise saying goes, 'We can't change the direction of the wind, but we can certainly adjust the sails.'

ABOUT MADEEHA

I was named 'Madeeha' by my parents – a feminine name of Arabic origin which is said to mean 'praiseworthy'.

Born in 1987 in a conventional Muslim household in the historic Pakistani city of Lahore, I've had a roller-coaster of a life and experienced joy and affliction in almost equal measure. My father was a chartered accountant and my mother a home-economist. My father was always playing with numbers and I could see how crucial the role of financial accountant is for a company. His professionalism, his persona, his charisma always inspired me to be like him.

My parents helped me unleash the power within me. Encouraging my dreams, they valued my growth. In their presence, I always felt seen. They instilled into me the drive to work hard and meticulously climb my way up to gain the best of both worlds, perhaps even more – I'm a homemaker, a chartered accountant and an entrepreneur.

My career started as an auditor in PwC and then EY. Having worked with the top firms for several years, I was not ready to stop for anything less. My career progression continued as I became an ACCA member and now a fellow.

In 2014, I moved to Australia. Fortunately, I landed a role in PwC soon after my arrival. I was contented with what life had given me and was going with the flow. What I didn't know was my life was going to go topsy-turvy very soon … I remember the call on 22 May 2015, and the words that shattered my heart to pieces and snatched away all my passion – my role model, my father, had passed away! I was eight months pregnant and couldn't to travel for my father's funeral in Pakistan. I quit my job and decided to just stay home to give birth to my baby.

The next few years changed my life completely.

I gave birth and saw my son taking his last breath in front of my eyes.

I gave birth and buried my daughter with my own hands.

But life goes on, it doesn't stop – it should not stop!

Today, I'm a content mother of two, Musa and Mirha.

I have learnt that you should always gather your courage and never stop learning. As I became a mother, I continued to study and got CA ANZ qualification and becoming a registered tax agent when my son was just two months old.

For me, impending motherhood was the impetus for launching my own business, The Kalculators, in 2016. Together with my husband Kaleem, I started my firm from a small garage. Today, we run eight offices across South Australia, employing twenty-plus professionals.

There were times when I worked seven days a week, and there were moments where I felt I had no more energy left, even days when I was in the hospital with my newborn in one hand and my laptop in the other, but today I believe all the struggles were worth it.

Today I am referred to as 'the tax lady' by over 20,000 people in South Australia.

Aiming to give back to the community, I founded Care Assure – a disability service provider, dedicated to helping people with disabilities live an empowered life. Today, Care Assure is trusted by thousands of people to provide disability support that inspires and enriches lives every day.

I feel blessed that our firm hasn't just grown, but has also received tremendous applause from the industry. I was honoured to be a winner of Ausmumprenuer – Rising Star for Customer Service, Business Excellence and Diversity and Inclusion program. I am grateful to APWA Australia for awarding me the 'Woman of Achievement award'. We were finalists for the Australian Accounting Awards (diversity and inclusion) and the Women in Finance Awards for Accounting Consultant of the Year.

But I can never achieve anything as empowering as my children. My son and my daughter are the trophies I carry more proudly than any other. I attribute my success to the strength they have given me.

I am Madeeha Usman, and this is my story.

www.thekalculators.com.au

KAREN Mc DERMOTT

It's my mission in life to share stories with the world, especially what I learn on this crazy journey of mine. I have been truly blessed in life. I live my perfect life, as a mum of six and a successful business owner, and I get to live my passion every day. I know the power of the 'pause' and treasure each moment no matter what hat I am wearing.

I like to hang out at the highest vibration, because when life's struggles happen I don't fall too far, and certainly not below the line. I learned the value of this when I endured a very low period in my life; a year-long stint with PTSD. It happened because my well had run dry. I call this my cocoon period, because when I awakened to life again, I saw it with a new and more beautiful perspective, owning every moment, and sharing what I discover so that others can benefit.

I recently had the privilege of sharing my seven life principles at TEDx Londonderry, and would like to share them with you now.

Seven life principles that will ensure you live the life of your dreams

How highly do you prioritise your goals? A study by the University of Scranton featured in *Inc.* states that only 8% of people achieve their goals. That's a whopping 92% of dreams not being realised!

I am honoured to share with you here the life principles that have enhanced my life beyond my wildest dreams, but first a story …

In 2008 I had just come through a rough period in my life, where everything that could go wrong had gone wrong. But then I had a wake-up call that shifted me back to my destined path in life, and everything began flowing again. Suddenly I was being gifted wisdoms beyond my years. I went on a bit of a spiritual journey and found myself living through seven key principles I now use as my foundation to life. I've had plenty of success in the years since, and I'm often asked what my secret to life is.

In 2012, I set a powerful intention to build a million-dollar publishing house. Big goal, huh! The seed was planted but my studies were in humanities, not publishing. So how was I to get started? Well, I set the intention, and things began to happen fast. What I thought would take me twenty-five years to achieve took just seven. I absolutely 'know' that working through these principles has fast-tracked my success, and all without compromising any of my values as a proud mum of six.

I am a great believer of leaning inwards for the answers and outwards for the support to make them happen. I believe the majority of the 92% not achieving their dreams are setting outward goals, but in my experience, when we set passion-fuelled goals, intentionally aligned with our values, there is no way we will fail.

So, I want to share with you a different kind of perspective; a perspective that ensures that when you set an intention, you set yourself up to win, not lose.

My seven life principles that will help you to maximise your potential in life are:

1. **Mindfulness**
2. **Knowing**
3. **Intention**
4. **Gratitude**
5. **Love**

6. Forgiveness
7. Belief

You may be thinking to yourself that they are just words; deep and meaningful words, yes, but still, just words. However, I want you to take a moment to consider that when you live through the essence of each one of these principles, you *will* experience life at a whole new level.

Let's first look at mindfulness

Becoming 'mindful' is when we are more aware of things around us; we see wider and deeper.

When you open your mind to becoming more mindful, something shifts within you without even having to try. Divine timing comes into motion and a greater awareness of self is mastered. With each of the seven principles to reach their highest potential, it is important to become more mindful.

My top tip to becoming more mindful, indeed with all of these principles, is to do it *consciously* for twenty-one days. This ensures the practice becomes a habit.

When you do something enough, it becomes part of who you are, who you come to be.

The second principle is knowing

Knowing is one of the most powerful things we can learn, or actually I should say *relearn*. We are all born with the ability to 'know', but we lose it along the way.

There are way too many people leaning outside for answers when really, it's an inside job. It really is as simple as that, but of course, as humans we tend to make life harder than it needs to be.

First of all, you need to realise you already have the ability to 'know', – we all do. I have a simple three-step knowing process that will help you kickstart your knowing.

1. Feel it
2. Think it
3. Action it

So you have set a powerful intention; it is now an energetic frequency, and you can be *confident* that the universal laws are doing their bit in the process to make it happen. Knowing ensures you stay on track when an inspired thought or opportunity comes your way, and most importantly, that you don't compromise your values in the process.

Feel it: When an inspired thought catches your attention, you are feeling it. Most people act at this stage, but I like to bring it a step further to the **Think it** stage where I ask the simple question, 'Is this aligned with where I want to go?' If the answer is 'no', or 'I'm not sure', I dismiss it straight away, with confidence! If the answer is a 'hell yes', then I have the courage to **Action it** immediately. If I don't, someone else will. The biggest things that have happened in my life have come from when I have actioned an opportunity or inspired thought immediately, as it absolutely feels like the 'right next step'. There is no fear in the process because there is no fear in knowing! I am able to make decisions with unwavering confidence, Knowing that my internal navigation system is working solely for my highest potential.

The third principle is intention

Setting a clear intention is an important part of living to your highest potential. How can you get what you want if you don't know what you actually want to achieve? This energetic exchange is important because it sets a ball in motion that can really build momentum in achieving your heart's desire. I have had a lot of fun in my life setting intentions and going on the journey to make them happen. There is a difference between an intention and a goal. With an intention, you set the target but surrender to the process of how it comes to be. Whereas with a goal often there is a step-by-step plan to achieve the goal and all focused energy goes directly onto each step, instead of on the unlimited potential of an intentional journey.

The fourth principle is gratitude

A secret not everyone realises is that gratitude is not only a wonderful virtuous quality to have, it is also a super-channel for manifesting.

When you take time to be grateful every day, your future self will also be grateful for it. It makes sense, as the results will outweigh any doubt in the faith you need to commit gratitude. To kickstart your gratitude journey, I recommend you get a gratitude journal. But the secret key to manifesting through gratitude is to think and feel what it would be like to have your heart's desire *right now*, in this very moment, and then sit in the essence of that moment.

The fifth principle is love

I like to call this the 'Law of Love' because when you put loving energy into something, it supercharges it. Not only do you get quicker results, the outcome is often more than you can ever imagine. I know this from many occasions of pumping loving energy into my intentions and achieving results beyond my wildest dreams.

It takes courage to live through love, but if you can find the courage within and have a passion for life and for your calling, just wait until you see how it works for you. Love life and it will love you back.

The sixth principle is forgiveness

Forgiveness is one of the toughest, but one of the most freeing, of all the principles. It is super valuable because if things hold us back in the past, how can we ever authentically move forward?

Not only do you need to forgive others, you also need to forgive yourself. When I talk about forgiveness I am speaking about an energetic disconnection to anything holding you back from realising your highest potential.

Everything and everyone in our past was there for a reason, helping us advance into the person we are today. They served a purpose for a season, not for a lifetime. There is no greater tragedy than a life entrenched in past hurt.

In order to evolve and reach your highest potential, you need to rise above and learn how to forgive.

We must understand that forgiveness is an almighty strength, not a weakness.

We have come to the last and final principle: belief

Quite often, belief can come through ourselves, but sometimes it is a gift from others. Our role is to open the door and let it in. Belief is a driving force in helping us open our minds to our highest potential. There are no limits, only the ones we impose on ourselves, so start believing today!

These seven life principles have been a catalyst in the exciting trajectory of my life. Should you choose to embrace them for yourself, I hope they will act as a personal dream activator for you too. You have nothing to lose and so much to gain. So if you are ready to be in the elite 8%, it's time to embrace a new perspective and live the life of your dreams.

ABOUT KAREN

Karen is an award-winning publisher, author, TEDx Speaker and advanced Law of Attraction practitioner.

Author of numerous books across many genres – fiction, motivational, children's and journals – she chooses to lead the way in her authorship generously sharing her philosophies through her writing.

Karen is also a sought-after speaker who shares her knowledge and wisdom on building publishing empires, establishing yourself as a successful author-publisher and book writing.

Having built a highly successful publishing business from scratch, signing major authors, writing over thirty books herself and establishing her own credible brand in the market, Karen has developed strategies and techniques based on tapping into the power of knowing to create your dreams.

Karen is a gifted teacher who inspires others to make magic happen in their lives through her seven life principles that have been integral in her success.

When time and circumstance align, magic happens.

www.serenitypress.org
www.kmdbook.com
www.mmhpress.com

HEIDI CONWAY

Learn and earn – from contention to connection

It had been an emotional night. *Ever had one of those*? I had called my husband back to our sunny Gold Coast home. He had left for a few days to a hotel room, at my request, because I just wanted space. Something inside me was feeling 'off'. I was twenty-seven, still no kids, yet two bull terriers, a great job, and still I wanted space! I just wasn't able to put my finger on why. I finally called my husband to talk and decided, 'Let's try this again, let's stay together … after all, we married for life.'

Well, that didn't happen, and after a heart-wrenching dream, I decided to end the marriage. It became somewhat clearer by age thirty-two, after yet another marriage, how I would finally find the freedom I was looking for. I had married for the second time at twenty-nine, hardly enough time to discover who I was and what I liked in life. No dogs now, but two wonderful teenage stepchildren whom I adored. An instant family: maybe that was what I had been searching for to fill the void and dispel the 'off' feeling? Turns out not to be the case, and we divorced, after establishing a coaching company where we trained coaches. I came home to Queensland, Australia, and now am a mother, stepmother, and wife to my third, hardworking, very intelligent husband. Finally! Married to a man who believes in my coaching ability and allows the space for me to be the mother and coach I felt possible; to earn from what I love to do and raise our children in a way that would help them learn to connect to their true selves. From ages eight and eleven, they followed a self-directed learning pathway, without really knowing what that was … it just felt natural.

Transition from Jennifer Lopez to Gandhi

In the words of Jennifer Lopez, 'If I wanted my kids to be great, I need to fix some things …' Yet, I know from my coach training and experience that nobody needs 'fixing'. But so much is 'wrong', isn't it? I mean, I go through tricky times, my heart knows things that my head disagrees with, so doesn't that need fixing? In comes the voice; 'You are not alone.' I breathe a sigh of relief as I write. So, if I don't need fixing, why is there still contention in my life? In relationships, work teams, in wanting kids to have their own minds and at the same time not wanting to worry about their preparedness for success in the future? I'm still confused if I am doing the 'right thing' and scared if family and friends will think I'm crazy. These are all the signs of contention: efforting too much, conflict within me and with others, competition, struggle and often feeling lonely (yet never alone). Again, I realise if I want my children to be great and have a great life by being empowered to be free, then what I really need to change is ALL that contention! In comes the paraphrased quote of Gandhi that I adore – 'Be the change.'

Why you might want to connect

This brings me to my 'why' for living, doing what I do in business, and why I surround myself with the people I do. What I was missing all these years before age forty-six (the year I started home-educating my boys) was the ability to educate myself too. I began teaching the boys to listen and notice things in their life; to listen within and listen to what was going on for others. To be aware, rather than be careful. Allowing myself to do the same was how I found my passion, my *ikigai* of coaching. It helped me to know how to allow others to see their own magnificence and connect with each other. So, my 'why' is to change the landscape within homeschool families, so they can learn and earn with joy and ease. To do this, I am 'being the change' as a mother. I have learnt we can teach the steps to connection no matter what trauma may have disconnected us from ourselves, and each other. When we connect with ourselves, help our children do the same, and also connect to God, the process of connecting with others is easy. However, there's been a change – in comes a global pandemic and we must learn to connect on a whole different level with our fellow human beings.

Tips for connection

At any time in history, we have been told life does not need to be a struggle – we can have it all. In the eighties and nineties, the gaps between where I was and what I wanted were about self-worth, feeling deserving and realising I could have it all. We were hearing that balance was achievable. So, if we can have it all, why then the contention? We have been given permission to have it all, we just haven't been taught how. We were taught compromise, poorly in my opinion, because it came with judgement. Even when the communication was not intended to be judgemental, the partner, friend or young person still hears it with judgement. At this point, I get curious; if we all know to the core of our being that we can be, do and have whatever we want, why then contention, bullying, struggle, divorce? It could be so simple, and indeed it is, if you are aware. Moving from a traditional school environment to home education often requires the space known as de-schooling, a time of letting go and destressing. There is so much joy and ease to be experienced when the communication is real.

Recognise the contention

Connection is central to changing the world in a positive way. We know that now, even if we are physically distant from each other. I think of the artist who loses her sight but gains her sense of hearing. In times of change, contrast, conflict and contention, ask, 'How do we stay connected to ourselves, and each other, no matter what?' It seems that change around the globe now requires even more skill for our positive connections to be influential. Even using the sustainable development goals as an avenue for change requires loyal and meaningful connection and expression of oneself. It's not only a village and a system required to raise and allow the individual learning pathway for our children, it's a mindset. This is very humbling, and I fully realise it is a privilege to be the support for many mothers and families, both locally and globally, as they learn this too.

Increase compassion

I had an emotional experience during the pandemic that really affected me. I have never, and still do not, claim to be an anxious person, and yet for a few hours on this day, I felt deep empathy and insight into how teens must feel when they start to express themselves, yet feel judged in the process. Although it certainly was not a pleasant experience, the push and pull of it woke me up to use my voice.

Have you ever felt the prompt to speak up, to write, to do more with your life, to care more, to sing more, to dance more, to be more of who you knew or know yourself to be inside? You've had dreams, visions, a prophesy of what was next for you or what you were born to do, and despite this, you're not doing it? Has God been knocking? If you, if we, haven't allowed ourselves to listen and receive the news and courage in a benevolent way, then the knocking gets louder.

Allow me to share an experience that happened recently. Some would describe it as anxiety although it was simple and crazy at the same time. I went into a chemist to pick up an item. I had a wonderful glittery mask on (because, hey, we may as well sparkle) and I did not tap for contact tracing. I choose not to contact trace because, for me, I feel it spreads fear, and I did not want to be a part of doing things out of fear. I stand for sharing love and kindness, and one cannot act fully with love and be afraid at the same time.

The people around me clearly wanted me to contact trace, and I was about to learn a lesson in vulnerability. There I was, surrounded by staff and customers yelling at me until I too yelled, 'STOP, STOP, get back!' All nine people did not back off until I fumbled and paid for my item and left – traumatised. There were no pleasant requests or compassion shown to me, and what saddened me most is that these people are most likely parents. This was the closest to trauma I have ever felt. I felt dizzy. I'm a woman changing the world – is that what it feels like sometimes? Dizzy, crazy!? I think so. So much contention. When I took some breaths and connected to self and God again, I leaned in to receive an answer regarding what the learning was here. I knew it was not about contact tracing. I did an exercise of asking – on a scale from zero to ten, at what level is the compassion for others in the community? I didn't mean the compassion level when we see an accident and we attend to help. I was asking about the compassion level, the grace, the space, the okay-ed-ness (is that even a word?) to be ourselves. I gasped – two out of ten level of compassion! I heard the answer clearly. Really? We allow others to be themselves two out of ten? Was this a real thing? I have since asked this question of many, and they all agreed. The level of compassion others in the community had for them to be themselves, the person they felt born to be, was two out of ten. That is so sad. This figure is what could prompt self-harm, and that is what must stop now.

Different communication

This is not what I typically experience in my inner circle. I knew I had to be the change and consciously listen. To communicate kindly to ourselves, our inner voice, requires more focus. Compassion and empathy can be taught, and this is how contention becomes connection at a whole new level, no matter what you are experiencing. Everyone deserves to be who they are, no matter where they are. They deserve to feel safe.

Commitment

The work we are committed to with our business is on track because we allow change-makers to be who they are. We are all change-makers. When I taught and audited health, safety and environmental performance in several industries, we addressed legislation. I used to say if we would just look after ourselves, look after each other and look after our environment, we would not need legislation. However, we are allowed to have our own beliefs and values, so hence legislation ensures that we are all cared for – or does it? If we were truly ALL allowed to be ourselves and show up in the world to discover who we are and live our passion and purpose, regardless of that high-paying job we may not enjoy, I am curious if all would be taken care of as nature intended. This requires trust, and that's why trust starts with us. Parents can hold the space for our children to allow them to discover who they are without judgement. Imagine if this was just as important as knowing our numbers and alphabet.

Changemaker Teens, and all children, will be the vehicle for this change, where we get to walk our talk. We are building the bridge for what it means to educate our children. Many are saying there is a revolution of education happening now. What brings me more ease instead is to stand for a natural evolution of education because we are building a community where there is no discrimination. And yet there is little (two out of ten) chance of being accepted for who we truly are and what we believe. So how do we close the gap? We choose, that's how. We focus on how we feel and allow others to do the same, holding the space for a better feeling, thought or behaviour to literally evolve, especially with teens and children. It's only when they have a foot in both camps that things get tricky; being themselves, and still trying to please parents, teachers and peers.

We are making progress. What's the saying? – 'It's all good.' If it doesn't feel good to hang on to things, feeling, incidents from the past, let it go and – as a dear friend once said to me – walk where your feet are. Walking where your feet are and encouraging the young ones to do this too will change everything for the better. We then get to choose and decide what will bring us freedom. Oh, and breathing helps enormously too.

We are now helping mothers hold the space for their young people as they discover, create and live who they are. When we get this 'right' as we cross the evolutionary bridge of education, this flows on to our partners and our families. We experience a whole new level of openness in our communication. We flow when these families walk out their door into their physical and online communities and two out of ten is no longer possible. Instead, it is the norm to listen and notice, and that is how we will begin to see ten out of ten.

Allow me to ask a laser question – what do you think we are afraid of that prevents us from being there already? For me, it was a fear of being raw … *ahh* nope, it isn't. That's a lie. My fear really? It's time! It's that I don't have time to hold the space for EVERYONE, which translates to I can't notice and listen to everyone like I do to my teens. Really, you are too busy? Too busy to care, to ascertain the direction of thoughts of another? Well, it's time to join the movement. Allow yourself, and then your family, and then your community to fully be in the flow of being themselves.

Enjoy the journey of discovering who you truly are and what you are passionate about. Breathe and hold your head up high and keep moving onward with ease!

ABOUT HEIDI

Heidi Conway, once life coach, once national manager in the corporate world – now a homeschool Aussie mum of teens. Heidi has been reviewed as being able to have a conversation with your mind whilst listening to your soul. It makes sense then that Heidi would listen to her sons and just know that in the traditional school environment their inner genius, that she heard and saw often, was not sustainably lit. Heidi sees herself as a change-maker mother, a global coach of change-makers, on a national and international mission with a deep entrepreneurial spirit and the drive of a true edupreneur. Heidi is co-founder of Changemaker Teens Global; a movement intended to revolutionise the outdated, unresponsive traditional education system. She is redefining 'school'. Heidi invites mothers and alternative learning educators to be the catalyst for positive change in the world by holding the space for teenagers to discover their innate change-maker genius, liberating them to find their own unique pathway where they show up, step up and give back. The vehicle for this transformation is the Changemaker Learning Dojo, a nurturing, safe place designed to encourage curiosity, creativity and compassion in each learner. Keeping home-based learning simple, self-directed and social is the goal of Changemaker Teens Global. Heidi has faith, that together, this vision and action will create positive, life-enhancing change – locally to you, and extending to the world!

www.changemakerteens.com

JACINTA WARLAND

'Cultural therapy' – the words I use for the work I do within Indigenous communities, along with my cultural heritage work. My journey to here has been a little unconventional. I have some vivid memories of my idyllic childhood in the green rolling hills and valleys of New Guinea, in the Western Highlands, where time stood still for the traditional native people. I lived with my family in this area for nine years. My father was stationed in the Highlands, where the vernacular for the local Indigenous folk was Oli (pronounced Au-li). Perhaps a derivative from the German language of the colonising predecessors of the region. They were collectively Kanakas, and for our area, Oli, and my *wontoks*.

My earliest connections with people from a different cultural background were the two wonderful figures in my life who cared for me and my older siblings. 'Haus Boy and Mari' – Anion, his wife Mary, and their two children, who lived in a small house made from traditional mud and thatch, at the bottom of the lawns, with a fire constantly fed to keep the cooking of their food staples on hand. As we played and ate those foods prepared from that small smouldering fire, we became familiar with the local dialect, and I was immersed in a very different way of life. My brother and sister, being older, showed me that friends came in every shape and hue of colour, a proper United Nations group. Everyone was accepted and included. We were colourblind to skin colour.

My fondest memories of those times were the Sing-Sings, which took place almost religiously every six months or so. The local tribes, and their travelling relatives, would amass at the showgrounds, being the flattest and easily accessed area, and perform their cultural dances, each having their own interpretation of the important events and learnings of their forefathers. As a child, I had no knowledge of these anthropological meanings, I simply delighted in the great spectacle of the vividly painted and feathered men, Mudmen and beautiful women who had adorned themselves with bright colours, beads, seeds, feathers and grass skirts.

Music, song, dance, vibration and laughter were the languages I grew up with. I would only talk pidgin but understood English as well. My ears filled with the rhythm of life, drums pounding, voices raised in unison, they called out, shouted, sang and mimicked birds, changed from joyful to fast-paced urgency, all using the space to celebrate and connect with others from the region. The smells of wild pig and cow-cow (a yam variety) cooked across the fires scattered around the perimeter, added to the always available fresh fruits, sugar bananas and sought-after salty plums for the kids.

I remember my feelings of absolute joy and excitement when I was scooped up into the arms of an Oli dancer, as he placed me on his wide brown shoulders and paraded around dancing and singing, showing off his catch of the day; a little child, a piccaninny, who was enthralled and just a little bit scared. These wonderful memories imprinted on me in such a way that my desire to connect with different people overshadowed any fear of the 'other' that most children were inoculated with by their very strict Eurocentric parents.

To say I had the best of both worlds would be true, not knowing prejudice and otherness, sadly when I left to come to Australia, saying my final 'me lookim you behind' to Mt Hagen, I was destined to be a little less accepting of the world, and a little more afraid. That's what growing up is all about, right?

At the tender age of ten, I was reminded I was a white girl, not to mix with the darker-skinned kids, and keep to my own kind. I found that skin colour was a badge most wore as a reflection, one of being better or more than others who did not possess the white skin colour, the belief of the race theory at that time. No longer was it acceptable to be friendly with the 'dark' kids. I was told, by the Catholic nun holding my small ten-year-old hand, that white girls must sit with the other white girls. As I progressed through my primary years, I created some firm friendships and to this day still have connection with those same dark-skinned girls. Our friendships endured through the school years. Yes, I flaunted the rules even then.

I went onto high school, moving every two years to new environments and states across Australia. This ensured I had to master any shyness and work on being accepted by many new people. My gift was the ease by which I made friends, living in three different states in five years. My first real boyfriend was an Aboriginal lad, a year older than me, and very resourceful. He was definitely a fun experience, taking me on adventures horseriding, fishing and skating. Oh my, the heady days of rollerskating in Darwin in the late 1970s.

My final school year was spent in the Catholic confines of boarding school, giving me structure and confidence to continue my later learning, and a desire to find my purpose. Freedom after finishing year twelve felt like an opportunity to live and go wherever I felt my passions take me.

In that first year of being an adult, I remember a quick succession of passions and pursuits, all leaving me breathless and wanting more. More adventure, more risk, more whatever it was that made me feel alive. I took some risks, learnt to dive, joined the army reserve and met my first husband through a mutual friend. His work led us to wed quickly and move to Western Australia where my desire to keep learning put me into technical college to learn some secretarial skills.

That year determined my next nine years, where I worked across many different industries. My first daughter was born, a gorgeous soul, full of wonder and a little livewire. In-between mothering her, my calling led me to training in massage, sports therapy and finally, Bowen therapy. Combining these skills led to securing reasonable income and direction. After three moves, we settled in Townsville where my next son was born. He was a blessing; such a good baby, full of smiles and beguiling. He still is at thirty. Sadly, my relationship was not meant to last, with my partner deciding to move away to his family in another state. That was a hard time. I was lost, hurt and confused, feeling much less confident in my direction, but the universe had another plan for me.

I found a friend, who became my love, my confidant and my rock, and helped me through. After a few years, we welcomed our son and completed the circle of love. We had hope, both having had unhappy first relationships, that we would make the effort in this one. My eldest son remained with his father, and my gorgeous daughter came to live with us and her new little brother. We held our lives together with adventures and moving around the state so I could experience my husband's previous life of ringer and property manager.

As my experiences grew, so did my unrest in my vocation. I wanted to do more, know more and be more. My husband was supportive, selling his prized boat to finance my first PC. I started studying business and tourism externally at Central Queensland University. Being able to read for purpose and be critical of different views and then explain my position was a freeing exercise, so I did well in my subjects. But it was the business development side that got my creative ideas flowing, knowing that an idea can become a reality if one applies their skills, great frameworks and solid foundations.

After four years out west, with the kids running naked to the chook pen and growing our own corn, we moved back to Townsville. I started working for after-school homework programs where I saw the younger generation of Indigenous children coming through the school system. I knew the program was under-resourced and poorly supported by the schools, but I felt every child should be supported. I could see these kids struggling to be heard, supported and encouraged. One young lady in the private school sector told me she was targeted daily by her teachers, particularly in the subjects she was trying to improve in. She said, 'I wish they were like you and could see us, Miss.' That comment was very insightful.

My brother had married a lovely lady from the Torres Strait Islands, so his children were identified as Indigenous kids by birthright. They were a very generous family, giving me opportunity to visit and experience the Islands and see the magic of the place through cultural eyes. I was honoured to be taken to places that held cultural and spiritual importance, and this was something I wanted to know more about. My real education had begun. Sitting with family on a deserted beach, eating turtle eggs and hearing the stories of the war and conflicts on the Islands, I finally had that aha moment of, *Wow, this history, these traditions, this is calling me!* I knew I had to learn more, so I could do more.

After a few years within the government sector, I branched out, and between working as a business development officer supporting small business ideas and community roles, I was accepted back to university to do my Bachelor of Archaeology. I had found my passion and my vehicle. Being offered to work in this area was a dream come true. My journey began with another government agency working towards better relationships with each traditional owner group within their region. One thing I learnt from this experience; I was not to be supported as a cultural broker or hope to raise the profile and exposure of the Indigenous groups in my region. The concept of recognition for Indigenous groups was viewed as a cost, a part of a public performance, and not a public relations offset; just lip-service.

My efforts increased to push recognition of our regional traditional owners and communities through 'Welcome to Country' signage, identifying the diversity of the groups along our main roads. The project hinged on relationship development, and after some great results, including the minister visiting as we unveiled the pilot signage, a backflip happened internally. A major program of inclusion was quashed. On my resignation from the role, the manager taking over was not able to replicate my rapport with the traditional owners groups, and to this day, we do not have that recognition and pride along our regional highways making the statement of who has custodianship of these lands.

I was earning good money but became tired of the internal policies pushing for ways around the legislation rather than embracing the protection of cultural heritage. I wanted to support the local groups impacted by the project into employment or business options, but it was not possible in that role. I saw the opportunity to encourage Indigenous contracts, with tenders for revegetation and water reclaim offered to outside companies. I showed my managers how they could use local Indigenous groups and get the same outcomes, but they were not keen. Were they being directed by the international decisions excluding Indigenous companies in their tenders? It was an uphill battle. I resigned after being 'requested' to sign documents that did not reflect the accuracy of my professional assessments, just so projects could move forward uninhibited.

My work as a heritage consultant eventually led me to ask why no-one had combined conflict resolution with anthropology, to help support the issues experienced by Aboriginal people in navigating the native title journey. I was excited to move into this area, finally settling on a Masters in Alternate Conflict Resolution to support my majors in archaeology and anthropology. This would make them (the naysayers) take me seriously, right?

I had become schooled in the histories, the heritage and the laws (lore) associated with Indigenous groups, and after the completion of the

Masters I could argue with confidence on their behalf. Time to get my Wonder Woman cloak on! Ha!

Yep, so it is said that learning comes from making mistakes. I made some good ones. I was ready to fight, armed with my accredited skills and social justice mindset. My mistake was thinking others wanted the same outcome; justice and fairness not based on prejudice, creating lasting peace and parity for all. Sadly, no government agencies wanted to be schooled in what they were doing 'wrong' where native title was concerned. It was costing them money, and creating major rifts within community groups and family clans. It was a huge area of frustration for many of the Aboriginal applicants and the solutions at the time were to continue the costly legal processes, or give up. Being recognised was a financial and emotional drain for many applicants on these claims.

Over many conversations with my Indigenous colleagues, I realised there was a huge misunderstanding of the collective idea of what *culture* is in Australia. I worked towards using my two passions, archaeology and mediation, and started my little group called Hands on Heritage. The concept was taking school students to 'camp on country', and opening up the idea of experiencing traditional knowledge and cultural experiences through art therapy, archaeology and story. My goal: teach them intuitive heritage, including stories of shared histories with our settlers and miners of the last century. On one site, the history and family connection of a settler family was intertwined with the known Aboriginal groups of the area, allowing discovery of the many wonderful relationships that were not written about by the Eurocentric scribes from the past. Our many shared histories are hidden – except for the stories that made headlines or helped the government of the day 'look good'. My research accidentally helped to find the scattered remnants of a legacy Aboriginal clan group associated with a specific area. Inspiration and connection is right in front of you if you are willing to recognise it.

My main inspiration was to get young people to understand themselves and truly find their personal connection to culture. This included activities where they could find a buried skeleton or two, hidden treasures and lost artifacts. I was given a space for 'Digs for Kids', and for a number of years I worked encouraging young people from all walks of life to explore their past. They experienced the skills, methods and thrill of archaeology, combined with the art therapy of several gifted Aboriginal artists and storytellers, who showed them how to capture a story through art, story and poems.

While holding onto my initial belief that young people are the ones who will change the narrative on race relations, I gained some great insight from these activities. Through understanding more of ourselves and being educated in cultural identity, cultural backgrounds and our environment, we all learn by doing, questioning and assessing our relationship to our environment, including family, friends and internally. By knowing our own cultural heritage, we can use these learnings as a strength to build who we are.

I have now included internal belief change in my work, using the skills adapted from cultural ways of knowing and neurolinguistic programing to achieve greater results in positive change for young people. Some of those involved seemed trapped between being an Aboriginal person and knowing who they are in the modern world. The system I have crafted may help find the next step to their personal destiny, respecting cultural frameworks as we learn together.

My work is now taking me into new directions, where I am delivering hope and healing programs, with my first partnership with a community started earlier this year. These programs assist with self-transformation and are developed in partnership with Indigenous Elders, using their content and solutions within their communities; a way forward leading to personal and cultural growth, peacebuilding with economic initiatives and business development.

The young girl who said, 'Wish they could see us like you do,' – she is my muse. I have grown, through this journey, to be a cultural therapist who sees the great potential within each person, encouraging creative ideas, and guiding them to pursue their passions and be successful. Yes, my girl, I still see you.

ABOUT JACINTA

Jacinta Warland is a qualified archaeologist, and cultural mediator. She has been working in the Indigenous space for some thirty years. She is a driven heritage professional, who recently reinvented her knowledge base, incorporating new approaches in cultural therapy, mediation and personal breakthrough programs to improve outcomes for client groups. Much of her life has been influenced by working with, and learning from, Australian Indigenous people. Jacinta has learnt much from her work, and strongly advocates for the recognition of the immense knowledge held within the song lines and dreaming tracks expressed through the oral histories of our Aboriginal story keepers. The intricate and sacred sites captured in the reciting of the song lines, connecting memory spaces, needs to be acknowledged as a valuable and complex way of knowing, to be replicated and celebrated while we can.

Jacinta's work includes the drive to assist new approaches to reviving cultural practice, through developing data repositories for creating a new library of oral histories and encoded knowledge. By creating alliances with

Aboriginal groups, the hope is that the resurrection of culturally important knowledge, sacred songs, dance and stories could be utlised as a novel approach to reconnect cultural practice and identity for young Indigenous people. Many of these youths are between worlds, struggling to make sense of their own existence. Her hope is to support the development of an Indigenous university in the Northern Territory that will revive the practice of Walking Country, teaching young people their stories, sites and rituals, as they build up a mental map of Country, becoming more complex with age and initiation, layering content over rituals. When finally schooled in this way of knowing, they would then be able to recite and recollect all the relevant elements and key histories in their clans' past, as well as encoded knowledge of resources and lifesaving water sites within their landscapes.

In the last ten years, Jacinta has developed some innovative approaches to educating young people in the field of practical archaeology and cultural identity. She recognised early in her career that across the board, the education system does not recognise the Indigenous perspective as a valid knowledge base for environmental and social sciences. To assist with this approach, she has created programs to bring young disconnected people into spaces where they can explore their legacy knowledge and their relationship to their cultural connections and identity.

Jacinta's primary focus is creating a shift in the perception of cultural knowledge in the mainstream vernacular. The real achievement is the change of values that occurs when the wider community understands the strength of cultural practice in practical applications. One example is the development of youth crime initiatives, where judicial practice is modelled on the Elders Court, where the whole community are involved in the interventions and community sentencing of at-risk youth. This gains respect for cultural authority and long-term change from young recidivists. Jacinta has positive connections with Indigenous communities across North Queensland and the Northern Territory, and the agencies and judicial system, and is working towards the solutions that will give hope for the future.

She sees a future where Indigenous knowledge systems and western science can find a path forward, to keep the sacred knowledge of the song lines, and make them accessible for the next generation of story keepers, who will be imbued with a deep and resonate way of learning, described as a rich, complex and intricately related knowledge system. Jacinta wants us all to imagine a place where Aboriginal learning systems could be used to create new ways of understanding, by learning and valuing different approaches, together.

CANDICE MEISELS

Your choices make you a change-maker.

I grew up in South Africa. A country that is bittersweet; an oxymoron of a country showcasing extreme poverty and wealth living side by side. A beautiful country flooded with sunshine and warmth yet plagued by darkness and death.

My childhood was filled with shimmering summer rays and the comfort of family and friends. My brother and I frolicked in our huge garden. We ran barefoot on the sunburnt grass, skipped through the hedges that lined the property walls and enjoyed play equipment that belonged to our mother's home day care centre. Our mother spent hours baking, creating and planning our birthday parties, with home-made cakes courtesy of *The Australian Women's Weekly* (a skill that I did not inherit). My Sunday mornings were spent at various soccer fields across Johannesburg, watching our Dad coach soccer and my brother play.

We grew up behind high walls lined with barbed wire, spikes and electric fences, yet we were oblivious to the dangers lurking too close for comfort.

Around the age of five, I started to realise there were things and people to fear. I look at my fourth daughter sleeping soundly in her child-sized bed. She'll be five next year and I'm filled with pain to think of such a young child experiencing the type of fear many children born in South Africa are exposed to from such a young age.

I used to dread bedtime and would fall asleep with the light on. I would listen to my heart beating and feel my clammy palms as I heard gunshots and wondered how close they were.

My mother would try to alleviate my concerns by telling me not to worry and that the gunshots were from Alexandra, a township at least twenty minutes away.

I cannot imagine the anxiety of children and adults living in war-torn countries, or in countries still plagued with corruption, crime and violence of any kind. My heart aches for the children and adults who have to live life in these conditions.

Anxiety plagued my childhood, teen years and adult life, but I have been able to learn to embrace it.

Some of my anxiety turned out to be a blessing in disguise. Of course, I would rather have not experienced the sheer panic as a child or the panic attacks I had as an adult, but I have chosen to see it differently and realise that anxiety has helped create and ignite ambition and change deep within.

Anxiety forced me to persist, to dream; to choose to make change and be a change-maker.

I could have chosen to always feel trapped, caged in by worry and constant negative thoughts, but after therapy, acceptance and reading many books, I turned my anxiety on its head and decided to embrace it.

No, I cannot go back to those sleepless childhood nights where I slept with a light on, constantly making my parents call the police, or literally frozen in fear when the gunshots exploded into the dark of the night. I experienced genuine fear in those moments.

I have no memory of walking in on a burglary as a five-year-old when I went to play at a friend's house after preschool. That event has been blocked from my memory, but I do remember when my best friend saw a man with a machete standing by her window as a teenager.

At twenty-five, I finished working at Disney's London HQ in Hammersmith and headed to see a show with a friend in the West End of London. On my way home on the tube, in a bright, yet empty, train carriage, a man sat nearby. He looked at me strangely before lifting his shirt to remove a knife. My flight or fight response helped me to get off the train at Baker Street (a busy London Underground station) before I even thought about what I was doing. What he wanted I will never know as I got off the carriage, just in time before the doors closed.

Anxiety warns us when a moment may be dangerous. Sometimes the flight or fight response helps, and other times it hinders.

I now use what is left of my anxiety to push me to be the best version of myself.

I knew my dreams were too big for Johannesburg. I craved more and my anxiety helped me to make choices that led to where I am today.

I knew I wanted to work, study and immerse myself in marketing. I loved glossy magazines as a child, persuasive messaging and just knew my heart was meant to be in marketing and business.

In school I excelled, achieving excellent marks in english and business, which looking back now, confirms my life passion and path.

I studied an Honours in Business and Marketing with so much devotion I picked up extra subjects so I could finish a year earlier.

I had a zest for life and knew the choices I made would impact my future.

I worked for a video game company in an entry-level marketing role and was privileged to work with some of the world's best publishers and studios in the film and video game industry.

My boss, at the time, saw my work ethic and perseverance and asked me to head up the PR department. The only issue was, I really didn't know how.

I was offered an open door and decided to walk through it; I jumped through the door of opportunity. I taught myself how, and when I got stuck, I researched the solution. I was soon made PR manager and I was only in my early twenties. I travelled to the US, UK and Europe and my eyes widened to the world of opportunities ahead of me.

As it happens with life, just when things were going so well, I started feeling bloated and lost a huge amount of weight. Being a petite person, I looked unhealthy and extremely thin. I thought it was gluten intolerance, but it turned out to be Crohn's disease. I remember my mother being devastated. I knew this would be a defining moment in my life and I had the choice to accept this life-long condition or become a victim and let it rule my life.

I could choose to be a victim or I could choose the way I would react to the diagnosis. Would I let it change my life, or would I choose to adapt my life and accept Crohn's is now a small part of who I am?

I have been unwell on and off with Crohn's, and of course, I have to ensure I take my medication, eat foods that work for me and see my doctors when needed.

Can I tell you a secret? Often, I forget I have Crohn's because I refuse to live with a label.

Once I was on medication, following the right diet and seeing my doctor regularly, I learnt to adapt to my Crohn's. My career continued to soar and I worked at trade expos, flew to events overseas, took press trips and really loved life.

I did have some setbacks with Crohn's, developing a life-threatening fish allergy, but again chose to stop eating fish rather than dwell on it.

At twenty-four I met my soon-to-be husband in South Africa. He was sent to Africa from London, for a work project after starting a new job and his colleague's wife having her baby early.

He chose to dive in and take the opportunity even though it was a new position and he'd never visited South Africa before.

Our romance was a whirlwind and within three months his contract had ended.

We got engaged and I contacted entertainment companies I had relationships with in the UK. I flew in for interviews and secured a job as European Associate PR Manager at The Walt Disney Company, which meant I helped with strategy across Europe and reported to the US.

I moved to London within six weeks. When you know something is right and you are on your path, you just know. You just need to listen to your heart or gut.

The experience was incredible. I learnt so much from my few years in London but deep down I knew it wasn't home. Again, when you know, you know, and it's up to you to make change rather than wallow in your situation.

I had visited Australia as a teenager and travelled after school with a friend. I knew my heart was in Sydney, I just needed to get the rest of me there.

We had our first daughter, now eleven, and there was no way I could stay in the UK and cope with the sun setting at 3pm. I felt like the sky was dimmed and I needed the bright sunshine and outdoor life I grew up with in South Africa – minus the crime.

My husband got a job offer for a two-year role in Sydney and we grabbed it, packing and moving within six weeks. This was another time I knew we were following the right life path.

When opportunity knocks, only you know if it's right to leap into the unknown, even if your anxiety of the unknown follows you.

We have now been in Sydney for just over ten years. I worked as a freelance journalist and for some PR agencies before realising my purpose is to help startups and small- to medium-sized businesses share their stories.

I love empowering others to share their choices which make up their story. Your choices and your story unlocks something in those who are meant to hear it. Your story allows others to acknowledge, step up and show up for our world by owning their choices and their story.

We are all here to serve and to follow our 'why' and our story showcases the challenges and opportunities that have presented themselves to us.

I have now been doing what I do since 2013. Listening to others' choices and stories, encouraging them to share with the media and with their audience. I act as a channel between founders, CEOs and brands, and share their stories with the media.

Many people I have worked with, or who I have mentored or taught, are nervous to share their choices and their story.

I encourage you to get over your imposter syndrome because you are not an imposter. You are truly the only person who has walked in your shoes and taken one step or word at a time through your own story's pages. I implore you to be vulnerable and to share your story. You never know the mark your choices and your story will leave on someone else's heart and mind.

At a business conference a few years ago, I met a woman who shared her story with me. She didn't have any of her own biological kids but at the time she was fostering five children. She also ran a local business as the CEO. She had chosen to become a foster mum.

I was in awe of her story. I contacted a magazine and arranged an interview to help her share her story. I wanted to inspire others who wanted to foster, so they too could help children who needed a home and family. I didn't realise I would inspire myself and my husband at the same time.

We had four young biological daughters when we started our course, applications and assessments for fostering. A couple of months later, we were all set to move to Melbourne for a tree change when we got a call. A baby girl needed short-term care.

We had said 'no babies' as we had a premature baby at the time. We had only recently qualified as carers, and we didn't realise the call would come so soon or that it would be a baby.

We chose to stay and help the child as there was no other match for her in her specific situation.

I am pleased to say that after almost three years of fostering this beautiful soul who literally arrived in our lives overnight, we have adopted her and she is now our official daughter. She has always been our daughter and has taught us all that love is not biological.

The foster mum who shared her choice and her story that day, literally inspired us and helped us to save a life.

Your choice and your story may inspire someone to make a change that they have needed to make in their own life. Perhaps it will even save someone from bad decisions or from heartache. Perhaps by sharing your story you will empower another to make a positive difference to our community, our country or even the world. We all know this is needed now more than ever.

Perhaps by sharing your choice and your story you will unlock something within and discover your identity, your truth and your power.

Maybe by sharing your story, you will be able to seek support on your journey or set boundaries and say 'no' to things that no longer serve who you want to be.

Most importantly, and why I am standing here today, is to uplift you and to ask you to share your story because you just never know whose life you will save. Just like the lady who shared her choices and her story, ultimately saving my daughter's life.

I need you to carve out an hour in your busy schedule, in your day-to-day lives – right now. The sooner the better. Pick up a pen and paper if you prefer to handwrite or type on your phone or on a computer, and write your choices which have made up your story in six hundred to eight hundred words.

Read your story back to yourself. Be proud of what you have achieved and the setbacks you have overcome.

Now use your choices and your story and share it with everyone and anyone; your friends, family, colleagues and your community.

By sharing your story and the life choices you have made, either through necessity or through desire, you may just save a life.

You have a duty to share your choices and your story.

Your choices and story flicks a light on those meant to hear it. Sharing your story can spark change and connection. Your choices and story can help others change their life. Sharing your choices and your story makes you a change-maker and we all know that our world needs as many light-workers and change-makers as possible.

Own your choices. Share your story. Be a change-maker.

ABOUT CANDICE

Your choices make you a change-maker.

Candice Meisels, thirty-eight, is the mother of five daughters. She lives with her husband and a host of rescue pets in Sydney, Australia.

Candice was born in Johannesburg, South Africa. She lived with her parents and brother in South Africa.

Candice visited Australia twice as a teenager and deep down she knew Australia was home. She met her husband in Johannesburg when he was randomly sent there for work after starting a new job. The couple had a quick engagement (three months), which seems crazy now as they look back almost fourteen years later. Candice worked at Disney as Associate European PR Manager and at another company in Milton Keynes. She remembers falling pregnant and walking in the snow to commute ninety minutes back to her home in London. She always knew London was not home but she is grateful for her time there with her husband, his family and the people and friends she met.

Candice, Mike and their firstborn daughter arrived in Sydney in 2011.

They were embraced by extended family living in Sydney at the time, and Candice is grateful to all the people who opened their hearts and homes to her family when they immigrated.

When her daughter turned one, Candice started freelance work for PR agencies and the media to understand how the Australian media worked. She soon fell pregnant with her second daughter and took some time off to be with the girls before starting a PR consultancy in 2013 on a part-time basis. The business grew as Candice specialised in founders, startups and scale-ups. Most agencies would not look at these businesses or brands because they were deemed too small to be viable. Candice looked at them differently.

She looked at them with empathy, with love, with passion and with a thirst to help them succeed.

Since 2013, CANDICE PR has helped hundreds of businesses, people and brands in Australia and New Zealand.

Candice has also had two more biological daughters and adopted another daughter during this time.

Candice is authentic and genuinely tries to understand the 'why' behind the business, the founder and the business story, before connecting them to the right media channels and their customers.

She has always been an entrepreneur, with interests in a few businesses from the age of eighteen. She encourages people to start their own business and backs women to back themselves, and to realise they can create their own lives, success and freedom.

Candice loves sharing value and knowledge with others. She studied a Certificate IV in Training and Assessment and has been teaching marketing and PR for fourteen years.

She ensures she gives back when she can and often works pro bono for feel-good PR campaigns. Her life purpose is to always be kind, to love and to serve, but she is happy to be a game changer and break conventional rules and labels along the way.

Candice Meisels is a publicist, founder of CANDICE PR, author, speaker, foster care and adoption advocate, philanthropist, mentor and tertiary educator. She is grateful for every person, client and opportunity she has been blessed to experience in the life which she now calls her story.

Candice continues to run CANDICE PR and can be followed on social media or found at www.candicepr.com

JOSEPHINE LANCUBA

Music can evoke so many feelings and create a deep connection to one's self.

The song 'Memory' from the musical *Cats* was one that resonated with me. As a child, I found myself drawn to the torturous soul of a character called Grizabella, the glamorous cat who once lived a life of grandeur. In Grizabella's old age, she lost her glamour and was shunned by the other cats, abandoned and forgotten. This song brings me back to my childhood.

My father, who we called Papa, wavered in and out of Christianity. He was Christian when it suited him, pinning bible excerpts on the fridge one day, then telling us God didn't exist the next. He could be fanatical at times. Papa would go as far as forbidding me, and my two older sisters, from listening to certain music and bands, claiming them to be evil.

It was the nineties and the Red Hot Chili Peppers were all the rage. Papa said it was the devil's music.

Even as a kid, I knew that was absurd. I must have been seven or eight years old. It was just another day in our turbulent lives. My sisters, mum and I had become accustomed to the chaos that was our norm. I recall grabbing my sister's musical score of *Cats* one day from the piano stand in our sunroom. Excitedly I ran to the backyard where I could be alone with the music. The notes jumped off the page as I studied them, desperately wanting to understand them all. With sheet music in hand, I sat on the grass next to the melted pile of my sister's burnt CDs that Papa had torched the night before. In the molten mountain of plastic, there was my sister's new Red Hot Chili Peppers disc. Another one bites the dust.

I knew the musical tune 'Memory' from *Cats* because I heard my sister play it repeatedly on our home piano. I will never forget the bliss I felt in the backyard that day as I read the song lyrics and sang. I would sing 'Memory' over and over, soft at first, then louder and louder, until I cried. I understood that old cat Grizabella. She yearned to be loved. We may have walked different paths, but I felt deeply connected to the character. I was her and she was me. It was from that moment my love for music was born.

I discovered early on that I had the gift of singing. Not only did I enjoy it, but I was good at it! The funny part was that no-one in my family really knew it. My parents certainly didn't, as they were absent in every way. They were busy running businesses, running from each other and busy running around.

Secretly, I dreamed of becoming a singer. I wanted to share my voice with the world. That would become a reality for me with confidence and time. Without the support and guidance I needed from my parents, it took me a long time to find my path in life and to find my voice.

My older sisters tried to help me where they could, but it was never their responsibility to raise a child. They were children themselves, after all, trying to make their own way in life. No, that wasn't their burden to carry. I was on my own.

I didn't have all the answers, but I knew one thing for sure; I didn't want to end up alone like Grizabella! I didn't want anyone to end up like that, I only wanted to be happy and surrounded by happiness.

As a survivor of domestic violence and neglect, I was out of home at the young age of fourteen and had to make my own way in the world. It was tough. There were times I didn't have enough food to eat. I would beg for help at the local charity or visit a friend who would let me raid the pantry when their parents weren't looking.

As a teenager working minimum wage and putting myself through school, there were times I couldn't keep up with the rent. I was fortunate enough to have friends who would let me crash on their couch for a few days, weeks or months until I got back on my feet.

When I reached nineteen years old, I decided to put all my chips into an interstate move from New South Wales to Victoria to pursue my passion studying full-time dance and musical theatre at an arts college in Melbourne.

I worked double shifts in the months leading up to the move, waitressing for $10 an hour and taking any odd job I could, even for small change. I saved a humble $1000 and was proud as punch! *That will keep me going for a couple of weeks,* I thought, *until I find a job in my new city.* Excited, I told a family member about the money I had saved. Shortly after, they asked if they could borrow my $1000 with a promise to pay it back in full before I moved. Well … they didn't. I was broke and off on my own (again).

I arrived at my prearranged rented flat with only the clothes on my back, a suitcase and $70 to my name. As I made my way through the empty flat for the first time, I noticed a beanbag in the middle of the living room. Score! *Somewhere to sit,* I thought. I dumped my suitcase on the floor and sat on the lonely beanbag. I then took a deep breath, buried my head in my hands, and cried. How was I going to survive? I had no money, no job, no food and no support.

It was in my sorrows that I had an idea. After all, I do love a good solution. I would go to the casino and double my money! Now, I wasn't a gambler by any means, but at the time, my teenage brain told me this was my only shot at making it through the next couple of days.

As you can imagine, I lost the lot.

At the time, I believed I was a victim of my circumstances. I blamed the world for my shortfalls. I blamed my parents for not giving me the start I wanted in life. I blamed my employer for not giving me what I believed I deserved. I looked outwardly for the reasons why I felt deeply dissatisfied and blamed everyone else around me for my failures. I was angry with the world, and I was hurt.

I was in the trenches of my own existence with no way out. Those trenches were deep. I soon realised no-one was coming to save me. I had to save myself. There is power in knowing that. I had more to give and was ready to make a change.

Slowly through self-reflection and time, my wounds would lessen. I would claw my way out of the trenches and rise above them. Positive visualisation and affirmations helped me move forward, and I began to create a life by design, not by default.

Having worked as a teacher and mentor to young people and creatives for most of my adult life, I understand what drives others in similar fields to give everything you have to others. Generosity and care is an essential part of the job. It's in our DNA!

I ended up forgiving my family member for not paying me back, however, it did teach me some valuable lessons.

Firstly, don't put everything you have into the slot machines.

Secondly, don't loan more than you can afford to lose.

Thirdly, never loan money to family. You are better off giving it as a gift and letting it go to avoid resentment.

Finally, I needed to take action in changing my life.

Empowering myself would lead to more resources and knowledge to empower others. Though my journey was bumpy and one I would never wish upon my own children, I remain proud of what I have achieved. I went from begging for food vouchers, to building a creative empire.

When presented with the opportunity to be a part of this book, *The*

Women Changing the World, my initial thought was … *My story isn't one that matters, I'm not a doctor or saving lives.* After some thought, I asked myself, *How do I change the world?*

I realised that changing the world isn't always about making headlines or a big splash. Positively impacting others' lives can change the world. It can be gradual and subtle. It can be made through the actions we take each day. Everyday people like us can change the world by living a life of generosity. We do this every day with our children and loved ones. We do this each time we service a customer who wants what you have to offer them.

After a mindset shift, I have come to realise that obligation in life gives me purpose. I have an obligation to serve others; my family, my students, my industry, my customers and myself. It is not what I 'have' to do, but rather what I 'get' to do. When I made this shift in my mind, I was humbled by the fact that I live a life of obligation.

Aside from living in obligation, I have what I call Immutable Laws that I live by. I bring those laws to my business and ensure I share them with my team so we are all working together with the same core values. One of those six laws is 'give to give'.

Not long after I started the Musical Makers Club, a fourteen-year-old boy walked into my studio to join a theatrical program. Sam attended our city-based club location in Sydney and trialled for a scholarship placement. Memorable because he had black ripped jeans, peroxide blond hair flipped over to one side with a pink streak through it, he was openly exploring his sexuality and was looking for a place to belong.

During the trial class and after the vocal warm-up, each student was asked to get up and sing solo in front of the group if they felt comfortable enough to do so. When it came to Sam's turn, he didn't hesitate. He got up in front of a group of strangers and went for it. He was great! He needed some technical guidance, as most kids do, but his self-confidence and passion shined. I awarded Sam a place in our scholarship program where he joined our production group and would play the role of Prince

Charming. A little rough around the edges, the group embraced him regardless. This sense of nurture and community that existed within my studio walls was no accident.

I worked hard over several years to create a safe space for young people and artists to thrive. Inclusiveness is important to me, and the idea of it is embedded in my team, my members and my branding message. It is a core part of who we are.

After five months of rehearsal, it was finally showtime! This is the day everyone anticipates. It is filled with excitement and energy.

It's 10am, arrival time. The cast and crew were flooding through the theatre doors to begin preparations for the show. Sam didn't show up. My team was surprised by his absence on the biggest day of the season. He was the lead of the show and yet a 'no-show', which is virtually unheard of in the theatre world. My team was surprised but I wasn't. I had come to learn earlier that Sam came from a home of abuse and neglect, a story I was familiar with. You see, I was him and he was me. I had predicted his absence as a possibility because with sadness comes instability. I already knew his family were not coming to see the show. I offered the family complimentary tickets in the hope that may entice them, or at least rule out the possibility it was an affordability issue. Still they didn't claim their seats. One would think that even if they didn't come to see him perform, they would ensure he made it to the theatre? As it turns out, they would not.

We always have a contingency plan for absent lead characters in case of emergency, as the show must go on! We have understudies ready to step in as we are fortunate to have multiple club sites and casts, where children often play the same role for another cast and show date. As a last resort, we also have very talented performance coaches who will throw on a costume and step on stage if needed.

I didn't want to move to contingency plans that day. I wanted Sam to have his moment, the one he deserved. This was the moment he had dreamed of. The one he had worked towards and travelled to rehearse every week, by bus, on his own.

Perhaps it was a bad day at home and his mind was cloudy. Perhaps he was scared and had a little stage fright with no-one to support him and tell him it would be okay. No, I wasn't going to let his fear or negative circumstances win that day. He was going to perform.

After many unanswered phone calls to Sam's home and guardian's mobile, I realised he needed me. On the busiest day of our season, I jumped in my car and went to his house to get him. I was confident my team had it covered onsite, and I was on a mission. This was his moment to celebrate the achievements he had independently worked towards and I was not going to let him miss it. I was obligated to get him to the theatre and that deeper purpose propelled me into action.

Prince Charming shined brightly on stage that day. He didn't have anyone in the audience to support him but I knew he was proud he did it. I was proud of him too. I have learned over the years I cannot control the actions of others, but I can control how I engage the world around me. I can 'give to give'. I expect nothing in return. I make this decision consciously every day.

Another immutable law I live by is 'be bold, be brave'.

Throughout my life I have had to be brave to survive. However, it is in being bold where I truly thrived. I also see that in the students and industry professionals I mentor.

I spent years hiding my past and became a master at masking my true self. It wasn't until I let go of the shame I felt that I was able to build a connection with others at a deeper level.

Be bold and be brave, as that is where true magic happens.

I love that I get to bring the joy of music, performance and arts to the world. I am grateful I have the opportunity to inspire the next generation of artists and guide them to their dreams. I believe a smile you bring to a young person's face can last a lifetime.

Change is in the dreams we facilitate in those who look up to us. Change is in the moments we create and the memories we make for our children. It is in the decision to give ourselves openly to our community and the world around us. Change is in our conscious decision to be kind to others.

I believe everyone has the power to change the world, one person at a time, one moment at a time and one smile at a time.

ABOUT JOSEPHINE

From a young age, I had to make my own way in the world. I went from begging for food stamps to successfully running several businesses and living a life of passion.

After a whirlwind career as an artist that saw me perform on a multitude of stages and on TV screens for over a decade, it wasn't until I was four months pregnant with my first child that I decided to hang up my microphone. I have not looked back since. I happily became the mother bear of two cubs and began my journey into business.

Now, I am an award-winning entrepreneur, talent agent, industry mentor and theatrical producer who is passionate about facilitating the dreams of others. Most of these roles are delivered through being the creative director of my arts companies, Musical Makers Club (where we provide quality performing arts youth programs and experiences Australia-wide), and talent agency, Next Move Studios.

One moment I hold dear to my heart is when I won the gold AusMumpreneur Creative Arts Award in 2020. As it happened during

Sydney's first lockdown (due to the COVID-19 pandemic), the win was monumental in continuing to spread hope and positivity throughout my community, by showing that anything is possible. Since then I have been selected as an AusMumpreneur Awards Judge – another great honour.

Obsessed with levelling the playing field for all performing artists, I focus on nurturing emerging talent and providing them with the resources and opportunities to showcase their skills and passion. I strongly believe in the social, emotional and physical benefits of the performing arts. I am an advocate for creating inclusive and positive opportunities for talent, industry professionals and arts businesses. Some of this work is done through my alliance with Ausdance NSW, where I am a part of the standing committee.

My core mission is to create happy and fulfilled kids. I strive to provide safe spaces where every child can be a star. Stardom to me means more than financial gain and fame. Being a star in your own life is about discovering ways to personally shine. The true path to stardom is in finding your inner spark. Helping others to glisten is my life's work.

Never shy of a new challenge, I am launching Studio Talent Collective, where I will educate and mentor industry professionals and performing arts studio owners in developing their own in-house talent agency and management company. My goal is to help studio owners increase their revenue, student retention and industry credibility. In turn, this gives them the tools to effectively manage and grow their emerging artists and students, whilst providing their students with fulfilling experiences and professional creative careers.

Though these days I very much prefer to work behind the scenes, I still do the odd performance job and work as a TV host on TVSN, Australia's number one shopping channel. The occasional gig keeps me current on industry trends and gives me a deeper connection to the creatives I mentor.

Keeping busy, I host a podcast called *Business, Arts and All That Jazz.* This platform celebrates the creative community and discusses topics related to business and the arts, which may support and inspire others within the creative space.

Throughout the ebbs and flows of business, I have come to realise that persistence is my superpower. Today I remain dedicated to serving my students, members, team and community in living a life that nourishes the soul and sings to them.

www.josephinelancuba.com
www.musicalmakersclub.com.au
www.nextmovestudios.com.au

KAREN DENNETT

If you could send a message to sixteen-year-old you, what would you say?

It was 1991. I was sixteen and just shy of 5ft, in what I remember was a blizzard in Snowdonia, North Wales. We were walking back to the campsite. I was wearing my uncle's extra large heavy fishing suit, a waterproof onesie, and I think it might have been an older boy's army boots. The sharp wind was bitter and while the walk was not too far, to me it felt like a trek to the North Pole. My nose was running like a leaking tap and every now and again the wind would whip the snot across my face where it froze on my cheek.

I was hauling myself into the wind, cocooned in a gigantic fishing suit, and every time my blistered feet met the snow I sank to my knees. My peers all had well-fitted Gore-Tex coats, waterproof trousers, thermal vests and their own walking shoes; they were happy. laughing and loving it. I was frustrated my family had no money, I was cold, tired and miserable, and I got shouted at by Mr G because I asked for a tissue.

To make matters worse, when we finally reached the campsite, aka a farm field, our tents had collapsed under the snow and we had to move everything into the cowshed to sleep for the night. Everyone got out the hypothermia blankets they had in their emergency packs for extra warmth. My emergency pack had bandaids, my grandad's torch, and some Kendal Mint Cake. So, after a dinner of heated up Heinz tomato soup and custard cream biscuits, I climbed into my thin sleeping bag with no hypothermia blanket, still feeling the chill from the snow. I felt totally isolated while surrounded by friends. I felt stupid and embarrassed that I had to wear an oversized fishing suit, and believed I was inferior to everyone because I wasn't fit enough and didn't have the right equipment. I felt as if I was a drain on the group.

At this point, we were joined by some university students also caught in the snow. They filled the cold cowshed with rugby songs and laughter, which lifted my spirits, and I learned the power of singing and mindset. Even though my peers were already happy, I had been comparing myself to them and felt hard done by. This external group brought the fresh perspective I needed.

Air Cadets gave me some of my best, funniest, most challenging, frustrating, tearful, rewarding and memorable moments as a teenager. I truly believe it instilled the little bit of self-belief I needed to find purpose and direction. I met friends who were going to college and had plans. Up until that point I had no expectation, no direction and no purpose.

At the age of two, due to plenty of persistence from my mum, the doctors discovered my thyroid gland had stopped working when I was around four months old. Due to a significant amount of time without thyroxine at such a critical period of development, my growth would be significantly impacted, according to my medical notes.

Naturally my parents were devastated and even though I did catch up, I now know I had, and continue to have, ADHD, which wasn't a thing back then. To everyone I was clumsy; a pest, a chatterbox, a nuisance. I was impulsive, never managed to focus on schoolwork and always seemed to get into trouble. My reports read that I would do much better if I could just focus my energy on my work and try harder.

Other children and their parents thought I was a bad influence, so I was often lonely, sitting on the edge of friendship groups.

By the time I reached secondary school, my divorced parents were still completely absorbed in their own battles about the money neither of them had. My parents worked hard, and like many, the goal in life was to get a job to pay the bills, have a few nights out and pay for an annual holiday. My dad, though, was entrepreneurial and started a business, taking great pride in his work. He did well for a while, but after a risk to expand his business didn't pay off, he returned to employment and never tried again. The only thing my mum said she ever wanted was to get married, have children, a nice home and to be happy. That was okay for my mum, but I wanted more, and no-one really understood why.

I love my parents and it has taken over twenty-five years to understand they did their best with the resources they had at the time. I am grateful for all they did for me, and I know they are proud of me now. However, I grew up frustrated, as they didn't encourage me until I graduated from university, and were not really invested in my future, other than suggesting I get a job that paid enough to get by until I got married and had my own family.

When I joined Air Cadets, I had no direction or purpose, and no idea of my value. When I joined, it was a baptism of fire; I struggled with the walking and had no idea that half a Weetabix was not enough fuel to hike up a mountain in a day. I complained about how unfair everything was, and like many teenagers I struggled to fit in, but something started to change.

I had no idea how to shine my shoes, identify aeroplanes by their silhouettes or use a compass with a map, yet I achieved my Duke of Edinburgh Award to silver level. I walked Mount Snowden and completed a three-day group expedition in the Windemere wilderness. I played the cymbals and the drums in the band for the Bristol Carnival, marching in many Remembrance Day parades. My ambition grew, and I gained a place in college with my friends from cadets, and I made friends for life.

Through Cadets, my self-belief increased, and as it grew, so did my courage to try new things. As I tried new things, my ability and skills increased, and I started to achieve. As I achieved, my self-belief increased, and my aspirations rose. A self-perpetuating circle!

You see, school and learning in a classroom, being tested for subjects, half of which I had no choice to learn, like biology, did not prepare me for my future. The system did not help me to achieve. In fact, failing in compulsory subjects that I found difficult and of no interest decreased my ability, confidence and desire to strive. I cannot recall a single careers discussion at school and although I had an incredible english teacher, who ignited a passion for creativity and writing by giving us fun and varied projects, it was my self-belief that helped me to engage in english and try my best.

My most important learning experience at school came when we were told our year group would not have a leaving party. Despite complaints from others, I took on the challenge of organising the leavers disco alone. I arranged the DJ, the venue, sold the tickets, arranged for teacher support and the event was a success. It was my confidence from my experiences at Cadets and seeing my dad's entrepreneurial journey that enabled me to take on the challenge.

At eighteen, my increasing courage led to organising my own work experience at the local newspaper and radio station, where I discovered a love for marketing, and wrote articles that were published in my local paper. As a result, I successfully applied for a place at university on a marketing degree.

I made friends for life at college, and we have continued to grow together through marriage, children and everything in-between. Then, at university, I found my tribe; the amazing Bournemouth University women's football team, my extended family, who along with my friends from college, have encouraged, supported and shared the laughter and tears for the past twenty-five-plus years. It was at university where I met my now-husband Wayne, and where our journey began back in 1995.

Even though I had increased my confidence and courage in my own abilities, and achieved success, low expectations and limited guidance or support instilled a strong desire to prove myself. For a long time I felt I was an outsider and not worthy. I felt lucky to have my friends and did not want to ask anyone for help because I didn't think they would be interested. I worked hard to overcome my challenges, often with two part-time jobs and vacation work, supporting myself through university. I made things happen, but I often took everything upon myself.

Fast forward fourteen years, a degree, a marketing job, and at the time, my first two children. I decided to become a teacher because I wanted to be accountable and teach high school business and enterprise.

I planned to be the best teacher ever!

I realised several things when I started teaching. Firstly, teaching is NOT a lifestyle choice; it drains your time, and you never switch off. I worked hard to build a good rapport with students and always felt the need to prove myself by working hard. After a shaky start where I misinterpreted the assessment criteria and was put on a stake and burned by parents, I endeavoured to become an effective teacher and worked to build understanding relationships with my students.

Wanting to give my students a better experience than I had, I strived to plan learning that was real, and create opportunities for students to achieve and see their value. I organised excursions to apply their business knowledge and created our school version of *The Apprentice,* as well as many other hands-on enterprise tasks. I was involved in initiatives that connected students with industry, and saw firsthand the impact industry activities and events had on finding purpose and direction. For many students, these activities resulted in increased self-worth, leading to increased engagement and raised aspirations.

I went out of my way to create moments which lasted in my students' memories for years to come. I could clearly see the difference when young people trusted the teacher to guide them and felt acknowledged and supported. Knowing the teacher truly cared about their success gave young people a stronger sense of pride, self-belief and a greater willingness to try.

Over the past ten years, I have witnessed students who struggle to engage with the written assessment structure. The focus on achievement of grades has led many to flounder and lose themselves. Funny, smart, kind and creative individuals can lose their spark as they struggle to perform in standardised tests, believing their worth is defined by a grade, when in fact, the grade simply reflects the performance on a particular test or series of assessments, on a particular day or timeframe.

The effort one student might put in for an A grade, might be the same level of effort required for another student to achieve a C or a D grade, and yet the comparison across grades minimises the celebration of the D. The perception that lower grades on standardised assessments indicates a general lack of ability and/or effort is detrimental to the mindset and capacity to achieve for our future generations.

The language used such as 'dropping down' from an academic pathway or 'dropping out' to go to college, suggest a different pathway as somewhat inferior rather than simply a different pathway. This demonstrates an elitism and promotes feelings of inferiority. How can we possibly expect young people to make decisions about their direction when they feel they are not good enough? The high achieving students often experience anxiety too, feeling the need to study hard to maintain their academic performance, at the sacrifice of other learning experiences.

When we hold achieving grades above all other endeavours, we only give credit to a limited set of skills and do not allow others to recognise, celebrate or build upon the talents and skills that make them shine. Even worse, when we hold teachers accountable and measure their performance against the academic achievement of all students, we minimise the impact teachers can have on preparing young people for the future. Instead, teachers begin teaching to assessment and not facilitating the ability to learn and build life skills.

I left teaching because I did not want to teach to assessment. I realised that as one teacher in one school, I could not create the change I wanted to see. If I was going to connect, engage and raise aspirations I had to step back and create wider opportunities to enrich the system, not be a part of it.

Five years ago, I nervously walked across town after a day of teaching, to my first networking event, where I met an amazing woman, who not only agreed to host my first student business conference at Murdoch University, but also supported and shared my journey to build a like-minded tribe of professionals willing to share their work and insights to guide the next generation.

The past five years have been extremely challenging. I have learned, pivoted, wondered why everything must be so hard, and felt isolated and alone with a burning need to justify my goals and direction to my family. As a solo female founder, I have had to juggle home and business, and at times, teaching. In a FIFO household, I had the responsibility of everything on my shoulders, while absorbing the criticism and frustration for my increased busy-ness and struggles with fitting it all in.

I love my children very much, and have worked hard to be the best mum I can be, however, as an entrepreneur mum, I have been judged for being late, having a messy house and always finding out about school activities the night before from Facebook. As women we are judged more for our 'performance' at home. At times the cognitive and emotional pressure of thinking about everything that needs to be done, along with the worry and emotional guilt of wanting to be and do more for everyone, is exhausting and self-care has been a challenge.

I am now the director of a growing education company that solves problems creatively and meaningfully, in a way that benefits everyone involved, with interactions and experiences that make a difference and create a lasting impact to the professionals, the educators and the students. I now have the challenge of taking these amazing programs and resources across Australia to begin engaging, sowing seeds and building mindsets full of possibilities.

I am in a position where I can learn from my own children and effect change for others through my programs. My own teenagers have shaped my understanding of the changing environments young people face today, and have enabled me to be mindful of their journey while creating meaningful impact. My life challenges have kept me grounded and authentic, remaining true to my vision.

I have discovered a way to invest my strengths to bring change and fulfil my purpose. I recognise where I need support and with ADHD this includes organisation, structure and execution. I understand that lacking in these abilities does not make me inferior or incompetent, it just means I need to seek those with skills to complement my strengths. I don't need to judge myself harshly for where I lack, as there are those out there who do this quite well for me! I have learned when I take my focus away from negative influences and put my energies where they need to be, my world starts to change for the better.

If I could speak with sixteen-year-old me, I would tell her she is enough. That her feelings of inferiority reside within her. That her insecurities are a result of imposter syndrome, and she is not alone in this feeling. I would tell her she is only defined by, and held back by, the limitations she chooses to accept. She holds the power to create and access the resources she needs to achieve her goals and she does not have to do this alone. I would advise her to give without sacrificing herself, and to take good care of and respect herself, in order to attract care and respect from others.

I would share the importance of mindset for financial security, to step up and lead with courage, to understand our differences and how we all bring value. I would encourage her to always listen actively and be open to the guidance and advice of others. I can't go back to my sixteen-year-old self, but I can pay it forward, to be the difference for our next generation of teens.

We cannot change the system, but we can enrich it and make the learning experience better for all students. To collaborate with educators and create opportunities that do not add to their workload and create extra pressure, but to add value and support.

The change I want to see in the world is where every young person can recognise they possess talents and strengths to bring value to the world, despite the challenges and restrictions they face. For them to have the opportunity to apply these talents and strengths, and go on to achieve and shine.

I believe this is a shared endeavour; I cannot do this alone. I am committed to collaborating with industry, educators and individuals who want to invest a little time and resources so our young people can take on and inherit the world with courage, tenacity and be the difference.

ABOUT KAREN

I'm a creative problem solver from the United Kingdom, who immigrated to Western Australia in 2015 to give my children an adventure, greater opportunities and the joy of living by the ocean.

I believe my purpose is to combine my creativity, problem-solving and ability to bring people together, to empower educators to enrich learning and create opportunities for young people to discover and harness their value, while building a possibilities mindset.

I do this as founder and director of Engaging Education: a company borne from witnessing the power of connection. A business recognising that seeds can be planted, horizons broadened and aspirations raised, when young people connect with and learn directly from industry professionals with meaningful learning experiences.

We are cultivating a tribe of dedicated professionals, passionate about guiding the next generation to develop one-of-a-kind programs that will make an impact.

When I realised the small impact I was making as 'just a teacher' could be amplified if I dedicated my time to connecting, engaging and inspiring students and teachers, I took the leap of starting my own business, determined to 'enrich' the system.

While continuing to work full-time as a high school business and enterprise teacher, I began building my professional network and organised student conferences and professional development workshops for teachers. With firsthand experience of the gaps, I set about creating memorable experiences which delighted attendees with insightful and interactive sessions, resources they can use again, and moments that sparked an 'I can do that' attitude.

I stepped out of the system to dedicate my time to encourage both educators and young people to build confidence, courage and a belief in themselves.

My workshops and programs include:

- Offering opportunities for vocational trainers and assessors with case studies, to prepare students for the workplace with professional discussions, and a different perspective to think critically.
- Building coaching skills and social, emotional and cultural intelligence in high school teachers to facilitate meaningful discussion and inquiry, in order to strengthen relationships and increase engagement.
- Introducing high school students to think critically about solutions to the life challenges they face and explore how these challenges play out in their world. With the guidance of a TEDx speaker coach, they learn how to find their story and deliver their perspective of what it means to make a difference with impact.
- Preparing girls aged sixteen to eighteen to be thoughtful, courageous, problem-solving leaders, ready to make a valuable contribution both now and in the future. Learning from experts, group coaching, professional mentoring and through the real experience of creating their own social enterprise projects.

Through fifteen-plus years of teaching experience, I have been dedicated to creating stand-out moments that make a difference and bring learning to life. These moments included excursions from theme parks to a call centre, from IKEA to market research at the local high street.

I passionately believe students should learn from experiences that give meaning and purpose to theory and teachers should always 'practice what we preach'. I have found myself doing press-ups with students on an army experience to demonstrate the value of teamwork, putting up tents at surf camp and preparing our in-house 'Alan Sugar' to fire candidates in our own version of *The Apprentice!*

In 1997, I was full of ideas, played football and was sociable; looking forward to taking on my first marketing role after graduating. I continued to work in marketing and communications for ten years until I began teacher training.

Fast forward twenty-four years and I now have the dream role of combining all my skills to guide the next generation and be the difference.

Connect with me on Linked In or email me:
karen@engagingeducation.com.au

EMMA ALLEN

Are we given a 'fair go' if we are born female or born into poverty?

'Meet me down in the lobby, I have a surprise for you.' I had been working with Samantha for a couple of years then. She was the incredibly passionate Global Village Housing (GVH) operations manager from Brisbane. Sam had been encouraging me to make the trip to see the houses I had sponsored and meet the families whose lives I had changed. It was my first day in Siem Reap, Cambodia.

Sokha, our trusty tuktuk driver who doubled as our interpreter, was waiting at the entrance of our hotel. We putted along the dusty laneways, then eventually along the main street near where the temple tickets were sold. He took a sharp turn. To get across a little canal, we had to jump out of the tuktuk and walk while Sokha navigated across a precarious dirt mound. Back onboard, we swayed and rocked along a narrow track venturing further and further out into tall fields of grass.

Then I saw it. Over to the right was a bright blue house on stilts; it was so familiar and recognisable. The tears started rolling, and I couldn't believe I was there. When we pulled up, the mother embraced us with a warm hug as if we were long-lost friends. She has two sons aged nine and seven years old, and a little three-year-old daughter, Pimm, who stole my heart. They are one of the few fortunate families with a small parcel of land, running water and some chooks. She showed us their old decrepit house which was now the kitchen, and the wonderfully strong and safe GVH house stood tall, with the Active Property Investing logo as proud sponsors.

This was one of the first houses we built with GVH, and the family greet us with big smiles every time we visit Siem Reap. We had just made lifelong friends.

* * *

My family migrated to Australia when I was just two years old and my parents worked tirelessly to build a successful business and a stable life for us. Every Christmas, Mum would buy beautifully painted Christmas cards which I remember admiring. On the back would be a photo of the artist. Some were deaf or blind, and others without limbs. I was amazed at how a person without hands could paint with their feet or by using their mouth to hold the brush. It was the beginning of my understanding that even without the things *you think* you need, you can still live a fulfilling life. Mum is the epitome of kindness and generosity. She saw a lot of injustice growing up, so she is socially aware and conscious of the welfare of others. Her mantra is that no matter how big or small, 'if I can help, I will', and that is how I live my life today.

Kindness is simple. It is showing that you have considered another person.

It makes someone feel valued. How powerful is that?

Kindness, even if for a fleeting moment in time, can change the world for one person. We can also take a cause we are passionate about and propel it forward by giving our time, skills and talents to create a multiplying effect of our actions.

A dear friend once told me that 'fair' does not mean everyone gets an equal share, it means everyone gets what they need, and she's right.

If we recognise we are a part of something bigger than ourselves, we may be compelled to create the change that breaks stereotypes, giving people a fighting chance or simply providing a basic human need of safety and security. When we are consciously aware of what needs to change, we just need to care enough to do something about it.

I am a ridiculously busy mother of two energetic kids, whilst running a successful property business which I created to bring a positive change to the industry. I have many causes close to my heart, but rather than trying to recreate the wheel, I believe there are people already driving change in causes that matter to you. These people are what I call the 'multipliers'. I know that if I invest my time, energy, sponsorship funds, skills or that of my team, it has a multiplying effect to reach and impact an even greater number of people.

Even in the face of sadness and adversity, there are many individuals willing to empower and give others a 'fair go'.

It's a girl

The sonographer announced with a smile, 'It's a girl.'

My husband beamed with pride, 'I've always wanted a girl!' An unexpected thought ran through my head. *Why do I feel immense pressure to protect her? How am I going to prepare her for a world that treats women differently?*

I was over the moon to have a daughter growing in my belly, but I had to fight my own prejudice. I sought advice from my mum who simply said, 'show her' and so I did.

I let my daughter see every strength and vulnerability of being a woman. How to be kind yet strong, to share your ideas, be creative and determined. I showed her how to run your own race, build a successful business, and collaborate with others whilst standing your ground. I surrounded her with strong female role models; her godmothers and mentors. She was even gifted my mother's name so she can inherit some of that *fire* that made me a force to be reckoned with.

Across our three generations, there has been significant change in the way women are viewed and respected in society and my daughter's generation has a strong sense of social consciousness. They are growing up in the digital age where information moves at the speed of light, and social pressures, pornography and ridiculous expectations are part of their everyday.

It makes young girls and women susceptible to sexual assault, violence and abuse. How does a society so advanced think it is giving our girls a 'fair go' when they are told 'not be rude', or 'if a boy is mean he likes you'? Girls put up with constant harassment only to find themselves in dangerous life-damaging situations.

Enough is enough. It is time to fight back. Literally.

A few years ago, I met and became friends with an incredible sensei and founder of Philotimo Jujitsu. Rose has dedicated her life to empowering girls, not just with self-defence combat skills, but the mental strength and ability to be modern warriors and win the war against bullying and domestic violence. She bears the weight of just how unfair life can be for girls from different social, cultural, religious and economic backgrounds.

I started jujitsu to be able to defend my family, to fight off the bad guy if we were ever in danger. Now, if someone threatened me, I would just break their arm. It sounds violent, but so is rape. It is not a glamourous cause to promote or seek support for; in fact, it is one of the uncomfortable truths that much of society turns a blind eye to, though hopefully not for much longer.

Even more unique is a predominantly female dojo, led mostly by inspiring female senseis, who are empowering hundreds to change their world. My daughter is surrounded by mentors of all ages in an environment promoting self-respect, discipline and compassion alongside elite athleticism. Sensei Rose Smith is a 'multiplier', and we need to support women like her in our communities, to change the narrative and give women a 'fair go' in defending themselves and thriving.

Born without a birth certificate

Most mothers in rural Cambodia have never been inside a hospital. Their children were born into poverty, with no clean sheets and no birth certificate. A 'fair go' on this turf would be having access to life's necessities like water, sanitation and a safe place to call home. Unfortunately, this is not the case. They lack infrastructure and must deal with corruption, and resources which are so scarce, ordinary charities can't even reach remote villages in dire need of help. Cambodia's history of genocide and turmoil has left the country as one of the poorest in the world. Jason Thatcher was an Australian living in Cambodia. After seeing the poverty and dire living standards, Jason designed a steel-framed house using local materials that can be erected in a day, gifting a life-changing home, safety and security. Global Village Housing (GVH) was born out of Australian ingenuity to empower Cambodians to help each other in a way that is socially, culturally and environmentally conscious. He found a way to reach the most remote and vulnerable communities. GVH employs a team of locals, providing them with valuable skills and tools to prefabricate the homes, which are delivered by truck and built onsite for an unsuspecting, albeit pre-qualified family. To the disbelief of these families, they have been gifted a home to keep, with no debt. For the first time in their lives, they have a front door, and they can sleep without fear of it collapsing. GVH homes sit high on stilts to keep dry from the wet season flooding and are well ventilated and fitted with solar panels to provide light at night. Just like that, their world has changed.

A conversation with Sam in late 2016 sparked a new vision. She had identified a school in a village where GVH was gifting homes that was in desperate need of fixing. With this newly identified need, I saw an opportunity to not only fundraise, but to bring together our generous community in Australia and create awareness of GVH and their important work. I co-founded Houses4Cambodia with three friends to build a community that could follow our journey from inception to delivery.

The response was overwhelming; our fundraising dinner sold out and exceeded all expectations, raising three times the amount of money we were aiming for.

As word spread across the village and materials started arriving onsite, what started out as sixty children enrolled, grew to 180 by the time it was built. We travelled to Battambang as team Houses4Cambodia and purchased the schoolbags, shoes, uniforms, hats and resources. We spent valuable time playing with the children, gifting bikes and getting to know the community. I remember watching them arrive at school the next morning proud as punch to be wearing their new uniforms. For most of them, this was the first time they had received anything brand new. Everything we set out to achieve was now being delivered and it was evidently life-changing.

Education is the key to giving these kids a 'fair go' to pave their way out of poverty.

It's especially important for girls. They are less likely to complete their primary education as they are usually relied upon to look after younger siblings. I'm talking about girls as young as seven looking after toddlers at home alone whilst parents work. If they are lucky enough to go to school, the dropout rate is high by the time they start menstruating, as there are no toilets or means of managing their periods.

For this reason, the school project encompassed building separate boys' and girls' toilet blocks. Toilets are more than just sanitation in a house or community. Imagine being a young girl needing to go out into the dark – it leaves them vulnerable to unimaginable things. GVH is determined to build more toilets within the houses so kids can go privately and safely.

Water is a basic human need, yet children as young as five years old walk kilometres to get to school with no food or water. The water well we built for the school is the centre for community health and wellbeing, as is the playground. I'm sure you can imagine the look of joy when a child rides a swing for the first time. By the end of the first year, a further sixty children had enrolled and classes were overflowing. It clearly shows that when given the opportunity, Cambodian children want to learn and be at school.

With the success of the first school, we took on the next school project. This time the location was only accessible by tractor, so it was more difficult and costly to build. Roads had to be built to access the area. The Tractor School was a project funded by the collaboration of five GVH global partners, one of which was my business, Active Property Investing (API) in Sydney, Australia.

The opening of The Tractor School became a major event, with the governor and key officials of the region in attendance. This time I was accompanied by my then ten-year-old daughter, who had fundraised throughout the year with two friends. It was incredible to share this part of the journey so she could experience Cambodia at this grass roots level for herself. Our friend Sam was awarded a medal in recognition of her work and GVH's contribution to the region. A well-deserved honour for Sam as she has successfully empowered Cambodian women with new skills and established microbusinesses like The Sewing Sisters in Battambang and Liza the Label in Phnom Penh.

We love visiting The Sewing Sisters. They are a GVH house recipient, and one of them is severely disabled, having no way of earning income until Sam taught them how to sew. She bought them machines and fabric and helped them to start a sewing business, which to this day, creates beautiful garments and bags sold in Australia. When you empower a woman, whole communities will flourish, and this is the case for their little village of women and children. On our last visit, they were trialling a sanitary pad design; another important project for the liberation of girls.

As humble as they are, Jason Thatcher and Samantha Townend are multipliers changing the lives of thousands of people with their ingenuity and dedication. I could not be prouder to be associated with their work, as they too believe that everyone deserves a 'fair go'.

Where to from here?

As much as I would like to think we are all born equal, the world is not 'fair' in its distribution of challenges and hardship. Life is indeed what we make of it, but some of us have a head start while others have more hurdles to overcome.

In any case, there are choices to be made.

If we can see what needs to change, we just need to care enough to do something about it. We can all turn a blind eye to the suffering happening around us or be courageous enough to speak up, spread a little kindness, or lead a movement with your time and talents to give someone less fortunate a 'fair go'.

For the people I call 'multipliers', you inspire me every day. I am grateful to have formed these friendships and also proud to say our collaborations are powerful.

If you are passionate about a cause, you don't need to recreate the wheel. Consider looking for people who are already trying to get the work done and gift your time, effort, money and talent to propel them forward. Leverage your skills and use your leadership to bring people together. Connect those who *need* help with the ones who *can* help. From this, your investment is multiplied and magnified to change the lives of many more people.

Since the pandemic, our Houses4Cambodia team has been unable to travel to check in on the families, schools and villages we have been supporting. Even from afar, we continue to help through GVH and Sam's network. My business, Active Property Investing, proudly co-sponsored GVH's 400th house, an outstanding milestone for this Australian grassroots social enterprise.

Remember the family at the start of my story? I was deeply saddened to hear that Pimm's mother passed away. She was a wonderfully happy woman who hugged us like old friends. Without her mother, Pimm is likely to be left at home alone as her brothers go to school and her father works to earn some income. I think about her all the time. I'm scared for her safety and wellbeing. She is a girl, born into poverty, vulnerable and naive, but it is still possible to empower her.

There is so much that needs to be done to give more people a 'fair go' and the simplest of human rights, safety, security, education and the ability to thrive.

ABOUT EMMA

As an award-winning entrepreneur and mother of two, I have shaped my career around helping individuals and businesses 'thrive'. I'm inspired to help people do things they didn't think was possible, and driven to help teams reach higher levels of performance, trust and business success.

I've had a long and successful career in corporate, carving my way through male-dominated industries and outperforming people twice my age. Interestingly, when I was ready to settle down and buy a home, I couldn't afford to a buy a house in the suburb I grew up in. This sparked a curiosity in me around property ownership and investing, which burst into a passion for financial literacy.

After the birth of my daughter, I left a multi-national corporation to follow my new-found passion into the property industry. A few years later and pregnant with my son, I decided to pursue my vision and established Active Property Investing (API) to help everyday Australians access information and support to successfully invest in property. My vision was to flip the script and make it a fun and empowering journey.

I had proudly woven together my previous skills and experience, creating a brand that aligned with my ethics, and delivering a high quality of service that would set us apart as a business. I created a unique culture at API where it is normal to learn, share and be transparent, and with that, our clients can make well-informed decisions. Our success is based on optimising the success of our team, clients, business partners and everyone around us.

We won the coveted Service Excellence WSABE Award for Western Sydney in 2020, a challenging year for many, and was dubbed one of 'The top fifteen Australian property experts to watch in 2021' by *The Australian Business Journal.* We have an incredible team who are proud of our brand, and continue to thrive even in the face of adversity.

The business has given me greater leverage to positively impact causes closest to my heart. I have taken my passion for empowering people beyond the boardroom and into the poorest villages of rural Cambodia, building houses, toilets, water wells and schools that will give generations a chance to grow out of poverty.

I am a bestselling author and philanthropist because I believe in the 'multiplying affect' of my actions. I invest in people; from everyone around me in the API business, to propelling those I call 'multipliers' who, with greater reach, are changing the lives of many.

My proudest achievements are the houses I have built with Global Village Housing (GVH) in Cambodia. I'm as dedicated to empowering families, especially women and girls, in war-torn countries, as I am in Australia. I'm a strong supporter of the Striking Distance Project at Philotimo Jujitsu, empowering women and girls to beat bullying and domestic violence.

As much as I would like to think we are all born equal, the world is not 'fair' in its distribution of challenges and hardship, but there are plenty of people who can spread a little kindness and create new opportunities, even in the smallest way.

It is along this path that I have met some of the most incredible people and made lifelong friends. Many have contributed to my personal and professional success, so I have a responsibility to ensure I invest in the success of others. 'If I get behind and support the people who empower others, this is the multiplying affect magnified.'

Website: www.activepropertyinvesting.com.au
Facebook: www.facebook.com/activepropertyinvesting
Instagram: www.instagram.com/activepropertyinvesting

Facebook: www.facebook.com/houses4cambodia
Instagram: www.instagram.com/houses4cambodia
Global Village Housing (GVH): www.globalvillagehousing.com
Samantha Townend – The Sewing Sisters Project & Liza the Label: www.samanthatownend.com
Philotimo Jujitsu: www.philotimojujitsu.com

YONA SIGNO

Our life experiences expand our perception of ourselves and the world.

Memories play a significant part in who I am, so I shall start by sharing my memories with you …

I was born in the Philippines and have many fond memories of living there. I remember my grandparents (Lolo and Lolas – Filipino for grandpa and grandma) who we visited often as they lived on the same property in the main house. I remember a fun birthday celebration, sharing a table full of cupcakes with my kindergarten class. On each cupcake was a letter, and together they read, 'Happy Birthday Yona'. I loved eating my favourite spaghetti from one of the leading fast food chains. My parents told me we would take that spaghetti with us even when we ate at other restaurants because it was the only food I would eat. I even remember seeing my dad in uniform for the first time. I learnt later in life that he served as an officer in the Philippine Constabulary. I have many fun memories.

On the other hand, I also have memories that have shaped who I am today. I remember the passing of my grandma (my Lola on my mum's side); an event that rocked our family. We were so close to her and I know she has greatly influenced who I am today because of the bond she had with my mum, whom I am very connected to. Another moment I remember vividly is lying in bed with my brother and mum as she prayed the rosary fervently, while helicopters flew over the house and there was gunfire in the distance. Years later, I found out it was during the time of a coup d'état in the Philippines. It was just a couple of years later when my mum, brother and I were on board a flying kangaroo (the national carrier of Australia) migrating to Australia. My dad was left behind in the Philippines to tie up loose ends before he too bid his military life farewell and hopped on a plane to join us in our new life in our new country.

Fast forward a year later, and it was the passing of my other grandma who spent her last years battling Alzheimer's disease and dementia. My parents brought my grandpa (my Lolo) to live with us in Australia. By then, he was my only living grandparent and he spent many wonderful years with us before he returned to live in the Phillipines. He would walk me to and from school, in his nice trousers and flannel shirt.

Years later I remember the excitement my family felt as we planned our overseas holiday, travelling back to the Philippines for the first time since we migrated to Australia. I was so excited because it was the first time we were going to see my grandpa, then ninety-two years old, since he had stayed with us in Sydney years before. But the excitement turned to heartbreak. The day we landed in Manila, the day before we were to see my grandfather, he was called by the angels and joined my grandmother in heaven. We had planned to spend Christmas and New Year with him, but as it turned out, we were there so my dad, who is the eldest son, was able to organise the beautiful funeral my grandpa deserved. Whilst it wasn't the holiday we envisioned, I was able to experience the beauty of my dad's province and felt the warmth of relatives who I met for the first time. Spending more than a month in the Philippines, which can only be described as an emotional roller-coaster, it was really a time when I was reintroduced to my heritage; one that is centred around family, food and emotion. This was a defining moment in my life as I felt a strong connection to my roots, and because of that, I began to travel to the Philippines as often as I could. I didn't realise at the time, but it was only the beginning of a powerful connection to my country of birth.

I am proud I was born in the Philippines and also feel blessed to be raised in Australia. Undoubtedly, both countries have greatly influenced who I am today.

Over the last ten years, I have been able to travel to many destinations with my husband, and even relocated to Asia for some time, due to my husband's work. We started our journey as first-time parents experiencing pregnancy while overseas, and returned home to Australia to give birth to our firstborn. We had the opportunity to live in the Philippines with our little family and even travel around Asia.

As my husband and I recollect our travel adventures, we are grateful we had the chance to travel as much as we did prior to starting a family, as travelling is definitely an experience that fills you with adventure, wonder and priceless memories. We decided to return to Australia with our almost-one-year-old to be closer to our family. And that year was one that was pivotal to where I am today. I had to decide between staying in the corporate world and starting my own business so I could work from home and have the flexibility to be a mum to our daughter. I looked back on my experiences for inspiration.

I have always had the desire to help people and be of service to others and my work experience in information technology in the education sector prepared me for the next chapter of my career.

Will my background in IT help me in this business? I wondered. I wasn't sure then – but I was excited at the thought of having the opportunity to be of service in a different way. I didn't have a business background but I had years of business analysis, project management and service management experience. The only way to know if it would work was to start.

When the time came for me and my husband to seriously look at business opportunities, we studied global trends and virtual assistance was the one that caught our attention.

As our business steadily grew, it occurred to me that there were only a small number of businesses that I could help *on my own* as a virtual assistant. I had to decide whether I would be happy helping the handful of clients I had or whether I could help more business owners in Australia pursue their passion. I decided on the latter, which meant I needed a team. After some research and conversations with local business owners, I received feedback regarding affordable staffing solutions.

As we had recently lived in the Philippines, I knew how skilled, dedicated and eager the people were. I was now faced with the opportunity to show the strengths of the two countries I loved dearly. I was excited about the possibilities.

Was this my chance to extend my purpose to serve with my heart and live out my *why*? Could I empower and support people who are passionate about helping others so they can be their best self and positively influence their family while also making a positive impact to communities both locally and globally?

We named our company Kaya Services after the Filipino word *kaya,* which means capable and 'yes, I can'. It was the perfect word to sum up the best qualities Filipinos are known for around the world. Kaya enabled us to marry our roots and live out our mission: Help entrepreneurs in Australia and beyond find feasible solutions for their growing business while giving Filipinos a more flexible alternative to the usual nine to five job.

The experience has taught me that purpose anchors and aligns your actions. Seemingly tough decisions and risks become easier to navigate when you remember to look into your heart.

At that point, we knew we would need a recruitment agency to make the process of hiring Filipino virtual workers more organised and professional. I've heard a few stories where Filipinos have been treated poorly by their agencies and companies so I was determined to showcase their talent in an environment that is supportive and nurturing from the moment they apply.

We initially established Empowered Virtual Services as our recruitment agency to serve as the platform for reaching out to Filipinos based in Manila. Founded on the same values as Kaya Services, which are empowerment, fairness and genuine service, we went to work straight away and spent a full week in the Philippines doing non-stop interviews. I had so much Starbucks coffee that week it felt like it would come out of my arms if you squeezed them! It was during that week we officially hired our first employee; a milestone for startup entrepreneurs like us, and just in time for a new project. Empowered Virtual Services has evolved so much since then.

Working virtually has been my way of life since I became a mum. I love that it allows me to spend time with my family while I serve our clients and community. When the COVID-19 pandemic started, I had to rediscover how my business would work for me and my team. I was most concerned about how my team was adjusting to the new normal, particularly those based in Manila because of the harsher lockdown measures. There was so much fear and negativity, and it made me realise the importance of having the right mindset, especially during times of great uncertainty. I began asking the question: 'What if there were a school that taught virtual assistants the right mindset?'

Mindset is not taught to us the way technical skills are, but I believe it's equally important in life and in business. When you have the tools to maintain the right mindset, you have something to fall back on when times are tough. You're more able to adapt to changing situations and extend your help to others. The right mindset is an empowering pair of lenses that can help you see opportunities to grow, and inspire you to keep asking: 'How can I show up today for myself and for others?'

Whilst the pandemic in 2020 brought much uncertainty to the world, including my own businesses, I recognised there were opportunities to develop as a person, especially during challenging times. We all have a choice. I enrolled myself into a certification program because I wanted to learn holistic ways of leading my team, and the things I learned have helped me infuse mindfulness into everything I do. The program showed me that I can do more beyond the realm of my business.

My experience on the program also helped me see my work in a different light. I've been meeting like-minded, passionate and heart-centred business owners in Australia and beyond, assisting them to scale their business by determining what can be outsourced in their business processes. This then allows them to maximise their time and energy towards tasks that are in their zone of genius and make their heart sing. I never realised I was a 'consultant' until someone brought it to my attention! Since then, my role has evolved from being founder and business leader, to a business strategist dedicated to helping entrepreneurs wherever they may be in the world.

I was inspired to also say 'yes' to becoming a Well-being Boost Program facilitator; putting the holistic tools I learned into action, even though I felt out of my comfort zone. One of the Well-being Boost Program's pillars is gratitude, and that's something that really resonates with me. I've always seen myself as a grateful person and having the chance to guide people into practicing gratitude is a privilege. I'm grateful to experience being in the same circle with people who have the same higher purpose. Their energy has amplified my drive in achieving my higher purpose, and I'm determined to create the impact I'm envisioning through my businesses.

Amidst all these changes, what remains the same are the values I've held on to. I've always believed in heart-led service, and we built our companies Kaya Services and Empowered Virtual Services with this in mind. We envisioned both companies to provide a supportive, transparent and empowering space for our team and our clients. My strong belief in the power of gratitude and positivity guided us through the uncertainties and challenges of the past year, and fortunately, I've received amazing support and affirmation from my family and 'success circle' (the individuals who are my sounding board and encourage me every day, whether it's personal or business). Whenever I set out to achieve a goal, I keep in mind I'm doing it for the people I love, for my teams and clients, I put my focus on heart-led service that creates a ripple effect with an an emphasis on community, collaboration and celebration. If I want to see a change, I need to be the change.

Life changes are inevitable, and it's comforting to know that whatever happens, I can go back to what's in my heart to guide me in making the next step. When I'm unsure about which path to take, I remind myself of the values that have brought me to where I am now and use them as a gauge to check if my heart is in the right place.

Everything I have learned and continue to learn has helped me to expand my self-perception and how I show up for my family, my team and our community. I'm now able to use my technical skills with the holistic tools I learned in a manner that's more spiritual and wholehearted. In a way, I see the world with new eyes and my heart has grown bigger in the process. I am thankful, grateful and blessed to be able to serve with my heart.

ABOUT YONA

My name is Yona Signo. I'm mum to two little ones, with a supportive husband, parents, family, and friends who have turned into family. Born in the Philippines and raised in Australia, both countries have a special place in my heart.

My background is in the IT space, with a Bachelor's Degree in Computing, specialising in Business and Information Systems and Project Management; certified PRINCE2 practitioner and ITIL Foundation in IT Service Management. I am also a certified Sacred Space Holder and Well-being Boost Program facilitator.

I'm a multi-preneur with a mission to make a difference both locally and globally. I am the co-founder and managing director of Kaya Services in Australia. Kaya Services employs a highly skilled and remote workforce to help businesses in Australia and beyond achieve operational efficiency so they can focus on growth objectives. I am also the founder of Empowered Virtual Services in the Phillipines; a learning academy for Filipino virtual assistants and freelancers. We empower them with tools for self-worth and skill-enhancement so they can live with freedom and prosperity while supporting a global clientele.

I live each day with gratitude and integrity. I love to laugh and travel, especially with my travel buddy – also known as my husband. On most days, I prefer coffee over tea. I enjoy white over red wine, especially the kind with bubbles. I used to snowboard (pre-kids), but now I love to scoot with the kids. I've bungee jumped in New Zealand and skydived from 14,000ft in NSW. I'm a creative at heart with an interest in design and handmade things, so much so that I spent a summer in Florence, Italy, experiencing life as a design student, basking under the Tuscan sun and making friends with people from around the globe.

I love to learn from and collaborate with like-minded individuals who continue to encourage the ripple effect of positivity to make the world a better place. I truly believe in continuous improvement and when it's feasible to do so, I join different programs and certifications that are in line with my purpose and my *why.* I'm passionate about supporting people who are also passionate about helping others. I'm a leader with a vision to empower others to be their best self so they too can make a difference in the world.

I'm a woman who is perfectly imperfect, striving to be the best I can be each day while harmonising being a mum in business. I hope to be a good example for my children, but more importantly hope they feel the unconditional love and support which I received from my wonderful parents. I would like them to be proud of my achievements, which in turn, will inspire them to live their best life. Through my challenges, I surrender my worries to Him and pray I can demonstrate to my children all they need to be faithful, compassionate and empathic humans who will stand firmly in their place and show the world the goodness of their hearts.

I believe in the saying 'right place, right time, right people'. I hope to be remembered for living life with my values intact, my ethical businesses that show strength in cultural diversity and heart-centred leadership, while infusing joy and laughter into all I do.

As I continue to discover what life has to offer me, I am grateful for all the blessings I receive and all those yet to come.

www.yonasigno.com

MEL HOMEWOOD

I wondered for some time why I decided to be a part of this book; could I really change the world?

Absolutely not the whole world, but if I could change the way one foster child can see their future, or help them to see there is hope and a wonderful life ahead, make them believe in themselves, or even become a mentor for a foster child, then my job in this world will be complete.

I never wanted to be a chef. I wanted to be a hairdresser, so I kind of chose the right profession because I believe I rock my mum/chef bun, the 'no make-up' look, and stinky uniform daily. It's so easy!

I was born in 1977 to a sixteen-year-old mumma, and a dad who was eighteen years old.

My childhood was not the norm. Even though I was incredibly loved by my biological family, trauma happened, and it hit hard.

What I do remember is this; my grandparents and my biological family were my everything.

When I was four, my mumma had a baby boy, my very first best friend. Mum and I were close but when my little bro arrived I remember feeling a sense of companionship like no other. I felt whole. He was so bloody gorgeous, and he was my brother, and we were a family of three that made my world complete.

But Mum got a boyfriend. I remember moving in; it was a great big house compared to the flats and duplexes we were used to. It had a massive backyard, sunken lounge – hey, for the eighties one might say it was pretty flash. But mum's boyfriend was a lot older than her, and I guess he gave my mumma the security and love she had always been looking for, which was wonderful.

But, he also liked me. From the age of five or six he did things to me that were not the norm. He told me if I ever said anything about what he was doing then he would kill my mumma and brother. So hey, I complied. I did as I was told; nothing was taking my world away.

It seemed it wasn't long before Mum confronted him and things went bad, real bloody bad. We moved out and it was just the three of us again. Things seemed fine, but it was far from that. How did she deal with it all, being a young lady in her early twenties?

Before long another man came along, and I remember my mum and my brother going on 'holiday' with him, while I was left behind with a 'friend' and her husband, two girls and a boy. I knew them so it all was good, but it was an eternity and I still wasn't going home. You see, I sleepwalked after the molestation trauma, so it was only logical I couldn't go on holiday, right?

I never went home. Mum's friend told DCP my mother was incapable of taking good care of me. Before I knew it, I was a ward of the state, fostered by my mum's 'friend'. I'm sure there is more to the story than my knowledge of it, but hey, I was eight and that is how I remember it.

DCP in my eyes were wonderful. I got to see my 'real' family every second weekend. I would get a taxi from my foster family's home to my grandparent's house. For some unknown reason, my mum didn't want to see me anymore. (Thanks for that, foster mother.)

My mum's friend seemed super cool to start with, but before I knew it, she had broken up with her husband for another man (who was lovely, btw), and we up and left, moving 50km away. This had a massive impact on me, but nevertheless, my school was awesome, and I made amazing friends who I still have and cherish to this day, year four was not all that bad, but year four was when 'it' started.

The physical, mental, and emotional abuse from my foster mother was horrid.

Through all the years of abuse from my foster mother, in my eyes, it seemed she did not hurt her own children.

She was super good at hiding all her horrible charm from her boyfriend; he was so cool, he brought a balance and joy to our lives. He was such fun. We would also occasionally visit her ex-husband. My first foster father is a legend. He loved all of us kids equally and never made me feel unloved or unwanted. He made me feel a part of the family and never let us go without anything.

Teenage years were heavy, having constant physical, mental and emotional abuse 'because no-one else wanted me'. I knew when DCP were coming for their routine visits because my foster mother would start being nice to me. In those times I felt like a 'normal human'. I wanted to be loved, and those times made me feel as if I was significant and wanted. I lapped it up, but they did not last long.

By the time I was a teenager, for some reason, the most important people in my life, my biological grandparents, were told by my foster mother that I was too busy with school to visit each fortnight. This was a lie as, at the time, we lived closer to them than ever. My foster mother was all about the dollar and how quickly she could make it. She conned a florist in our new town to start a florist/catering business and guess who did all the cooking … yep, me! It was mostly Red Rooster and Woolworth's buns, but my part was tiring, with all salads made by hand until the wee hours of the morning. Her friends in my teenage years even called me 'Cinderella' as every time they came around, I was cooking or cleaning.

My high school friends were my saving grace. We laughed, we had fun and it was time away from home when I was not being harmed. My foster mum hated that I loved high school and all the fun associated with it, so the abuse just got worse. One morning around the age of fourteen, I remember her dragging me around by my ears for not putting a load of washing on or something equally ridiculous. At school a friend asked why the back of my ears were bruised and bleeding. It was embarrassing but I was still trying to hide the abuse, as hey, 'no-one else wanted me', right?

In year ten I had a pretty good knowledge of food from the catering business, so when it came to my work experience placement, I worked in a hotel for two weeks. I really loved being in the hospitality world. I lapped up everything I was taught because I wanted to be accepted. The next thing I knew – I was an apprentice chef!

I met the most amazing people in my first year at the hotel; one of them is still one of my best friends today. I entered apprentice chef competitions and adored my lecturer at TAFE who always helped me, and my struggle with confidence.

I had my apprenticeship transferred and ended up at a hotel in Fremantle. It was the best thing to ever happen to me professionally. I worked brasserie, cold larder, sauces, functions, cafe – you name it, I learned it. That job made me who I am today, knowing all elements of the culinary sector.

By the time I was eighteen I decided I'd had enough of the abuse at home. One morning, my foster mother slammed my head against a brick wall so hard, over and over again, that I thought I was going to have brain damage. I moved out that day. I caught the bus to work despite having my own car, as I was not allowed to drive, and told my boss my abuse story. He was very helpful that day and I wish we had kept in touch.

In 1999 I followed a boy to New South Wales, where I was privileged to work as a chef at the Sydney 2000 Olympics.

After a few years of trauma with NSW Boy, I caught a bus to Queensland, cheffing and partying hard, before I met my husband who put me on the straight and narrow. He has supported every inch of my being and helped me to become the successful chef, businesswoman, wife and mumma I now am.

In 2003 our baby boy came along and I was more in love with my boy than I have ever been with anyone else in my entire life. I made him! Somehow I had lost my mother along the way, but this baby made me have all the feels I never thought I would ever have. I loved him and my partner more than life itself and felt more emotional than ever. I literally cried the first three months of my son's life because I was now a mum and it was all I ever wanted. I was a mum! I was able to be the mum I never had, to give the love I had never had; to LOVE like I never had.

Baby boy was challenging. I often tell people he came out strong enough to hold a knife and fork and want a steak! He was strong and determined, and by age of four was diagnosed with ADHD. As parents, it was emotional realising he needed help but not knowing how to give it. We wanted to have more kids, growing up close together, but after three years of trying REALLY BLOODY HARD, we gave up. However, we moved to the Pilbara and were pregnant within two weeks. Something about the red dirt, I think! I cheffed throughout the three years of our firstborn's life and it was super tough, but we did it. When our girl came along life was truly complete; I had always wanted a baby girl of my own. I remember my mum loving me endlessly and I wanted to be that person for my daughter. I hope, despite the hormonal teenage years we are experiencing now, she understands how much I love her.

We have moved from state to state since the kids were little and had the privilege of seeing so much of Australia; our chef careers have also taken us through south-east Asia several times. We finally settled in The Great Southern of Western Australia twelve years ago, and have made so many amazing friends. We have connected with a family we chose and even reconnected with the old. We are truly blessed to have those we choose to be in our lives and make this world a better place for us, for me, for my family.

Deciding to buy the business we have owned for the last three years has BY FAR been the most challenging time for our family. With our son now eighteen, and our daughter reaching fourteen while not feeling her place in the world, it has been super tough, to say the least. But every day I get up, I go to work, and I do what I love and love what I do. I used to think I was 'just a chef', 'just a mum' or just a 'DCP kid', but it made me the determined woman I am today, despite all the bad things that happened. I remember my foster mum telling me one day history would repeat with my children. I remember thinking at the time, *You're a nasty piece of shit.* For a very long time, my success was to prove her wrong, but at the end of the day my success is because I choose to make my life better. I choose to be a better mum, I choose to make my marriage work no matter how hard it gets, and I choose to be the chef I am, to make my family proud.

My business idea came from my family's allergies and intolerances. It inspired me to cater for everyone who has an intolerance or food allergy. I wanted to create a space just like my nana's home, full of wonderful furniture and knick-knacks, comfort foods and smells. I wanted to be surrounded by green plants to clean the air, a garden to grow my own produce, to recycle, reuse, relove and repurpose; to help our Mother Earth by doing all I can whilst producing great food and welcoming customer service. I wanted to create a comfortable safe space where anyone can feel welcomed and loved, a place where history is relived, a place where old meets new.

We brew our own kombucha and switchel, make nut milks and nut-free butters. We make cold-press juices and smoothies whilst keeping all the pulp to create our own dehydrated wraps. We dry our seeds for our seasons and support local people, products and produce.

The cafe is vegan and coeliac accredited, which is a hard challenge but one I personally thrive on. In less than three years, I have created a business that has not only won the hearts of coeliacs and intolerant folk, but many awards including Albany Chamber of Commerce and Industry Businessperson of the Year in 2020. Even though I had no speech ready, I am still blown away that little old me did this. I have struggled with my personal and business growth since COVID-19 hit, and with the fear and uncertainty, it has bought up issues and trauma which I thought I had dealt with and buried.

Still, moving forward I hope to conquer a lot more. With staffing being a massive issue since 2020, I have had to work in and on my business. For me as a cafe owner and chef, I have had to do the lot, which is often very hard work, and I have become greyer by the day! But I have survived and keep pushing on despite the impact it has on me physically and mentally.

My children have suffered with my absence, yet despite all their challenges, they understand why I am not as present as I could be. My family (biological, foster and chosen), all understand and know I am on a mission to do what I love and love what I do, no matter how upset or frustrated they see me at times.

I am grateful for those I choose to be in my life and who have made me the person I am today. After years of depression and issues with self-worth, now my struggle is balancing what I love and who I love without sacrificing one or the other. I believe in time, at exactly the right time, all my questions will be answered. I will always strive to be the person and mentor I never had, while being grateful for the good people who made me who I am today.

I am Mel. I am a mother, a wife, a boss, a chef, a business woman and an award winner; and all of these things are something to be super proud of. I am learning to be proud, I am learning to love myself no matter how damaged I feel, how insecure or how little self-worth I have. This life is a journey where every day we can learn from the bad, turn it into good and choose to make it better. It may not always go to plan, but hey, 'it is what it is'. This is life.

ABOUT MEL

Western Australian born and bred, I am Melissa Homewood.

A chef, cafe owner, boss, wife, friend, family member to many, and mum to two children with allergies, intolerances and different abilities.

From a very early age, I remember strolling with my young teenage aunties down the quiet country streets of Mundijong to Mrs Lightbody's farmhouse. We would milk the cows, collect eggs on Anstey Street and deliver them through neighbour's yards to Nana Pete's house. I remember years of skipping and running down the back lane to visit Nana Worthy and smell the goodness of her endless treats from the Metters oven, devouring the goodness she made, picking the mandarins off the tree, and waiting for the Cottee's soda truck to deliver refreshments.

Mundijong has always felt like a safe place to me. My true home where love began, where the love of food began and where my heart will always lay with wonderful memories of my youth.

My childhood led me to believe I wanted to be a hairdresser, but my teenage years proved otherwise, and with a young childhood full of wonderful family gatherings, with what I consider the best foods I have ever eaten, it was inevitable my love of food would lead me to an apprenticeship as a chef at a hotel in Perth, at the tender age of fifteen.

By seventeen, I had transferred to a much bigger and brighter apprenticeship at a hotel in Fremantle. I excelled, with great support, in many aspects of the culinary industry including Apprentice of the Year Award events. Just after my nineteenth birthday, I was fully qualified and one of the youngest to do so in WA. Running a 120-seater restaurant and function center at this age was a massive achievement, before starting my travels. In 2000, I flew to Sydney to be an executive chef at the Sydney Olympics.

In 2003, I became a mum to a beautiful boy, who was diagnosed with ADHD at the age of four, and my love and knowledge for food changed. I educated myself on how foods affect the body and mind. With my son being dairy intolerant, our family found a whole new way of eating. However, in 2007 I became a mum again, to a darling daughter, and being a busy, working mum of two, the dietary requirements were left by the wayside and somehow, we returned to 'easy' foods, which reintroduced behaviors, increased weight and even altered moods.

In the late 2000s I was diagnosed with a gluten intolerance, and my son was now histamine as well as dairy intolerant. Life needed to change. The more I researched and learnt how many people were affected by allergies and intolerances, the more I felt I needed to cater for those in need, so again I researched about food education.

I started my own catering business named Custom Catering, customising each catering event to those who needed my food knowledge on intolerances and allergies. I loved it!

By 2018, the stars aligned for me to buy a cafe.

My cafe is now coeliac accredited, vegan, and refined-sugar-free, with a focus on intolerances and allergies, growing my own produce, and a 'no-wastage' policy, as well as recycling and reusing historical furniture.

It's a cafe where you are surrounded by an abundance of green plants and fun memorabilia.

In 2020, I was nominated for and won Businessperson of the Year at the Albany Chamber of Commerce and Industry Great Southern Business Awards.

In 2021 and now with many awards under my belt, I am proud to be a part of the AusMumpreneur community and this book.

www.facebook.com/thealkalinecafe

KRISTY FAIRBAIRN

Women changing the world is such a powerful thought.

My life has been surrounded, and shaped, by many women who altered the course of my life and impacted my world as a daughter, a sister, a wife and as a mother.

Sadly, I've lost some very special women, and despite their passing, their influence continues to guide, comfort and drive me.

My birth mother was a loving, caring young woman who lost her battle with addiction and mental illness when I was just a toddler. She recognised her struggles. She asked for help, and received it many times. When I was just eleven months old, after speaking with her family, she asked her brother and sister-in-law to look after me, alongside their three children. She sought help and tried to get well but sadly, when I was two and a half years old, she died. This was the moment my world changed course.

My childhood and adolescence were challenging. I never thought I'd amount to much. Some days, surviving was enough. My past does not define who I am, but every moment and challenge has shaped my future. As I get older and more reflective, I can acknowledge, with gratitude, the people and opportunities that have come my way.

My birth mother's selflessness ensured my safety and security in a loving family home. As a mother myself, I now understand the sacrifice it took to make such a difficult decision and I'm truly grateful for my mother, and the aunt who took me in, raising me alongside her three children. She too changed my world. She gave me siblings I might not have had, with whom I've shared laughter, joy, grief and disappointment. I always knew of my childhood beginnings and of my first mother, whilst being nurtured and loved by my second mother. I was free to ask questions, and maintain a special bond with my extended family. I lost my second mother to cancer in 2016. Knowing how to show up and be with her through her final journey was very empowering for me. As I raise my own children, I catch myself in small moments telling her, 'I understand now, Mum,' and, 'You were so right.'

When I reflect on what I wanted to do when I was younger, it was always to serve others.

I was interested in social work. To me, this was a wonderful opportunity to connect and help others. Not being a high-achieving school leaver, I felt it was a level of education I could manage. I never felt smart enough to attend university.

As I got older, the want to pursue a social work career waned, but my desire to serve and support people didn't. Teen years are tough, and school wasn't for me. That's why I was drawn to hospitality. Hospitality taught me a lot.

I learnt how to actively listen and engage with people; to speak with them, to hear them and understand their needs. I also learnt how not to engage with people. Working on a restaurant floor requires a knowing of when to be quiet and when to be the life of the party – and those moments are not up to you, they're up to guests you serve. After leaving high school, I was fortunate to meet a remarkable woman; another who would alter my course and help steer my ship to calmer waters. This woman that changed my world was a restaurateur and in me she ignited a passion that blossomed into a hospitality career. Her mentorship taught me to serve without being a servant, and to impress upon others care and attention, no matter how brief the interaction. She was a force of equal parts of kindness, determination, spirit and drive. We maintained a special bond and loving friendship long after I moved on from hospitality. She was taken from us in 2015, a year before my mum, but she continues to steer this ship when it veers off course.

After years of treading the boards, I took the skills I'd learnt and applied them to real estate. This was a new opportunity to support people through what is often referred to as one of life's most stressful events – moving house. Through attention to detail and unflappable customer service, I worked my way into a client care role and I'd never felt more at home! I found assisting clients with their individual needs powerful. I was lucky enough to build meaningful relationships with clients who shared stories of joy, grief and new opportunities.

Working and caring for small children is a juggle that plays with your emotions. It's hard to make the right choice, if there is such a thing. I'm an all or nothing kind of person, and unfortunately, I was giving all to my work. I decided to step away from a role I really enjoyed.

Being a stay-at-home mum gave me precious time with my children, and immensely valuable moments with my mother before her passing. Yet, I felt sidelined. The rewards of work and discovering my potential were sailing by, and I was observing my own life from the shoreline.

It's easy to lose yourself when immense grief is followed by immense grief. It's as though you're sailing uncharted and turbulent seas. My ship was slowly sinking and the crew I was used to relying on to help me navigate these challenges were lost. I needed time to grieve and heal, and time with my children, but I also needed a source of income. I wanted to contribute to something bigger than myself and my abundant emotions.

It was then that another woman sailed into my life. She owned a bookkeeping business and wanted someone who could work for her remotely. We connected from the moment we met, and I felt so supported as she took me on and nurtured my skills and confidence. Her small business is now mine; I bought it from her in 2017. As I look back on the last four years of running my own business, I'm filled with immense pride on what I've achieved. While reflection is important, it's the looking forward that really excites me! This was another moment my world changed course.

As an adopted child I've felt insecure, an imposter – narratives that can control you. Doubt is crippling.

From the women in my life I've learnt that believing you are enough is empowering. I was fortunate to be raised by two loving mothers, and blessed to be surrounded by treasured friends and mentors.

Since becoming a business owner in 2017, I've been on a momentous personal and professional journey. I've attended conferences, locally and nationally, and I've spoken with inspirational people who have helped me to gain clarity on how to set goals for myself and my business. I feel supported to achieve these goals and to dream big. I understand my value, my worth, and my potential impact. I am driven to aim high because I continue to be inspired by amazing, strong, smart women. Most of all I know I am enough, and I'm forever grateful to the women of my life.

The gift of one more day with each of the women I have lost is a selfish ask. I'm grateful for the awareness each one has given me; for the lessons I've learned in their presence, lived in my everyday life and taken from the grief of each loss.

It has been a gift to have some amazing women in my life who have taught me how to nurture my desire for success and to be clear on what I want. I use my vision board as a compass to determine what I want to attract in my life. I dreamed of being able to afford a private school education for our children without it being a burden on our family; to provide them with the best educational outcomes. I am proud to say that our daughter was enrolled in her new school this year, ahead of starting high school next year, and our son will make the move in a couple of years when he's ready for grade five.

My husband is a wonderful provider for our family, but this has come at a sacrifice too. He has worked away as a fly-in fly-out steward since before our children were born, and this has seen us regularly juggle life without him for up to five weeks, and sometimes for as long as three months during the challenges of 2020 (COVID-19). At other times he has been home for weeks or months, not knowing when his next work placement will be. There are, of course, benefits to this lifestyle, as when he is home, he is completely home and available to us. By growing my business, setting goals and looking at my vision board, I am building a business that can support our family without his income, which will give him the opportunity to stay home and pursue his hobby and passion of farming, and to be at the dinner table every night with us. I am proud to say in my first four years, my business has grown by 444%, from a team of one, to a team of seven incredible women.

We work with some amazing clients, who we support and empower to grow and thrive in their own businesses; to create a business that supports them to be financially free, and allows them to spend time doing the things they love, with the people they love. This has come through grit, determination, and mapping out a path to follow, whilst still embracing unknown opportunities, and valuing myself to invest in my future.

I'm growing my business to empower other women, to offer them opportunities, to support them and to drive them to aim high. I'm investing in myself, my business and my village of amazing, inspiring people. Through working with business coaches I've gained such clarity in my personal life, and have been able to work through some of the self-limiting beliefs and negative narratives that have followed me through life. Now I consider situations before reacting, and respond with purpose. I'm more open to curiosity and seek alternative perspectives to find the lessons and opportunities in every situation. I'm empowered by my experiences, not defined by them, and this has added value to the challenges I've faced in life. A new motto I've adopted from one of my coaches is, 'We never have business problems, only personal problems reflected in our business.' By valuing myself, and investing in myself, I have been able to let some extraordinary people into my life who have guided me to make powerful moments from challenging situations.

I feel blessed to have learnt so much in the past few years, and to embrace the lifetime of learning I have to draw on. Through my personal growth, I have developed a desire to support other women in business, beyond the transactional financial health of their businesses. To dig deep with them, and help them harness their passion and ability to succeed, and help guide them, just as I have been guided.

I'm embarking on an amazing journey that's peppered with tangible and achievable goals. I'm sure there will be stormy seas to navigate, but I'm stronger, more agile and far more resilient now than I once was. The 'imposter syndrome' ebbs and flows; that's natural and it helps keep things in perspective. I attribute so much of my growth and personal awareness to the crew of women I've had guiding and preparing me for life's challenges. Now it's my turn to give back, to be one of those women for somebody else. In addition to building my business services, I'm becoming a coach to help other women catch the wind in their sails – we all need a little help to know how to get where we want to go. If it takes a village to raise a child, it takes a crew to build a business. We need experienced mentors to help us navigate the challenges, coaches to help us find the answers within, and others to believe in us. All are essential for our business and personal growth.

One last sailing analogy – it's okay to find yourself looking for safe harbour. There are times in our lives when we need refuge and protection, just don't drop anchor for so long that you find yourself moored there. As women we can second-guess ourselves, we can undermine our strength and capability, and we can hold ourselves back from achieving everything we've ever dreamed of. I'm investing in myself, because I am worth it, and you are too.

Women change the world for other women, and I'm looking forward to being one of them.

ABOUT KRISTY

My name is Kristy Fairbairn and my journey towards building The Business Oasis starts in a small town in Tasmania where my father used to make a living as a fisherman. Growing up in a household with a seasonal and lumpy income, I have always known the pressure that it can place on your family when you're not certain how much cashflow you will have this month and you're not in control of your finances.

At the early start of my career, I worked across multiple industries, including hospitality, real estate and administrative support services. These allowed me to approach client work from a few different angles, learn about the various elements of the industries and learn about the importance of varied revenue streams, as well as the importance of building strategies to develop steady income.

I started a flexible bookkeeping role in 2017 that allowed me to work from home and spend time with my young family. The owner chose a new direction in 2018, and I decided to buy the business and The Business Oasis was created.

From working in the hospitality industry to becoming a founder and CEO, I have indeed gone through many challenging yet wonderful and life-changing experiences that have definitely shaped my values, principles and who I am today.

It has taken a great amount of strength, dedication, delegation and trust to get to where I am now, and I couldn't be more absolutely excited and grateful to share with everyone my journey and how The Business Oasis has become a safe zone for my clients and how it can be one for my future clients.

I am passionate about helping small business owners

My qualifications include Cert IV in Bookkeeping and Accounting; BAS Agent Registration, Xero partner, MYOB partner, Pure Bookkeeping Licensee and Mastermind Facilitator, ICB Member and Facilitator, ABN Member, undertaking study to become a Credentialed Pro Coach with The Coaching Institute.

My achievements include being a finalist in two categories in 2021 Women in Finance awards and finalist in multiple categories in the 2021 AusMumpreneur awards, an entrant in the 2021 Accountants Daily awards, 2021 Roar Awards, and an entrant in the 2021 Telstra Business awards.

I have also had the opportunity and privilege to work with fellow bookkeepers and accountants to mentor and coach them in achieving their own business goals and successes.

If you'd like to connect, you can find me on Instagram: www.instagram.com/thebusinessoasis or my website: www.businessoasis.com.au or send me an email kristy@businesoasis.com.au

I have an amazing team around me so if I can't respond straight away, my team will, and I look forward to connecting with you as fellow women changing the world.

www.businessoasis.com.au

LEAH CHANDLER

It sure is funny how life can lead you to your purpose … your passion … the one thing that makes you so emotional it cuts you up inside. To be honest, telling my story on why I do what I do is one of the hardest things I've done. Why? Well, I will tell you.

When I was a teenager, I knew I wanted to have a positive impact on kids and families' lives in some way. I thought I would be able to do this by studying to become a lawyer to represent families in need. However, after working in a law firm, I decided rather quickly that the law was flawed and I knew I was not in the right place to be of value to the families I wanted to help, let alone feel fulfilled myself.

I decided to work in school sport and loved it! I got to work with parents, volunteers and educators who gave their time to provide school kids (both primary and secondary school age) an opportunity to compete in a sport they loved. They learnt how to be part of a team, and had the opportunity to travel and meet new people. After this adventure, I worked in the fields of sport and recreation, youth, fitness and wellbeing. I enjoyed it, but I only really found my passion when I had my own children.

My husband and I have three children (two boys and a girl) and we love being parents. Our kids are unique, and I know all three of them will contribute positively to our world in their own way, but we had a few rough years where life was very difficult, especially for our two younger children.

My passion for establishing inclusive communities was born from my experiences during this time in my life. This was the start of my journey of acceptance and compassion, not only for children and families like mine, but also for parents like me.

Our middle son started to display signs of Asperger's syndrome and attention deficit hyperactivity disorder (ADHD) when he was around three years old. My husband and I had no idea what we were seeing, only that our very loving, witty and intelligent son was prone to huge emotional outbursts, which often led to hurting others (meltdowns), was not able to regulate his tone or loudness of his voice, could not read facial expressions, suffered anxiety and had sensory issues. He had trouble relating to his age group or younger, and preferred to talk with older children and adults.

When he went to school, he was branded the 'naughty child' and often ended up on behaviour plans. He was teased at school, and some educators did not treat him well. The best thing we ever did was to seek help from the 'right' professionals to assess and diagnose his conditions, which meant those behaviour plans changed to individual education plans (IEP). He was able to get some help at school, however we noticed his teachers often didn't have the necessary education, help or support to work with kids with additional needs. They had so many kids to work with in a classroom setting, it was difficult for some kids to get the individual help they needed to learn and be happy.

We did everything we could to help our son cope. We learnt about his conditions and the strategies we could put in place for him. We would go along to school and help him with these strategies, until eventually he began to take responsibility for self-regulation. We learnt how to communicate with his educators and health professionals, and ended up having a great relationship with a few key people who really wanted to help our son succeed. We definitely were 'those parents' who fought the school on the 'unfair' things, however, we also worked tirelessly with the school to create an inclusive environment for our son. To this day, we are very grateful for the key people who were instrumental in building a strong support network. Without this network, I don't know how we would have coped, as parents or as a family.

Our daughter was diagnosed with autism at about four years old. She walked on her toes, had low muscle tone, was not coordinated, was very delayed in her milestones and displayed signs of impaired cognition and auditory processing delay. Our daughter's school journey began in the same mainstream primary school that both her brothers attended. She was so quiet that when she became anxious or bored in class, she was able to find a way to leave the classroom without her teacher noticing, and wander around the school by herself. This was scary as she had no sense of danger or direction! Often her brothers would see her from their classrooms and take her back. The stress for my daughter became too much, as she knew she could not learn the way most of the other kids could learn. She had so many sensory issues that she would disengage and go into her own world, ignoring everything around her. She could not relate to other children and would play alongside her peers, which often resulted in bullying. Again, we worked with educators and health professionals to establish a supportive network, however, we needed more! We pushed for a cognitive assessment, and when our daughter was finally diagnosed, it was deemed she had an intellectual impairment, allowing her to go to a special school where her individual needs could be catered for. Within months of starting at her new special school, she came out of her shell. She is a very visual learner so she excelled when able to learn in an environment that was conducive to her sensory and social issues.

My experiences with my kids made me notice how many kids were struggling in a school and social environment. I realised there were other families out there, just like ours, who needed help. I also saw how many educators burnt out early on in their careers due to the overwhelming number of children who need support they are unable to provide.

My biggest 'light bulb' moment was when I sat in my son's class and saw he was not the only one struggling! It was apparent at least one third of the kids were not coping, and I observed that the teacher did not have the necessary tools to deal with what was happening in the classroom.

Despite thinking I was a 'strong' person, I suffered severe burnout and was shocked when I found myself bursting into tears and sobbing uncontrollably in random places! It took a huge toll on my mental and physical wellbeing. I was constantly fighting for my children's rights to be supported and happy; trying to shelter them from bullying, educating support people on how my children should be treated, and helping our family to cope. We had to create strategies for our oldest son too so he could understand his siblings and have a good relationship with them. And of course, we wanted him to feel happy too.

It was around this time I began my yoga, mindfulness and meditation journey, and it was the best thing I ever did for my wellness. I was able to start moving through my grief and see a sliver of silver in the lining of my life. The hardest thing I had to work through was the guilt of not being able to protect my children from the stressful situations they should not have had to deal with at such a young age. I believed it was my fault they had these conditions, and the burden and guilt related to that was always in the forefront of my mind. I still feel emotional when I recount these feelings.

Having discovered the value of meditation, I decided to approach my children's school and offer yoga and mindfulness programs, as well as fun fitness programs, to offer a solution to the issues I had observed in both my children and their peers. The reception was incredible! We started to really help young children connect their mind and body by using mindful moving techniques. Children were starting to learn how to self-regulate their bodies and emotions. We also made our programs FUN! This was how Kids-Fit Australia was born.

We took our programs to mainstream early learning centres, primary schools and high schools and realised our programs were filling a need within our community; a need to keep kids fit and well for everyday life and to start the conversation of building an inclusive community for kids and families with additional needs.

We recognised these kids had amazing people around them; people who cared and wanted to assist in a positive way. These were the parents/carers and educators who also needed support and tools to be well, so they didn't hit burnout and were able to move through hard times, just as I had. We wanted to lead the way in providing support to these three core groups, so they could be part of a respectful, supportive community.

So where did that lead us? We began trialling a practical session for educators. We had such a wonderful response from the attendees that we built this into our core programs and decided to offer a similar program to parents and carers as well.

Our educator sessions have been designed to provide tools for educators to help children find their focus and calm when they arrive at school and at times of learning. Self-care tips and techniques for educators are also provided to help eliminate burnout.

Our parents/carer sessions have been designed so parents and carers can help their children to find their calm. We focus on teaching mindfulness for busy minds, self-care for both parents/carers and children transitioning through meltdowns, and relaxation ideas before sleeping.

We encourage both educators and parents/carers to support and listen to each other so they can work together to build an inclusive community for their kids.

We love combining these sessions with our kids' programs to provide solutions for kids, parents/carers and educators. In this way, they are all supported and given the tools to be fit and well for everyday life. This is what I get most excited about! Seeing kids self-regulate, educators and parents/carers getting along and communicating well, and knowing these tools and techniques will stay with them for life.

It's funny, when I look back on the heartbreak and stressful times, I am grateful for the lessons learnt, although I could do without all the grey hair! I now see we all had to go through these lessons to get to the present day. My oldest son is kind and caring, is fabulous at reading people and works hard to include everyone when working with others. He has proven time and time again that he is a leader. Our middle son is in senior high school and works hard at everything he does. He is constantly developing his coping strategies and cares about people in need, always standing up for others when they can't stand up for themselves. He is a great conversationalist who can talk to anyone! My daughter had major spinal surgery this year due to severe scoliosis, and as always, is amazingly resilient. She speaks her mind and is aware of where she wants to improve, working hard to achieve her goals. She has learnt the art of asking for help, which is fantastic for someone with communication issues.

All three of them have a strong desire to connect with others and we are so proud of that!

My parents and parents-in-law have also had big lessons in how to deal with our family, especially when we had no idea ourselves what to do next! We are grateful they wanted to be part of our village, as this has made our lives much easier. Our children (and us) adore them!

As for myself … well I have learnt humility and resilience. I have learnt you can turn hard things into good things. I have learnt there is always a silver lining in everything; to see it, you just need to take some time to work through the process. I have come to the realisation that grief and guilt are very real, and it's okay to feel these emotions. The process of working through these feelings is important and should be acknowledged more in our society.

As parents we often forget to look after ourselves when things get tough, or remember to ask for help when we need it. Asking for help and getting the support we need allows us to build an inclusive community. If we show our children we can be vulnerable and sometimes need help, they understand they can do the same. It really does take a village to raise a child! Brene Brown has a great quote which sums up how important it is to accept being vulnerable – *'Vulnerability is not winning or losing; it's having the courage to show up and be seen when we have no control over the outcome. Vulnerability is not weakness; it's our greatest measure of courage.'*

So how can you help build an inclusive community?

Well, it's quite simple! Have compassion for others who you see are struggling or displaying stress. Life can be challenging, and you never know what others are going through, especially those children with emerging behaviours and additional needs, their families and sometimes the educators who support them.

Be appreciative of our differences and acknowledge that we all belong in this world; we all deserve to be treated with respect.

Show your vulnerability and ask for help – after all, that's how we influence others to do the same.

Be kind. Find the silver lining. Be well.

ABOUT LEAH

I'm a lover of people and find humans fascinating! I love seeing and celebrating the differences in others, finding ways to help us all be part of an inclusive community.

I am married, a mum of three children, and we live in Brisbane, Australia. Our family dynamics are interesting as we are touched by autism and ADHD – amongst other things! We have a great family who work hard to understand and respect each other, and I must say, this is my greatest achievement.

The story of my family and its challenges has shaped my life both personally and in business. Many experiences have been hard, yet rewarding, and have contributed to my resilient and compassionate nature. These experiences have enabled me to see how I can help to build an inclusive community; a community where we support each other, especially those who are touched by kids with additional needs.

I have always enjoyed working with kids and families and being part of the wellness industry. I've been able to combine these two 'loves' and now provide programs so kids and their support people can be fit and well for everyday life. My company, Kids-Fit Australia delivers targeted wellness programs for kids of all ages (including kids with additional needs), and educational and self-regulation programs for parents, carers and educators.

I do enjoy being fit and currently compete in Olympic weightlifting. I love the social environment and pushing myself to continually improve while staying fit and strong. I also love to practice and teach yoga, mindfulness and meditation. I find this keeps my mind and body healthy, especially when life gets a bit full-on! I'm also a yoga therapist and a fitness and strength coach, and find my work with kids and their support workers extremely rewarding.

I love to learn new things, my latest hobby being stand-up paddle boarding (SUP). I often fall off and if I do get to stand I wobble all over the place, but that's the great thing about learning anything new! I love being in the water, outdoors and just out there enjoying life! You can often find me on my deck or hanging out down at the Brisbane River to get my rays of sunshine, and generally admiring nature. It's so good for your soul, not to mention your mental wellbeing!

If I can be of any help to you in anyway, please get in touch!
My details are:
Social media : kidsfitaust (Instagram, Facebook and LinkedIn)
Email: leah@kidsfitaustralia.com
Website: www.kidsfitaustralia.com

Wishing you a fabulous day!
Leah

AINSLEE HOOPER

'She will probably only live for three weeks, or if she does survive, she's going to be a vegetable for the rest of her life.'

I was born in the late 70s with a disability. Nearly five decades on, I think it's safe to say those doctors got it wrong. My childhood was fairly typical; doing kids' usual stuff, hanging out with friends and parties. Physically, I did what I could, and what I could not do, I didn't. Even in primary school, when others were doing their bike education and I learned touch-typing on my own, I didn't question it. Accessibility and inclusion were not topics of discussion, so things just seemed normal. The only reminders of my disability were hospital stays and school bullying. Everywhere else, I was just me. It would not be evident to me until much later in life that I was allocated the 'disabled person' role from birth, with many negative consequences. However, this label would eventually become my power and ultimately inform my purpose in life.

I travelled through school life with mediocre grades. While I enjoyed classes like media studies, I did poorly in most other areas, especially critical subjects, so I was never really engaged with my studies. I had no sense of direction in life. When choosing my Victorian Certificate of Education (VCE) subjects, coordinators deterred me from pursuing photography, with integration aides refusing to assist my physical needs. Photography didn't align with a suitable career path for someone like me. I had no aspirations, as anything appealing appeared unrealistic or out of reach. The only notch on my belt was holding the second-lowest score in my year twelve graduating class. Life was similar as a young adult, filled with parties, pubs and TAFE. Upon discussing my academic progress with one of my TAFE teachers, we decided the Certificate IV in Information Technology I was doing was not for me. Ironically, this course had been deemed perfect for 'someone like me' by those same people from year twelve. I transferred to a Certificate II in Multimedia and found something I enjoyed. After completing this certificate, it was time to venture into adult life and find a job.

Never having a part-time job like most of my teen peers, my only work experience was in high school. Having a disability, I decided to sign up for a Disability Employment Services (DES) provider. At my first appointment, my employment consultant asked me to tell him about myself and what work I was interested in. I explained my recent TAFE studies and skills in web design and wanted to find a job in that area. My consultant proceeded to look me square in the eyes and say, 'You need to take a long hard look at yourself and realise what you can do.' Looking for a job in an area I was skilled in and sparked my interest was the wrong approach. My consultant organised a job interview with a government agency, advising he would attend and do all talking, except for me to acknowledge I understood everything. At twenty-one, I found myself in a full-time call centre job with the Australian Public Service (APS); supposedly a perfect job for 'someone like me'. Used to having people dictate what I should be doing, I didn't question the status quo; I was living my life on autopilot. It would take another twenty years with some pivotal moments in-between before I switched from autopilot and began to take control of my life.

My life between 1999 and 2002 was pretty mundane. I did the nine to five grind, coming home, sleeping and repeating five days a week. Suddenly in early 2002, I began getting severe migraines multiple times a day, every day. They would come on without notice and make me violently sick. I had been a chronic headache sufferer since I was fifteen, spending a whole term of year nine in hospital, but these migraines were different. Hospitalised, my neurologist advised me to lie flat on my back until they could determine a reason for my migraines. Three months of tests with no answers meant three months of lying flat on my back. Due to my disability, I am paralysed from the waist down with no feeling. As a result, I ended up with a grade four pressure sore on my backside. My mysterious migraines quickly took a back seat. I spent the following twelve months in bed, both in and out of the hospital.

At the age of twenty-five, I fell into my first major depressive episode when my specialist informed me I would spend the rest of my life in bed. Nine months from the original injury, a nurse took me aside to suggest I needed to change specialists. It became apparent my specialist was treating me like one of his aged care patients, not a twenty-five-year-old woman. With a new specialist and a fresh approach, I was up and back at work just shy of twelve months from the initial injury.

Over the next couple of years, I returned to the same daily grind I'd been living before becoming ill, but this time things were different. During my year of strict bed rest, I had a powerful fear my brain was turning to mush. Although I was now back at work, I was very aware I was taking eighty calls a day, all with similar enquiries. I would knock off at 5pm only to eat, sleep and return to do it again. I needed more, but I didn't know what as I'd become accustomed to life happening around me. At this point, a colleague suggested I enrol in university as a mature age student and study something that interested me. I had always wanted to study philosophy, however, the idea of enrolling at university sounded laughable. Still, I investigated it, and I was eligible, so decided to take my colleague's advice. At twenty-seven, I was a part-time university student studying a Bachelor of Arts at Deakin University, undertaking a philosophy major. I was finally doing something for myself.

In my first year, I received average grades on par with what I expected. Receiving my first grade back the following year, I opened the envelope and pulled out my assignment to find a 'D' scrawled on the front page. I burst out crying. Why did I think I would be any good at university? My tears quickly became tears of happiness and excitement when I learned a 'D' meant I had received a distinction, the second-best grade you can get. With this newly discovered talent, I perused the unit guide to see what would spark my interest to complete my degree. I discovered a unit about humans, cultures, and how we make and relate to our worlds. It reminded me of all those documentaries I loved to watch. Five minutes into the first lecture and I was hanging on every word. I had found the one thing that sparked absolute joy, completely changing how I saw the world around me; I had found anthropology. With this newfound passion and sense of belonging, I decided to throw myself entirely into university life and became a student association representative.

With swine flu making its way through Australia at the time, my work colleagues and I were taking calls for the Swine Flu Hotline. A week later, I received a phone call advising that students who had attended the recent student association retreat were required to get tested. By week's end, I was in bed with the worst flu I have ever experienced. As a result, my pressure sore from all those years ago broke down again. My specialist clarified my body could not handle another breakdown and my orders were, once again, to stay in bed twenty-four seven and alternate from side to side. The difference with the second injury was I had two things to focus on in my life that I hadn't previously; firstly, my degree, which I continued completing while in hospital, and secondly, my partner. My partner, whom I met a few months after I commenced my degree, would entertain me with plans for what would become our home. The injury, like the previous one, took a year to heal. However, I wouldn't return to life as I knew it. As my specialist had said initially, my body could not handle another breakdown, therefore life as I knew it had to change. Not only did I have to give up my beloved King Koil mattress for a hospital bed, but I also had to give up independent transfers. Giving up these transfers meant support workers coming into my home for the first time to hoist me in and out of the shower. As if my dignity hadn't already taken a huge hit. The process of becoming a disabled person was in full swing.

I've had some fantastic support workers over the years, however, some of the worst examples of ableism I've experienced have come from the disability sector. The very people who are tasked to care for marginalised people continue to discriminate in favour of able-bodied persons. At my most vulnerable, I experienced support workers talking to me in a manner I refer to as 'talking at me'. These people used a tone of voice akin to talking to a child. In addition to injury, support workers voiced their surprise when they found out I worked, studied and had a partner. Their surprise spoke volumes; I, a disabled person, was not meant to have any of those things. With the belief others knew better than I still deeply ingrained in me, I did what I had always done to cope. I repressed my feelings and internalised all my frustrations until they were buried deep inside. Throughout my second period of strict bed rest, I threw myself deeper into my studies. It allowed me to mentally escape the confines of the four walls surrounding me, even if my body could not. As a result, my passion for anthropology grew. I saw how anthropologists helped solve problems faced by the most marginalised and vulnerable populations worldwide by bridging gaps in understanding. I was now clear what I needed to do. My injury healed and I returned to work with an invitation to complete an honours degree. Work became the necessary tool to get me through my degree, not the other way around as it had been for years.

Although I had clear goals to attain my PhD, one vital detail was missing from my life plan. I did not hold the self-belief I could do anything outside of what I had been doing since I was twenty-one. While some people came into my life telling me I could do more and be more, the voices closest to me, which I had heard from such a young age, echoed the loudest. Those voices discouraged me from giving up a steady, secure job, 'ideal' for 'someone like me', and combined with my inability to see my true worth. I had been doing the same job day in and day out for so long. What if I did try something else and fail? Surely those voices knew better than I.

Then came the event that changed my life in more ways than I could imagine. I had a complete nervous breakdown resulting from workplace bullying. Occurring over a period of two years, it would eventually result in my questioning my sanity and identity. With the voices echoing in my head about job security and being full of self-doubt about my ability to do anything else, there appeared to be no way out; the coping mechanism of self-destructive behaviours took hold. A mental health professional made it abundantly clear that if I did not get out, I was going to die.

So, with the permission I had never been confident enough to give to myself, I left the only job I had known. It was a chance conversation with a friend at the gym (a place that has become part of my mental health therapy), which serendipitously brought all the bits of my life together like pieces of a jigsaw puzzle. She asked me what I wanted to do with my life. It was at that point my purpose, although already clear to me, became even more so. I knew I wanted to help solve problems faced by marginalised people. However, my experiences of ableism (even those experiences I didn't realise were a result of ableism until much later) crystalised my purpose. I was part of a marginalised population; the 20% of Australians with a disability, the largest minority. So, in 2019, I commenced Ainslee Hooper Consulting, helping a wide variety of businesses and organisations reduce the risk of ableism and increase inclusion throughout the community. Utilising various research methods and policy analysis, I have been able to help businesses and organisations ensure positive outcomes for both their businesses and people with disabilities. I use my experiences to raise awareness through writing, my podcast and speaking engagements, to empower individuals working in the disability sector with the necessary interpersonal skills to provide quality services. I was deeply honoured to receive the Employment Award in the Geelong Awards for People With a Disability in 2020 for my work. While being labelled a disabled person had resulted in negative experiences throughout my life, it is now a label I wear with pride.

I want to leave readers with two messages. Firstly, no-one has the right to dictate the life trajectory of another person, no matter how good your intentions may be. If you are in a position of power, use your privilege wisely. Everyone has the opportunity to positively influence a person's world, which will inevitably change someone else's world. Secondly, if you are reading this and my story resonates with you, know it is perfectly acceptable to follow your dreams. Do not allow anyone else's perceptions or ignorance to limit your potential. To quote Bell Hooks, 'I will not have my life narrowed down. I will not bow down to somebody else's whim or someone else's ignorance.' This is my story, and it has only just begun.

ABOUT AINSLEE

I'm Ainslee, and I'm a disabled person. It's taken me a long time to say those words, and my story will explain why. From Geelong, I live with my partner and our fur baby named Sheldon (and yes, he is very much like his namesake, Sheldon Cooper from *The Big Bang Theory*). I'm also a sci-fi loving nerd with a thirst for understanding humans and lifting heavy weights.

I didn't realise it until much later in life, but I was put on this earth to help people see the world through other people's eyes, to remove invisible barriers and bring an understanding of disability.

As an applied anthropologist and founder of Ainslee Hooper Consulting, I am dedicated to helping reduce ableism and increase inclusion for the 20% of Australians living with a disability. I work with all sorts of businesses and organisations – from councils, disability service providers, and sustainability services firms – just to name a few. Doing this kind of work allows me to adapt my approach specific to client needs. I get to meet many amazing people who share their stories, which in turn helps me inform solutions for the client. Hearing these accounts have left a lasting impression on me.

I never believed the saying 'do a job you love, and you'll never work a day in your life' until I started my consultancy.

Founded in 2019, I've provided consulting services and speaking engagements for clients, including:

- City of Melbourne
- Point Advisory
- genU
- OC Connections
- Geelong Gallery
- Disability Leadership Institute
- Bree Gorman Consulting

Hearing so many amazing stories through my work inspired me to start my own podcast, *Ainslee Hooper Chats with* … I get to interview people from the disability community across the world, who share their stories on how they experience their disability. You can catch it on Spotify, Apple Podcasts and Google Podcasts.

Before starting my consultancy, I worked in a call centre in the Australian Public Service (APS) for twenty years, connecting the Australian public to financial assistance from welfare payments to disaster relief and early access to superannuation.

If you met me in 2018, you would not recognise me as the person I am today. Although I am an introvert and most consider me to be a quiet person, my ex-colleagues, who have attended some of my speaking engagements, are astounded at the confident and talkative person they see today. After an anthropology conference dinner, even my partner commented that it was the most he'd ever heard me speak; a stark difference to the person who would go to work every day with barely a peep aside from answering customer enquiries.

In 2015 I completed an honours thesis in anthropology examining the public policies implemented as part of the Northern Territory Intervention and the negative stereotypes of Aboriginal Australians they perpetuated. In 2021 I commenced a PhD in Anthropology researching the experiences of people with disabilities in my hometown of Geelong during COVID-19.

In 2021, people with disabilities are still forty years behind the women's equality movement. However, I look forward to a future where this gap no longer exists, and disability inclusion is the norm. It's a slow process, with many inspiring disability activists fighting for our rights since before I was even born, but it is a fight we must continue to ensure future generations don't have to.

If you'd like to join me in the fight to address the issues which perpetuate ableism and hinder inclusion, you can connect with me on LinkedIn (www.linkedin.com/in/ainsleehooper) or email me: info@ainsleehooper.com.au

KYLIE-LEE BRADFORD

As a child, my mornings began hearing the wild birds calling and the smell of a smouldering fire, as my mother woke early to prepare her coffee on the campfire.

The memories of growing up in a small Aboriginal community, in Kakadu, Australia, are filled with joy and laughter. As children we would be swimming in waterholes with towering magical waterfalls, bathing in billabongs flooded with native birds and wild lily pads, and the evenings were filled with tranquil sunsets. Growing up, I was surrounded by family, culture and knowledge, and these are treasured memories I will keep forever. This wonderful life experience of growing up in Kakadu has moulded and guided me into the person I am today.

My mother Sheril, my best friend, teacher and advisor to many young Aboriginal children, was my inspiration for starting my business journey. We grew up with the connection to land and respecting all that our land gives and teaches us. Guided by our mother's wisdom and advice teaching the girls everything she could about women's business and native foods, I knew never to ask when my brother would disappear with my uncles for weeks on end.

As kids we never knew the craziness of a city and were sheltered from the toxins that city life can bring. Even our treats and sweets were wild native berries and bush honey.

I would follow my mother through the bush in search of the perfect gumnuts to make her handpainted earrings. We would walk for hours; I loved to follow Mum. We'd carry back our bag of nuts and ochre to camp and I would play in the dirt while I watched my mother spend day after day sanding, painting and preparing the most beautiful earrings I have ever seen! When she was done, we would drive over an hour to the local shop to sell them to the owner, who would later sell them to tourists.

It was the first time I witnessed entrepreneurship in its most raw form.

Now I have grown, I'm a mum of four beautiful children. It was time to start my own story. The decision to leave country was extremely hard for me and my heart and spirt often aches for the calmness and tranquility of Kakadu, as it's a place where time truly stops and I only hope my daughters are inspired, in a small way, from the journey we have all been on.

My business journey started around six years ago when my mother and I were invited to go on the show *Shark Tank Australia* to showcase our idea of creating organic baby clothing which featured handpainted art and dreamtime stories. At this stage, I only had a few sample runs I had designed to take on the show; we hadn't even made a sale yet.

It was Mum's first time in Sydney. She felt so deadly in the green room getting her make up done for the show. She was so proud that she cried on national television when they asked her to come out and meet the Sharks. My mother's comment walking out the door was, 'Not bad for two girls from the bush.' I remember shaking so badly when walking through the large double doors to face the Sharks. All I could think of was, *It doesn't matter what happens, you will have this experience with your mum forever.* On the show we were offered two investments which sounded very exciting for a small startup, but through due diligence we soon realised the investors did not have the same vision and mission we had for the company. For that reason, we turned down the investment and walked away to conquer the organic baby industry alone, with community at heart.

To be honest, everyone thought we were mad. I would get comments like, 'You're crazy to turn down investment. How will you ever make it coming from Kakadu?' But for my mother and me, staying true to culture and protecting our community was everything. I am so proud we stayed true to ourselves, and more importantly, believed in us and doing it *our way*.

Looking back six years ago, there were not many Indigenous businesses around, especially with women founders, so I made it my mission to inspire as many Indigenous women as I could.

'It really doesn't matter where you come from, if you have a dream and you want it badly enough, the world is your oyster.'

I can't tell you how many times I was knocked back on my business journey. Regardless of the knock-backs, I truly believed in our vision and knew if I held onto that and didn't give up, then the noes would eventually turn into yeses … and that's exactly what happened!

As the environment changed and the world was becoming more conscious of buying eco-friendly and organic products, our brand very quickly became recognised for exactly what I had worked for; as an Indigenous business producing wellness products for mums and bubs with community at heart.

We stayed in our lane, committed and focused on what we specialised in, even if we didn't appeal to every customer, and yes, we lost some sales in the process.

One thing I have learnt is that not everyone is your customer. The sooner you can understand your brand's DNA, by identifying exactly who your ideal customer is and what they look like, you will see your business truly grow.

Building trusted relationships and surrounding myself with inspirational people in business helped me to stay on course and reach my end goal.

I focused on our wholesale sector, growing to over one hundred stockists in two years. I put the profits back into mentoring and coaching Indigenous women in business and their startup business entrepreneurial journeys. I even had the privilege of travelling to Papua New Guinea on a cultural exchange with an incredible bunch of Indigenous women.

Not only was it important to grow my business, but it was equally, if not more, important to grow myself. I attended women's business school, investor bootcamps, MURRA Indigenous business school, countless networking events and made sure I stayed connected to country, and returned home to Kakadu any chance I could.

I started speaking and was paid to speak at events across Australia. This was the most doubting experience for me; there were always negative thoughts racing through my mind. *Did all these people really want to hear my story? What makes you so special or unique?* I was filled with self-doubt. It is incredibly confronting to stand in front of a crowd of people, especially women in business, and tell them your story with a hope it inspires even just one of them.

Although I was terrified every time I spoke on stage, I knew the more I did it, and the more people that heard my story, the easier it would become. My confidence grew, and with every speaker request came a crowd of incredible women that I, in return, learnt from, collaborated with and am still friends with today. What really helped me to overcome the nerves and stresses of public speaking was to realise this is my story and if I mess up, no-one will know. The more I became confident in telling my story, the less I worried about messing up and even if I did mess up or fumble, I just moved on and no-one in the crowd noticed a thing.

Speaking at events opened many different avenues and led to me being nominated for awards. I was amazed when I won the Indigenous excellence award. I often look back and think, *How the hell did I get here?* The answer is hard work, and most importantly, my family, who are my biggest supporters. I'm glad I included them in my journey; the champagne moments as well as the sad moments of tears and fear.

My fear, the fear I speak of, is not the fear of losing money, but the fear of letting people down who look up to me. My daughters would say, 'Look at Mummy on TV,' or my nieces who live in Aboriginal communities call me to say, 'Aunty, can you help me start my business?' But most of all, I don't want to let down my mum. She is my inspiration.

My mother was the bravest, most courageous Aboriginal woman you could ever meet, with the biggest heart in the world. The foster children she took in and cared for would say the same. We were so lucky to have a caring mother and she welcomed babies Felix, Joe and Koda, and had them with us to adulthood. She was my biggest supporter of all. I am grateful and blessed to walk in her light and legacy. Knowing she is proud of me is what keeps me from ever failing.

These are the strengths you draw and call on in your darkest moments, and through many years of grit and determination to succeed, I now have a very successful ecommerce store producing Indigenous wellness products for mums and bubs, which I run with my family and an amazing team.

I have an incredible social mission to help mums from Aboriginal communities and their newborns. I have proudly produced a 'welcome to the world' pack with relevant culturally safe information, including a list of Aboriginal health centre connections for the community, along with everything mums need to know to help in the first twelve month after bubs' birth. We also include our handpainted jumpsuits, wraps and a range of products provided by our amazing sponsors!

With over one hundred wholesalers and corporate partnerships around Australia, and our new organic wellness and juice bar in Samford Valley, Brisbane, we not only sell our Indigenous wellness products, but we also showcase and educate people on our native foods with a range of quandong and Kakadu plum smoothies and cold press juices.

I am proud to continue to work in our Aboriginal communities, especially mentoring and training programs aimed at teaching young Indigenous women entrepreneurship. My first, very special women's retreat in Kakadu is commencing soon, and we are hoping to make this an annual event.

Success, for me, has come with many challenges, tears, laughter and rewards. When my mother passed away suddenly I was broken. I spoke to her one morning and that night I answered the most horrifying phone call from my younger brother, who said Mum was gone. The grief was unbelievable. The hurt just wouldn't stop and I felt so alone, with my mother and best friend gone. This chapter of my life almost killed me. I fell very quickly into a self-sabotaging depression, and the overwhelming feeling of grief flooded me with sadness and anger. I knew the only way I could truly move through this difficult time was to go back to country in Kakadu, which was calling me in my dreams every time my head hit the pillow. I spent six months back in Kakadu being cleansed and connecting with my country and Elders.

The hurt will always be there but through my spiritual connections I can feel my mother and I talk to her every day. My Elders were able to cleanse a small part of my grief to allow me to connect again. I thank my mother each and every day! I thank her for giving me the wisdom and cultural knowledge to showcase our beautiful products to the world. She walks beside me every step of the way and I miss her more than she will ever know.

Now I share her wisdom with my own children, taking them home to country in Kakadu for ceremonies and important milestones and spiritual connections.

I'm extremely lucky that my children will always have Kakadu, Nana and their ancestors to guide them on whatever journey they choose to take.

But always remember this is your journey. You tell your own story and make your own path; you choose the people you allow in your life and the people you let go.

ABOUT KYLIE-LEE

Kylie-Lee is a proud Murrumburr woman who grew up in a small Aboriginal community called Patonga in the heart of Kakadu National Park. Kylie's mum is a traditional owner of this region and a well-respected Elder. In 2016 Kylie-Lee began her company Kakadu Tiny Tots, an Indigenous-owned company from Kakadu NT creating beautiful organic baby and children's clothing that features handpainted Indigenous art and designs. Every little piece created comes with its own Dreamtime story.

The company has grown from strength to strength, stocked in over eighty boutique stores around Australia as well as domestic and international airports. Their ecommerce store has tripled in sales year on year. With a very exciting social media campaign to be launch before Christmas promoting beautiful products made from Indigenous women around Australia. Growing up in the bush is incredible but also comes with many challenges especially when trying to start an Indigenous business!

www.kakadutinytots.com.au

MARIA FAALAFI

Change the world? What does that even mean? Is it possible for one person to *really* change the world? I believe so!

Change does not come from a single action but rather a chain of actions which creates a reaction; a reaction that inspires and influences family, friends and your community to trigger a wave of change. To change the world, we first need to create change within our home, our immediate family and ourselves.

By telling you my story, I hope to share my reasons for believing we all have the power to change the world. For generations, my family has been underpinned by strong, independent women who empowered me, and gave me the confidence to fearlessly follow my dreams. Each of those women had a different kind of influence over me. My mother, my greatest mentor, has always been a go-getter. She believes if you want something, you need to work hard for it and achieve it yourself. My dad left before I was born so she had to withdraw from university to work twelve-hour days just to make ends meet. When we moved to Australia, she worked day and night to save for a house and finish her accounting degree. Her efforts paid off, and now after two decades, she has the job of her dreams and owns multiple properties. Another woman who influenced me with her great strength was my grandma: a breast cancer and domestic violence survivor, she had the greatest sense of humour and always knew how to put a smile on my face. While my mum worked long hours, I was cared for by my great-aunties and cousins. They were all women and inspired me in surprisingly different ways. One cousin, a very talented artist whose passion sparked my quest for creativity, taught me how to expand my imagination through art. Her mum, one of my great-aunties, was an amazing cook. She loved making cakes and would always let me help her in the kitchen. Her culinary influence encouraged me to open up my own cafe. Another cousin was a fitness fanatic; she would do aerobics every night and call me in to be her fitness buddy. Together with her sister, we would have so much fun dancing and moving to the music. This ignited my passion for movement and fitness from a young age. Without realising, these amazing women changed and shaped my world. They lovingly planted seeds that would later bloom to guide me on my journey. I felt safe in my bubble, guarded and guided by this wonderful group of women.

However, in 1997, my wall of security came crashing down when we moved to Australia from Uruguay. I arrived with nothing but my suitcases and two words of English in my vocabulary; yes and no. Life was hard in my teenage years. Not only was I dealing with all the typical hormonal changes and emotions, but I had no friends, was unable to understand anything or anyone, and most of my family were 12,000km away! At that point I realised I had two choices. I could either feel sorry for myself and cast a shadow on my bubbly personality, or I could amplify my best traits and try my hardest to rebuild my world. Thankfully I chose the second option, and in no time, I had created a plethora of wonderful friendships. Ten years later, I was sure the hard times were behind me. I moved interstate, had a great job as an engineering drafter, and was in a long-term relationship with the man of my dreams. I'd purchased my own home and had a head full of aspirations of starting my own drafting business, and travelling to exotic locations. I was a perfectly healthy, happy twenty-something-year-old … or so I thought. One day while studying for my Bachelor of Business (alongside my full-time position), I suddenly got a terrible throbbing migraine, so powerful I couldn't move from the bathroom floor. My boyfriend (now husband) picked up my limp body and took me to the emergency department. On arrival, they pumped me with strong painkillers, but as they failed to work, the doctor decided to do something experimental and injected my scalp with a local anaesthetic to rapidly lower the debilitating pain.

Little did I know this event would be the first of many to kickstart my health journey. Within a couple of months, my health began to rapidly deteriorate. I went down to 42kg, losing 6kg in just two weeks, developed digestive issues, chronic fatigue, dizziness, daily panic attacks, brain fog, heart palpitations, blurry vision, phobias, severe anxiety and depression. I quickly realised something was terribly wrong, and my body was shouting at me to stop everything and do something FAST. As the depression and anxiety worsened, I felt trapped within my body and mind. It was as if something had taken over my every thought, my personality and my life. My happy personality was overshadowed by fear and negative thoughts. I was scared to go out anywhere as I didn't know how my body would react. I was also tired of pretending everything was okay in front of friends and family.

My life turned upside down in a matter of months. I had to quit my job and sell my home to be able to stop and heal. After years of doctors' visits, trips to hospital and countless referrals to specialists, I still had no answers but a growing list of symptoms. They would give me pills to mask those symptoms, which often made me feel worse as my body was too weak to handle the side effects. I felt defeated and exhausted. I didn't want to do it anymore. It was at that point I realised I was standing in front of another fork in the road, this time much tougher than the last. Once again, I had to make a choice. I could either give up, or pick myself up and gather my last shred of hope and energy to seek answers for myself. So that's what I did and my healing journey began.

I put my busy life on hold and with the help of my amazingly supportive husband and family, I started searching for answers. I read healing books, spoke to numerous health care professionals and closely followed incredible survival stories. It was then when I started to realise what I'd been doing to my body for so long. My body was simply crying out for help. I now believe mental or physical struggles are an internal alarm for our bodies to give us the wake-up call we desperately need. It's like our body's handbrake, so we can stop, reflect, learn and change our ways to start the transformation into our true self. To start my healing journey, I needed to make some drastic changes in every area of my life.

I saw a naturopath who recommended a gluten- and dairy-free diet to heal my gut. I started drinking green smoothies, which I call my liquid vitamin pills, so I could replenish the vitamins and minerals my body was lacking. I gave up all high GI sugars such as corn syrup, cane sugar, honey, maple syrup, and all artificial sweeteners, as I knew they were affecting my blood sugar levels. So I wouldn't feel I was missing out, I replaced these sugars with more nutritious, lower GI alternatives such as coconut sugar, stevia and rice malt syrup. I later found out I had reactive hypoglycemia; a blood sugar condition that ended up being the culprit for my severe anxiety, heart palpitations, depression, food intolerances and panic attacks. I proceeded to get rid of as many chemicals as possible from my life. You don't realise how many chemicals are in our everyday products until your start to read the labels! I replaced all my beauty, household and food products with ones that were all natural and mostly organic. It was then my mind's turn to heal. I started to practice meditation, removing anything causing unnecessary stress in my life. I saw the people I loved more often and started doing things I used to enjoy again. I also started volunteering. In time, my symptoms began to dissipate and I slowly started to take charge of my life.

During my healing journey, my friends and family started to notice positive effects from the changes I was making. They asked me how they too could improve their health and lifestyle. When they began to see their own positive outcomes, they also started to help others to make positive changes. I realised I had a new purpose in life; I felt compelled to share what I had learned and wanted to help others on their journey of change. As I was cooking everything from scratch, I developed a passion for healthy cooking. I become obsessed with replacing the unhealthy treats and meals I missed so much with healthy alternatives. A year later I opened a healthy, organic cafe in the quest to change people's perception of what healthy food should taste like. At the cafe, I met many amazing people who would tell me of their health journey and how they had healed in similar ways. After the birth of my daughter, I decided to sell my business to concentrate on motherhood and my health again. One day, while changing my daughter's nappy, I realised the amount of waste my tiny baby was making in such a short amount of time! This led me to research ways of minimising waste for my daughter, which progressed to finding other ways to live a more sustainable life. We started to compost all our organic waste, giving new life to anything that could be reused or repurposed. We changed our electricity provider to 100% renewables, and chose to buy items made from natural fibres. We bought an electric vehicle, which turned out to be the best and most economical decision ever!

Those small changes would lead me to a brand new part of my life journey. I became passionate about sustainability and wanted to make it easier for busy people to find environmentally friendly products and businesses. I created an online eco-friendly marketplace called ECO Marketplace and a directory for all things natural and healthy called Eco-Healthy Finder.

In the past, I had wanted to be more sustainable, but did nothing, as I could always find an excuse to convince myself my actions would be so small they would never create the impact needed to make change in the world. Let's be honest – most of us are aware of the urgent action needed to ensure the survival of not only the human race, but also all other species. At times, it's easy to feel a sense of hopelessness and lack of power in making a difference in the fight for our future. But there is no better time to create change; now is the time to evolve, adapt and revolutionise. The choices we make with every service or product we buy is what truly drives change. We can use our consumer power to show businesses and governments we are serious about change. As the saying goes, 'If we don't buy it, they won't make it.' In order to initiate change in every aspect of our lives, it is first necessary to go through a metamorphosis process; to look within, find our true purpose and grow our wings to guide us into our journey. Change begins within and starts with self-awareness. Ask yourself a simple question with everything you do, *Will this help me be part of the problem or the solution?* Ask this question when you think about your career, or before you purchase anything. This question will facilitate self-awareness and increase your clarity when deciding which path to take.

We are undoubtedly creatures of habit. Let's create good habits to replace damaging ones. When we develop and implement positive habits on a daily basis, we feed our body, mind and soul. Start by doing something you care about, practicing gratitude when you wake up and before you go to sleep, have a green smoothie instead of a coffee (trust me it will give you a lot more sustained energy!), use meditation to clear your mind, and make space for encouraging thoughts. An important habit, and one that helped me greatly with depression, was to volunteer. Making a difference in the community, whether through money, items or your time, or simply performing random acts of kindness, is an amazing way to heal a broken, discouraged soul. You can help your neighbours, friends and family, a homeless person or sign up to an organisation. You can share your story to help others, or start a business that fulfills your purpose and helps those in need. As a little girl I used to believe we needed superpowers to save the world, but now I know we all have the power within us to be a superhero and change our world for the better. And just like every superhero, we must learn to understand our power and how to use it. Every action we take, no matter how small, can implement a force that will not only change your life, but the lives of those around you.

When you use your mind to manifest what your heart speaks, anything becomes possible. I hope my story can guide and encourage you to take the first step in changing the world. It doesn't matter where or how you start, what matters is to start somewhere and build from there. Change can start with YOU. You can be the drop of change that creates a ripple effect of positive reactions. Because change is not scary, but a future without change is!

ABOUT MARIA

These days, when I wake up in the morning, I feel refreshed, relaxed and excited to meet the day (well, when my daughter lets me sleep!). But it wasn't always that way. Ten years ago, my life changed forever when I suddenly became ill.

Let's face it – modern society does not exactly encourage healthy living. We prioritise success and achievement above all else, often at the expense of our health and the health of the planet. In my twenties, I fell victim to this vicious cycle myself. On the surface, things looked great! I had a thriving career as an engineering drafter, owned my own home, was engaged to a wonderful man and had a great social life. But deep down, I knew something was wrong. It felt like my body was fundamentally unwell. At first it was just a creeping suspicion, but after a while, my body began screaming at me, warning me that my way of life needed to change – and fast.

I began to lose weight rapidly, had terrible migraines, developed food allergies and digestive issues, dizziness, heart palpitations, panic attacks, double vision, severe anxiety and depression. And they were just a few of my everyday symptoms.

Before long, I had withdrawn from both my social and professional life. I spent my days in bed desperately hoping for answers.

My doctors struggled to find a diagnosis. None of the multiple tests could pinpoint anything critically wrong, yet I felt I was at the end of the rope. Despite my symptoms, I had a powerful will to live and I was determined to fix myself, no matter what it took. I had no option but to question everything.

I started with food. I had read stories of people dramatically improving their health through diet changes so I researched all I could, and set about putting together an organic, all-natural, gluten-, dairy- and sugar-free diet.

I guess we all know the average modern diet is unhealthy, but I was totally shocked when I realised how unhealthy the food I had been consuming was.

Just reading the ingredients on some of the packaged foods I had in the house made me feel sick; chemical after chemical, and not a single nutrient in sight. This was the first part of my wake-up call. I replaced all the junk with quality, nutritious foods. That was just the beginning.

I started looking at the other products in the house; beauty products, cleaning products, things I used everyday.

Not surprisingly, each one was made up of an endless list of impossible-to-pronounce chemicals. And to think – I'd been rubbing these substances all over by body and using them to clean the surfaces where I eat. I had no choice but to approach the situation holistically and rely on my new change in lifestyle in the hope it would make a difference.

Slowly my symptoms diminished. I felt human again. I felt healthy again. I felt like myself again!

I suspected that countless others were suffering in a similar way with unknown health issues. This inspired me to create my businesses ECO Marketplace – a one-stop shop for all things eco-friendly, and Eco

Healthy Finder – an online directory for eco-friendly businesses and healthy food outlets. I wanted to make it easier for busy people to live a healthy, chemical-free lifestyle.

My vision is to continue to help people to take control of their lives and their health, while contributing to a more sustainable, eco-friendly future!

www.ecomarketplace.com.au

TARA McKEON

'You only get out what you put in,' is something my grandfather said to me many years ago when I was just a child. It didn't resonate then, but today it is heard loud and clear. It's taken a while to appreciate the sentiment behind the comment and what it actually meant. Thinking back, it's probably a statement I resented, not only as a child, but as a teen and an early adult. You see, nothing really came easy for me. I often looked around and silently thought, *Why can't someone just help me*? I grew up with a single mother. Mum had me when she was just a baby herself and my biological dad had a family of his own. My first stepfather, who I loved immensely, was taken away and died behind bars. The second was abusive. For a long time, I felt I had no-one to turn to. I quickly learnt the only person I could rely on was myself; bouncing from couch to couch, sleeping in my car, living out of a suitcase at times. To this day I still have one bag I never fully unpack. I well and truly knew what it was like to be at rock bottom. It wasn't a place I wanted to stay.

I always had a passion for the fashion industry, but the romantic idea of studying full-time for some kind of fashion degree with no guarantee of paid work at the end of it, was simply an unrealistic dream for me. Often unable to afford groceries, sanitary products or petrol, I needed something that would pay the bills and give me a steady income. I was drawn to nursing, not only because it was a stable income, but I wanted to help others in need. It took me seven years of stop-starting what should have been a three-year degree before I was finally able to complete it. Again, with the degree came weeks of unpaid placement. Although I loved the course, survival came first, which meant I would have to defer and return to multiple hospitality jobs to get by. It was only when I met my now-husband, Paul, I was able to have a bit more security and support, and was finally able to finish my degree. My first year of nursing was spent across palliative care and emergency, and my love of helping others grew. I advanced and completed postgraduate studies in critical care and loved it. I know what it's like to be vulnerable and in need and in a way, by helping others, although in much different circumstances to my own, I was also helping myself to heal from the trauma of my past.

Time went on and so did life. My father, who I now had a beautiful relationship with, suddenly became unwell and passed away on the very same palliative care ward where I once worked. This was extremely hard for me to process. We had spent so much of our lives distant, once we came together again I truly feel I lost my best friend. Throughout his illness I had begun to succumb to the pressures of study, emergency nursing, living off hospital food at his bedside and began to gain weight. Thirty days from diagnosis to death wasn't long enough for me to process what was happening. I tried to protect him and never said the final things I wanted or needed to say. Saying those things would only have highlighted to him the inevitable. Once he left this earth, I was strong for a little while, but it soon caught up and I fell in a heap. Depression and anxiety began to creep in and that was the start of my weight gain issues.

Like so many of the difficult situations I had found myself into in the past, I learnt to block out the pain and keep going. Although a piece of me was gone forever, survival mode was something I was no stranger to, and just like old times, it seemed to kick right back in. I went back to nursing and to caring for others, but forgot to care about myself. Falling pregnant with my son was the piece of happiness I had been longing for and I prepared to embark on my most important role yet, becoming a mother. Brodie was born in January 2018. Although without a doubt the birth of my son was the happiest moment of my life, the lack of a support network around me, a husband who had to return to work and a baby with multiple undiagnosed intolerances and what appeared to be an allergy to sleeping beyond twenty minutes at a time, eventually started to take its toll. I didn't have a close group of girlfriends others seemed to have, so no-one was coming to see me or my new baby. I felt sad and alone.

I recognise now I was probably suffering from postnatal depression, but at the time it was just an unexplainable loneliness and immeasurable sadness. The stigma that seems to surround such things made me feel that if I admitted to how I was feeling, I would be seen as a bad mum, a failure. Always having to be fiercely independent for my own survival, I couldn't bring myself to ask for help. I had an overwhelming fear that even if I did ask for help, who would come? It had always been just me. And so the weight crept on. I stopped weighing myself when I hit 140kg for fear of the scales no longer recognising my weight. From 80kg to 140kg and 168cm tall, I was unhealthy and unhappy. I remember squeezing into size twenty-two, refusing to acknowledge I was any larger than that. My anxiety was at an all-time high. The thought of going to the shopping centre and bumping into someone from my past was mortifying. I simply couldn't attend social situations I was brave enough or even wanted to go to, because I felt I had nothing to wear. As a new mum, clothing should have been the last thing I needed to worry about, but the fact was there was nothing for me and therefore it was the first thing I thought about. Although I had always loved the fashion industry, it was apparent that it no longer loved or welcomed me because I didn't fit the social or advertised mould of 'what a woman should look like'. My heart was broken.

I remember sitting with my husband many times, watching women walk the streets with little boutique shopping bags and saying, 'I wish I could shop like them.'

His response was always, 'One day.' He loved me no matter my size; the issue was I felt I could no longer love myself. Society didn't want me. Everything I had achieved seemed to become invalid due to my increase in size. It just wasn't right. About a year after my son's birth, my father's estate began to be finalised and with my inheritance I decided to invest in my health. I had a sleeve gastrectomy performed. I was morbidly obese, a shell of my former self with no confidence or will to go on; it really was a matter of life and death. Choosing the surgery was probably the hardest and scariest things I have done, yet I have no doubt it saved my life. The weight began to come off and the lights of my soul slowly began shining again.

I remember walking into a women's clothing store, terrified. I had lost over 30kg, but was still ignored by the shop assistant as I hesitantly walked in. It was the first time in years I had walked into a standard clothing store, and felt completely overwhelmed. I remember hunting the racks for a size twenty, reaching straight to the back automatically for the largest size, but they all seemed to stop at a size fourteen or sixteen at most. Then, like a needle in a haystack, I struck gold and found an oversized, loose-fitting dress in a size eighteen. I couldn't believe it. I remember hesitantly asking the shop assistant if I could try it on. She didn't look up but gestured me towards the fitting room. I could barely squeeze the door closed past my body, but finally I was alone in the fitting room, with the dress. As squished and uncomfortable as it was in that tiny little cubicle, I managed to get the dress on and the pure elation that consumed me is something I will always remember, because you will never believe it, but the bloody thing fit! It was hideous, but I didn't care! It was mine. I remember taking it to the counter and paying, trying to explain my happiness to the shop assistant but again, she seemed not to care. She knew the only thing I could purchase from the store was already in my hands, so for her, any time spent with me was wasted. I walked outside the store with tears in my eyes, finally with my own little boutique shopping bag. I was just so, so happy my husband took a photo.

Once the initial joy of being able to purchase something from a standard store had subsided, I began to process what had happened. Again the joy turned to sadness as I thought about how sad a world it is, when a size eighteen/twenty female can't easily purchase clothing. The fact was, I had found one piece of clothing in an entire store that would fit, and it was such a big deal. The only piece of clothing in the store that would actually fit me was the most hideous shape and colour, yet I was so grateful for its existence. It just wasn't right. But it was the social norm. As a society, should we just accept that the fashion industry only really caters for those sized six to fourteen? Even though the market is there for bigger sizes, the clothing options are not. My maternity leave was coming to an end and I found myself faced with a now or never moment. Either I returned to night shift emergency nursing, or combined my love of fashion and helping others in a different way. I decided to take a leap of faith, back myself 100% and make sure no woman ever felt the way I did, ever again. Basic clothing is essential. Options should be a right. Clothing of the same quality and price across all sizes, prints and shapes should be a given. The harsh truth seemed to be that many clothing brands didn't want to be associated with women of a certain size. I decided I was going to be the one to change that. Everyday women, people just like me, need to be represented and given a choice.

It was funny when I floated the idea to a few people, everyone seemed to have an opinion on what I should be doing. They didn't care when I needed their help, yet the negativity flooded in when I shared my idea. How stupid could I be to leave nursing to open a store? What was my store going to sell? Just dresses? It was clear to me they had never felt the anguish of not being catered for by the fashion industry. They had never felt the pain of literally having nothing to wear. Tall poppy syndrome was strong. They were quiet and content when I was a sad, lonely new mum, but the second I wanted to be something more – to do something more – everyone had an opinion. The old days of relying on myself had made me strong, strong enough to back myself. And so Proud Poppy Clothing was born.

From that moment, I set out on creating a brand that was more than just another clothing store. I wanted to build a community. I never wanted women to feel alone or unwelcomed, either socially or in a clothing store. I wanted them to know they are not alone. They didn't have a problem, it was a problem with society, and I was going to change that. By unapologetically putting myself out there, I wanted every woman who saw me to be able to relate to a normal body, a normal person and be brave enough to be themselves unapologetically too. At times I am scared. At times I am embarrassed, but I think back to the sad woman I used to be and how she would feel if she could see someone like me now, telling her that there is absolutely nothing wrong with her. I wonder how much easier things would have been for her. So for her and for every woman like her, I will continue to grow the beautiful community that is Proud Poppy Clothing, so no-one ever has to feel unwelcome, ashamed or unable to be themselves ever again.

ABOUT TARA

My name is Tara McKeon. I am thirty-five years old, a mummy to my beautiful son Brodie, with another babe on the way, wife to Paul, my ever-supportive husband, and a fur and feather mum to my three dogs, two cats, rabbit and chatterbox eclectus parrot, Pablo. An animal lover from way back, they keep finding their way into my home! I am also lover of travel, longing for this COVID-19 pandemic to end so we can get back to what we do best as a family; exploring. Fine wine and delicious cheese are my best friends.

If you had to look back at my professional history you would see I am qualified in many things. From handing out yogurt samples at supermarkets, selling raffle tickets at the MCG, hospitality gigs on Hamilton Island and all over Melbourne – you name it, I've done it. Hard work has never been something I'm afraid of, in fact, it was often essential to survive. Later in life I trained as a nurse and completed a postgraduate diploma in critical care nursing and worked several years as an emergency nurse. I am now the proud owner of Proud Poppy Clothing – a women's clothing retailer which has become so much more than just a store; it's a community of supportive, like-minded women. Ironically the only job I have been fired from was managing a women's clothing boutique and the only interview I went for where I didn't walk away with the job, was a women's clothing retailer. That was lucky because now I am building my own empire with an army of Proud Poppy supporters cheering me along.

Proud Poppy Clothing was launched in August 2019 as an online-only retailer – a one-woman band, a new mum working from a laptop with two tubs of clothes. A mere two years later, we now have a bricks and mortar store in Doreen, two warehouses, a styling suite and eighteen staff. We ship hundreds of orders globally each week and have thousands of followers across our social media platforms. I am passionate about bridging the gap between mainstream advertising and the fashion industry; the gap between what is shown as the social norm of what a woman should be, and what we are in reality. I am passionate about celebrating women in all their forms of beauty and realness.

As the winner of four AusMumpreneur awards for 2020, I have been featured across several media outlets. With our global reach expanding rapidly, we can't help but feel that things are just getting started for Proud Poppy Clothing and I am so excited to see where the future takes us.

LAURA ELIZABETH

You are here for greatness.

You already identify with the change-maker archetype and possess an understanding that your purpose is to co-create a new world, ripe with opportunity, prosperity and abundance.

This path is messy. My own role as a change-maker and thought leader is definitely not for the prim and proper, or straightlaced conservative minds.

In fact, the very thought of it, for some, is so deeply confronting they refuse to engage with me at all. But here I am, ready to disrupt and create ripples alongside other fierce-gentle leaders.

(*Fierce-gentle:* definition: fierce with your boundaries, gentle with your worth – Fleassy Malay, writer).

Coulda, shoulda, woulda will not launch epic change within your reality and the world that needs you. So what are you going to do?

Here is what I have learned stepping into the path of the change-maker.

Disclaimer – everything I share here is purely based on my own experience and understanding. I encourage you to soak up whatever resonates as truth and allow anything else to fall away. My perception of truth is mine alone and not intended to be gospel for you or anyone else. I simply offer what I know, to ignite inspiration for your own potential.

You do you, babe!

You need to start

Where you begin may not be where you end up, but none of that happens without starting. Intentions are actions waiting to happen and that vision board isn't going to manifest itself. Be open to new opportunities for growth (if they feel aligned) and allow and accept all possibilities without attachment to outcome.

If you knew me twenty years ago, I was timid and super awkward amongst crowds; riddled with anxiety, desperate to fit in. I wanted to help the people around me and friends called on me for support, but I never knew it was possible to live from a place of self-worth and authentic truth.

I didn't even know my industry existed back then. There's a high chance I would have baulked at the mere suggestion of it!

I had no idea how my life would twist and turn. That I would lose everything, more than once, and have to rebuild. That I would emerge stronger every time, not just surviving but thriving! Eventually being thrust into a world where I am showing up loud and proud, right here on this deeply sacred mission.

Back then, even as a teen, I made a commitment to be of service to the conscious evolution of humanity. To use my natural gifts for good. From memory, there were some pretty candles and maybe an oracle card or two set up around an altar and I wrote super specific intentions that I wanted to be of service in any way I could.

At sixteen, I began sitting in a spiritual development circle (before it was cool). We practiced meditation, learned how to read tarot cards and other types of psychometry and how to tap into our intuitive gifts.

It was the medicine I needed at the time, in a world I didn't understand.

It gave me hope. I sat in that circle approaching ten years, taking short breaks during the births of two of my three children, before our lives meandered along different paths, and the women's circle organically fizzled out. I am grateful for the connections and lifelong friendships I still have with many of these women. Our time together shaped the woman I am today.

During that decade, I spent more time defending my spiritual practice than celebrating it. I was the brunt of many jokes and people around me would often be super uncomfortable. Stepping into my growth zone meant ruffling a few feathers, and now twenty years later, I've been known to ruffle entire flocks! I was labelled a 'witch' and a charlatan, amongst other unfavourable names, by those around me who never actually took the time to ask what intuition is all about.

Instead they let their judgement get in the way and felt entitled to ridicule and judge, rather than meet their own discomfort with curiosity and exploring for themselves.

I learned (albeit slowly, remember I was only in my late teens/early twenties) to stop defending myself. To find compassion for where they were on their personal spiritual journey, or lack thereof. It's not everyone's cup of tea, and that's okay. However, my choices to walk my own peculiar path definitely drew attention.

It didn't stop me – if anything, it fuelled me.

I went on to learn reiki (again, before it was cool), reflexology and several other holistic healing modalities. There's too many to list as my hunger for learning grew, but you get the picture I'm conjuring for you here. I had found my areas of passion, my *lane*. The things that lit up my soul. Each certificate expanded my toolbox, paving the way for the next level of personal growth and professional service.

It is in the past few years, however, of unapologetically stepping up, that I have really had to hold compassion for myself, trust and stand proudly in my lane.

Know your why. Psst! Changing ONE person's life is enough

Ask yourself: What would the world be like if you lived the life you dream of and what would the world look like if you didn't?

I began this work not to change the world, but with the intention of helping one woman at a time on her journey. Yet the ripples it has created within client's families and communities is beyond anything I could have imagined, and now I've tasted what is possible, I can't help but be curious of what else is out there.

So right now, (I say right now, because heaven knows I will keep evolving) my contribution, my service to women, includes, but is not limited to, yoni massage. (Yoni – its literal meaning is 'female genitalia', but it also encompasses other meanings such as 'womb, origin and source'. In some Indic literature, yoni means vagina, and other organs regarded as 'divine symbol of sexual pleasure, the matrix of generation and the visible form of Shakti'.) In a nutshell, the yoni is the entire female reproductive anatomy.

Or if you really need me to spell it out, I massage vaginas.

But it's so much deeper than that (pun intended!).

Willing women work with me to push beyond their perceptions, limiting beliefs and shame, to be held through a journey that facilitates their most vulnerable and transformational healing using all my combined skills.

And no, for the record, I am not a lesbian. Not that it's relevant when it comes to being of service, but for some reason, I get asked that question a lot. It just affirms how there is a lack of information about what this work actually entails, and how we perceive our bodies and sexuality.

Anyway, why do I do what I do?

Be led to where you feel you are meant to be

As far as I am concerned, this is exactly where life has led me and exactly where I need to be. Right here is where I can best facilitate change to co-create a better world for all. Imagine if every woman had access to the support and tools necessary to let go of all the generational conditioning that made her feel less than? Imagine if we all knew how to love and appreciate ourselves unconditionally?

Wherever you are led, focus on being here and present for it. Enjoy this moment in your journey and be curious and open to explore what else is possible.

Enrol in the school of unlearning

The secret to progress and making a difference in this dynamic world is knowing the responsibility lies within you to do the *inner work*.

The what-now? That's right! It is up to you to surrender all that you thought you knew in the grand school of unlearning before you can effectively and successfully unleash your big ideas into the world. Your outer landscape will be a direct reflection of your inner landscape, so let go of all the crap that holds you back. The fears, the saboteur. All. Of. It!

Inner work will be required

There are few of us courageous enough to step into the magnitude of this work and I really own that. The inner work I have done to get to this place of understanding is worthy of acknowledgement in and of itself. I know why I am here.

So if not me, then who?

And if not now, then when?

Can you imagine what the world would look like, if all women celebrated their bodies, honoured their voices and led from a space of compassion for themselves *first*?

This is the reality I am here to create. This is the reality I choose to invite into my world.

Every single day is a different experience but comes with the guarantee that I will witness women remembering how to love, honour and understand themselves like never before; remembering their worth, honouring their birthright to exist simply as they are, and knowing that is enough.

Co-create to change the world

You may have noticed I use the term *co-create* when I refer to our roles as change-makers? Because, babe, we are better together! Trust me, I spent years thinking it was solely my responsibility to save and change the entire world and ran myself into the ground (several times), trying to navigate that bullshit.

My advice? Your vibe attracts your tribe. So find your lane and gather those like-minded queens like an army! Surround yourself with the kind of company that lights your soul on fire! There are enough of us here committed to making a difference that it doesn't all have to fall on you.

Sit Deeply In Your Own Lane

Here is the fun bit: *Weed out anything that doesn't light you up.*

Where does your passion run deep?

What can you talk about for hours on end and never get tired of it?

What brings you the most joy and excitement?

Answer these questions and you've found your lane, babe! Let everything else go for someone else to thrive.

Maybe it's two lanes, but definitely don't commit to more than three lanes or the freeway is going to get congested really quickly. Hello road rage and burnout! Remember you're doing this with your people, even if you haven't met them (yet!). Give yourself full permission to ONLY do what you love. If you dedicate your time, energy and money (which are all the same vibration, by the way) to wherever that passion is, I guarantee life will move mountains for you in exponential ways.

Trust that the deeper you sit in your lane, in your truth, in your passion, your peeps will find you!

Once they do, for God's sake, check your posture, drop your shoulders and breathe! Stop being hard on yourself and give yourself a moment to celebrate all that you have already achieved.

Change is a byproduct when we dare to be different

This pisses people off. And that's okay! Let me repeat that. Once you find your lane and drive momentum forwards, it is not your duty to make sure everyone else is happy. Trust your intention. Find your courage. Lead from your heart.

If someone is challenged by your progressive concepts, that is their issue, not yours. Keep your head high, pick up your tits and show up as the miracle you are!

Show up & believe

If you're serious about co-creating change, you have to get comfortable with being uncomfortable and be prepared to disrupt the status quo.

I know it's not always easy, but it is so important to back yourself 100% of the way. Girl, you've totally got this. Because if I can do it, so can you!

You do not have to explain yourself

Fierce-gentle change-makers and thought leaders do not need to explain themselves. It is likely they've spent the best part of their foundation years fumbling over their words, afraid to show up as their authentic self, not wanting to offend, or desperate to fit in. I was that person. There comes a time, however, when the fruits of your labour and your radical self-acceptance will outweigh the need for validation.

You do not need anyone else's permission to be great!

Read that again.

Simply believe it with every cell of your being, and it manifests (remember, like attracts like).

Courage and visibility is so much easier when you are aligned with your passion and purpose. Remember your intention, connect with your tribe and build the foundations of a better world together. Those you seek shall find you.

I am Laura Elizabeth, women's embodiment coach and storykeeper.

These are my go-to code words I use to ease the general public into what I do. The watered-down version before the big truth bomb follows the mysterious introduction.

My role at this time perhaps isn't the *be all and end all*, but it is most certainly a missing link in how to learn to love and accept ourselves unapologetically and live in a kinder environment. For this reason, I am here, doing this courageous work without the need to explain.

Here I am folks! Oh so grateful and blessed to be trusted to hold a non-judgemental, safe and transformational space for women to release years of conditioning, pain and suffering.

I've started.

I know my *why*.

I am led by opportunity.

I am constantly maintaining my *inner work*.

I am surrounded by my tribe.

I stay in my lane.

I dare to be different.

I show up.

I dont waste time explaining myself.

Together we rise!

ABOUT LAURA

Hi, I'm Laura Elizabeth, a trailblazing change-maker and advocate for women's empowerment. Author of *Loving Herself Whole, Back Yourself!, Wild Woman Rising, Rising Matriarch* and *Heartcentred Leadership*. Director at Maven Press, creatress of Kuntea, and owner of Laura Elizabeth Wellness/Erotic Maven Medicine.

I am dedicated to creating intimate experiences for conscious women ready to step into a deeper layer of understanding of themselves. I assist them to embrace and embody their sensuality, reclaim their voices and own their personal power.

I offer womb and yoni massage therapy, reiki attunements and a catalogue of workshops, education and training events online and in person with a focus on women's health.

I am also the woman behind a steadfast, handcrafted organic product range topping it's tenth year, including the risqué yoni steaming brand Kuntea for reproductive health and wellness.

My love of writing and being a keeper of women's stories has led me most recently to create Maven Press Publishing. I am delighted to be able to doula storytellers through the conception, gestation and birth of their books into the world as they step deeper into their truth as change-makers.

A naturally gifted psychic medium born on the east coast of Fife, Scotland, I immigrated to Perth, Western Australia, as a pre-teen in 1999. With two decades of experience cultivating my skills as an energy worker and holding space for clients, I offer the safest and most profoundly intimate containers for women to encounter deep transformation.

A boundary-pusher and taboo smasher, I am best known for my real, quirky and honest guidance, ensuring the deepest empathy, understanding and non-judgement. I believe it is important to keep a healthy sense of humour to stay grounded and authentic.

My service to clients is most definitely a niche I believe is the real missing link in human connection and healing for women. We are programmed to think, feel and do based on the needs of others. But we unleash our real magic when we set aside time to explore honouring, nurturing and loving ourselves back into a belief of radical acceptance and remembering our magnificence.

A passionate solo mother of three, leading by example, smashing goals and living with purpose, I hope to be a positive influence and for my own children to reach their full potential and inspire others to do the same.

I hold your hand and love you, while you remember how to love yourself.

www.lauraelizabeth.com.au
facebook.com/eroticmavenmedicine
instagram.com/eroticmaven_medicine
instagram.com/kuntea_by_le
www.mavenpress.com.au
www.instagram.com/mavenpress

MEL JAMES

The OG – my origin story

I didn't really know what a social worker was or what one did when I decided to start my degree back in 1999. I knew I enjoyed helping people, sitting with them to listen to their stories and trying to assist. I had learnt which classes at high school I could skip without being noticed and where to sit with friends or peers who seemed low, sad, depressed or flat, so we could talk in peace without getting into trouble. I recall sitting in class one day and seeing a friend drawing pictures of a coffin, her name and the letters RIP in her book margins. With the limited knowledge I had about suicidality, given my own fairly protected and sheltered upbringing, I instinctively knew she was in dire need of, at the bare minimum, a conversation with someone safe.

I initially wanted to be a counsellor because of these sorts of experiences, but early into my social work degree I suspected I didn't have the patience or skill set to do that sort of social work.

Now, as a mum of three, I am certain of my lack of patience; anyone who has tried to hurry a two-year-old out the door when they insist on putting on their own shoes knows of my struggle!

My first year at uni was very much about finding my feet, figuring out what I liked and didn't like, and working out what on earth this social work business was all about! I knew I wanted to work with children and young people, and other communities of vulnerable, marginalised peoples, supporting, empowering and advocating for them, to help improve their lives in their own way. When I realised genuine social work is about being present with someone, working in partnership with them, walking alongside them, rather than doing something *to* or *for* them, it started to make sense. With values steeped heavily in social justice, human rights, ethical practice and professional integrity, I started to find my calling.

To be perfectly honest though, it wasn't a 'calling' for me at that stage. There was no lightning bolt or grand sign from the universe – it was a job, a role, the start of a potential career. In those early years of practice, it was about learning just enough theories, frameworks and approaches in order to fulfil the tasks of the job I held at the time. It was when I moved overseas and worked with vulnerable children engaged in the child protection system that I started to find my own 'way' of working. I admit, I only moved to the UK to feed my travel bug, but it was the best move of my early career, building my skills and knowledge quickly, and being exposed to different backgrounds, cultures, people and experiences.

I had a number of teenagers on my case load when working in Essex children's services. I was barely out of my teens myself, and to be honest, fairly arrogant and cocky. I couldn't understand how mums and dads could hurt their own children and had minimal empathy or patience for them. I was quite judgemental too, with limited knowledge of the depth of poverty, trauma, domestic and family violence cycles that affected the families I worked with. But then I met a young person, Carly, who called me on my privilege when she challenged me, asking why I wasn't a mum yet. I was mid-twenties and childless, and for her, with her own mum having four children by the time she was my age (and her grandmother the same!), I was the one who was falling far short of expectations. It took time, humility and respect for Carly's story before she began to open up, talk with me about what she might want to do (finish school, move out of the borough, even travel and work aboard, like I was) and I began to realise my own views and biases needed to be challenged.

Carly, like so many of the diverse clients I had the privilege of working with, was inspirational, confident and encouraging. They were all, in their own way, eager to break the cycles that held them back – poverty, generational trauma, abuse, drugs. Carly taught me more in the five months I worked with her than the first five years of my career. I had thought I was a professional simply because I had the privilege and opportunity to earn a degree. It was eye-opening to realise I knew very little about 'the real world' despite being allowed out in it as a so-called 'expert'!

Returning to Australia about four years later, I continued my career in child protection, growing my passion and commitment to improve the lives of children, especially those in care. I wanted to truly hear young people's voices: to listen to the experiences of the clients I worked with and for; to be innovative and creative in meeting their needs, while remaining humble and respectful of the privileged position I had being involved (sometimes involuntarily) in their lives.

While working in management with a non-government organisation, I started to see the 'system' failing kids while purporting to be helping them. In desperation to get more foster carers approved, some would be assessed as 'suitable' but perhaps they were financially motivated, or had a limited support network, had complicated trauma histories themselves, or just had such busy afternoons with their own children's sports and activities, so placements would end when they could not take a child to family contact, medical appointments or therapy sessions. This sort of mismatch would result in yet another placement breakdown for the child, with them often feeling it was their fault, retraumatising them if they'd already experienced rejection and neglect, which was often the case. It would let down the carer as well, leaving them to feel they had failed or were devalued by their support team.

There were sadly too many cases of people becoming carers who shouldn't have been assessed as suitable because their own traumatic childhoods were not acknowledged and left unaddressed, resulting in harmful responses and actions towards the very children placed in their care for protection. There were so many – too many – of these cases, that I contemplated leaving the industry and becoming a librarian, a florist or some other role that didn't put me in the face of trauma every single day.

Taking risks

By 2009, I realised I was done. I was done just 'having a job' in the industry. I couldn't simply accept inadequate carer reports; poorly written, superficial and completed with a woeful 'tick-box' approach. Especially when I could see their direct, detrimental effect on children. I had a supportive partner and a dream of becoming a mum myself, so I knew it was time to take the plunge into working for myself so I could sleep well at night knowing I was trying to address the gaps that led to children being harmed.

It was absolutely terrifying, leaving paid employment (with the perks of a car, laptop and phone thrown in for good measure) to start a business where I wouldn't know the next time I would get paid – the nature of contracting. But as a daughter of a house painter and child care worker, both of whom had worked for themselves when I was growing up, maybe taking that risk was somewhere in my genetic make-up? I had no idea how to run my own consultancy business, so failure was absolutely an option. Xero and MYOB, digital and tech, marketing and comms … these were not in my vocabulary.

So I started Social Care Solutions, small and safe. I reached out to those I knew, who knew my practice, to see if they would hire me for assessments, one by one. I began to be recognised as a quality practitioner, who listened to what the client (the agency, the department) wanted, but who would stand up for my ethical views and practice integrity. I gained a reputation for saying 'no' to carer applicants who weren't suitable, even when this resulted in difficult, awkward and downright abusive conversations. I've never been thrown out of a client's house but I have come very, very close! I worked by the values of being transparent, honest, respectful and professional and I have supported people to make the choice to withdraw their application to be foster carers, rather than progress through a whole assessment and be denied. Even when faced with pressure from clients to recommend carers due to the dire need for them in the system, I kept at the forefront of my mind that my real 'client' was the vulnerable child in need of a safe home. I would often think, *Would this be good enough for my own child?* and if no, then why would that be acceptable for a foster child? I decided I would work with integrity and not bow down to pressure; if this meant I didn't work, then I wouldn't work.

As my reputation and workload grew, I had the opportunity to meet a number of amazing people who went on to become mentors. One such mentor, a client named Steve, told me if I said 'no' to work, then others would 'get their foot in the door'. He suggested I subcontract my work to others in the industry like me; people who I trusted and respected, who I could oversee, supervise and ensure were committed to the same values. He took the risk and offered to be the first company to allow me to subcontract to others and as they say, 'the rest is history'.

Delegating work, trusting in my team, putting my 'brand' and reputation into others' hands was a huge risk. Child protection is a delicate, sensitive, high-risk business, so I took my time and ensured the people I hired shared my vision, values and passion. Regardless of who paid my fees, my client was always a vulnerable child or young person, just like Carly. This commitment to integrity of practice saw the business become a company and start to grow exponentially.

It's about more than just me

The first few years in business as a company, with a team rather than as a sole trader, were a mixture of trial and error, and often involved a growing sense of imposter syndrome. I would look around and think, *When will people realise I'm not grown up enough to be doing this?* I still have those moments, even today with my CEO title. Perhaps a little of that self-reflection (second-guessing?) and humility (fear?) has been good though, as it's made me keep questioning, *Am I staying with my values? Am I truly living my vision?* I have come to realise it is now more than just 'me'; I have a team. I had to learn how to delegate and oversee the work, not 'do' the work myself. I had to be 'more on the balcony, less on the dance floor'; more a leader than a manager. This involves ensuring the team are as passionate, driven and committed as I am to child protection. I tried to ensure they were smarter and more skilled than I was. It became a key to our success – I hunted for practitioners with high standards and a passion for improving the lives of children in foster care. I sweetened the deal for them to come work for me, rather than as going out on their own as independent contractors, by providing professional development opportunities, supervision and mentoring, quality assurance processes, and a connection to a steady flow of work.

It was by having a team around me I was able to take time to build my other 'team' – my family. One by one, my family grew and so did my company. After seven years of working in Social Care Solutions, I came to a point of no return and had to ask myself, *Do I embrace all these new opportunities and grow, or do I let the company go, and return to the stability of a full-time employed role, now my children were getting a little older?* In order to make this decision, I did something I really should have done at the very start of my company. I reached out to like-minded business experts for their guidance and support.

I connected with a customer service expert to work out how best to approach my customers about their needs and how we could meet them.

I connected with a business advisor to consider how to grow my company structure. I connected with a financial advisor to work out how I was steering my company. And I reached out to other mentors, social workers like me, who had gone on to develop, run and oversee big companies or organisations and could help me figure out how to wear my dual hat of social worker and business owner. I joined networks like AusMumpreneur and learnt about marketing, digital technology, brand awareness and PR.

Utilising brilliant and skilled people to guide me when I had a gap in learning or skill enabled me to expand and grow my business. We added consultancy and training services to our list of offerings. We loved influencing and improving the lives of each individual foster child who would be cared for by the individual foster carer we assessed, but training other practitioners to improve their assessment skills (and supporting agencies to have improved practices, structures and policies within this space) ensured we were building capacity with a wider sphere of influence. I'm proud to wear the CEO hat at Social Care Solutions, where we have directly had a positive impact on the lives of thousands of children across the country.

Trying out the entrepreneur 'hat'

I started my business to fill a gap I found in the foster care sector. As it grew, I realised there were plenty more gaps to fill, so we adapted where we could. Some gaps were not suitable to address in my first company, and a serendipitous meeting with a former child in care led to starting another company, assisting people to understand what fostering actually is and guiding them to make informed choices about which agency to foster through. When my co-founder threw the word 'entrepreneur' into a conversation one day, I laughed it off. Me, an entrepreneur? No, I'm just a social worker who has two businesses. It took others to remind me this was no small feat; especially during the COVID-19 pandemic of 2020. While many businesses are failing, my two companies have continued to grow and meet the needs of our customers, and I realise I'm privileged and lucky to have reached where I am, but it hasn't been without hard work, dedication and commitment. With an idea for a third company forming, still in the infancy of development and idealism, this is clearly a 'hat' I am ready to embrace. Or maybe I'm just embracing more grey hair and more wrinkles!

This journey has not been without its challenges; rogue staff, difficult clients, an under-resourced and underfunded sector, people paying peanuts but wanting caviar. But the joy, pride and satisfaction I feel at knowing the many thousands of children's lives my team have touched and improved in some way makes it all worthwhile. I no longer doubt my choices; I move forward, my hat rack full, and I'm excited about whatever lies ahead.

ABOUT MEL

My name is Mel and I'm a social worker, practitioner, business owner, and entrepreneur. I have so many different 'hats'; some I'm very comfortable with, like being a social worker as I'm very proud of my profession; others, like 'entrepreneur', have taken me years to wear proudly and comfortably. None of these in isolation accurately describe who I am now though. It's a hybrid of all of them, as well as the titles of which I am most proud – wife, and mother to my three beautiful kids – that capture who I am and my identity as a person … And probably explain the grey hairs and wrinkles!

I had no idea I would end up working in the child protection industry, or that I would come to be passionately driven to improve it. I completed my Bachelor of Social Work and Criminology in my early twenties, thinking I would start my career working within the justice system. However, as sometimes happens, I fell into a residential youth worker role, got excited, passionate and hooked on the work, and never left child protection. After a few years working in frontline child protection in the UK, I returned home to Australia and began to throw myself into roles within the foster care system. It was there I quickly became frustrated, disheartened and angered by the distance between best practice and the lived experiences of so many in the 'system'. So many children were being hurt or harmed by the system, with placement breakdowns, carer burnout and high staff turnover the 'norm' resulting in inconsistent care of children. I realised I needed more knowledge to help me grow in my career, so I continued my learning through completing a Masters Degree in Social Work. I didn't want to just work 'in' the system, I wanted to work 'on' the system. I did not want to be a manager – I wanted to be a leader.

When working in a management role in a non-government organisation, I saw a gap in best practice and felt it was something that needed to be addressed. Foster and kinship care assessments were being written poorly, without analysis of evidence, without depth, without the voice of the children in placement truly being heard, and this was affecting the outcomes of vulnerable children. Children were being placed with carers who weren't the right 'match' or who shouldn't have been carers at all. This was leading to many placement breakdowns, children being hurt unnecessarily, with an 'oh well, that's the system' unapologetic approach. So, I left my permanent, secure, stable full-time job and decided to work for myself.

Just as I had no clue I would end up working in the child protection system, I absolutely hands-down had no idea I would end up working for myself. Traditionally, social workers do not have their own companies. In the beginning, it was terrifying to leave the security and stability of a permanent income and step into a world of self-employment.

Now, in 2021, I own a thriving child protection consultancy company called Social Care Solutions with sixty staff across four states in Australia, delivering high quality work with integrity and professionalism as our driving values. I am also co-founder of another business, The Tribe Project – a digital experience platform built with a colleague who lived through the foster care system and experienced firsthand the inadequacies that demanded change. I also have a third business idea starting to form. It is my passion to see change in the sector that drives me, no matter which 'hat' I'm wearing.

www.socialcaresolutions.com.au

KARTHIKA SIVARAJAN

Who am I?

We know neither how our journey started nor the destination, but one thing I do know is that I am inspired by people I meet every single day.

Life is a beautiful journey for us to enjoy, accept, reflect on and realise the purpose of our existence.

This is the story of my search for an answer to the question, 'Who am I?'

I was born in a south Indian Tamil-speaking family, who nourished me with love and affection, and anchored me into a strong value system. A few incidents in my childhood have impacted me greatly, motivating me to investigate the many possibilities of life and our existence.

The ray of light

Deepavali is an Indian festival of lights which symbolises the spiritual victory of light over darkness, of good over evil.

I vividly recall a childhood memory one foggy November day, on the eve of Deepavali, when I was relishing sweets and savouries prepared by Mum. The air was full of joy and excitement. My friends were having fun, bursting firecrackers in the front yard. Through the smoggy air, I sensed a pair of eyes staring at me with a sense of longing.

A famished rag-picker boy, about ten years old, was looking at me with piercing eyes full of questions and emotions. His countenance triggered a feeling of sadness and guilt within me and I spontaneously felt like sharing my happiness with him. When I ran in and told my parents what I had seen and how I felt, they asked the boy to come in. We shared our special meal with him and asked him to join in our celebrations, bursting a few firecrackers.

With a small but dignified smile on his face, he left soon after, but the incident triggered me. I drilled my dad with so many questions: 'Why is he working today and not having fun at home? Where are his parents? Does he live on the streets? Why is he poor? Why is there such a huge gap between rich and poor? Why can't we get rid of poverty?'

Here was a child of my age, struggling to survive through no fault of his own.

To this day, I am still in search of answers to those questions. The boy was the spark of light that removed the darkness of ignorance in me. He helped me to realise how thankful and grateful we ought to be for the life we are living and how we can help people around us.

I am reminded of some verses from the ancient literary work in the Tamil language, *Tirukkural,* composed around 400AD and known for its timeless wisdom on ethics and morality.

'It is compassion, the most gracious of virtues, which moves the world.'

'Although an act of help done timely, might be small in nature, it is truly larger than the entire world.'

A vision for life

The school I went to provided me with several opportunities to serve the community. Together with the local Rotary Club, our school would organise free cataract surgeries for the elderly from poor and disadvantaged areas of our society. On one such occasion, I was part of a group of volunteers assisting doctors to screen patients for eye cataracts.

A gentleman in his seventies came in, haggard and a bit unsteady. He was screened promptly and the doctor discovered he had almost fully lost vision in one of his eyes. He was offered free surgery and post-surgical care. He asked the doctor how long it would be before he could get back to work, if he went for surgery. The doctor told him it would be two weeks. The old man thought for a moment and politely declined. He was a daily labourer and the sole breadwinner for his family, putting food on the table for his frail wife and school-going grandkids. He couldn't see them go hungry for two weeks. His words and actions brought tears to my eyes. It still moves me greatly, whenever I recall the event.

To me, he epitomised compassion and selflessness, on top of his independence and hard work. His commitment and love for his family, despite his own frailty and vision loss, has never ceased to amaze me. This incident brought me to think about all the parents and grandparents who make untold sacrifices for the wellbeing of their kids and grandkids. The respect and gratitude I have for my own parents and elders has continued to grow since then.

Hierarchical society

During my teens, I attended a festival at an ancient temple in our ancestral village; an agricultural village surrounded by verdant green fields. It was a temple ritual meant to synergise the mystic powers of the temple deity. Our entire extended family had gathered for the occasion. Soaking in the freshness of the village greenery and the chatter of people around, I felt so much joy. On reaching the temple, my feelings of happiness quickly evaporated when I saw several people and their scantily dressed kids waiting at the entrance. I knew they were not allowed into the temple because they belonged to the lower castes. They were only allowed inside after the rituals were completed.

I felt so much anger and disbelief that in these supposedly progressive times, people were still discriminating against others in the name of religion, caste, tradition and culture. A girl who has a rebellious nature, and questions discriminatory traditions is considered arrogant for not respecting her elders and traditions, so I felt powerless to raise my voice against what I thought was a grave injustice to the less fortunate in our society. Fear of earning a bad name for the family made me stay quiet, but I was in no mood to participate in the rituals that day.

The only thought to occupy my mind that day was: how can a ritual, supposed to synergise the mystic powers of the deity, achieve its purpose by excluding our fellow humankind?

However, it was some consolation to see those poorer, 'lower caste' kids smiling and waiting eagerly for their *prasadams* (offerings made to God, like sweet rice or fried chickpeas).

All they needed was acceptance and kindness. I thanked God/supreme power for enabling this experience to realise and accept life. The event brought about a change in me.

To change their standing in society, these kids need to be educated, so as to improve their socioeconomic status. A few years later, our family – my brother and dad – helped provide some of the basic needs at the local primary school, indirectly helping these kids receive a decent education. Every small help to society is a drop in the ocean, but every drop is unique and valuable.

Everyone's presence and thoughtful action, no matter how small, is a valuable contribution to society. Let's play our ethical and moral part in it.

Gift of love

In the early years of my marriage, we employed a housemaid to help us in our household chores, as we both worked full-time. She called me 'Didi' or elder sister. She was getting married to someone she liked, and was excited and looking forward to her wedding day, but I noticed her happiness fade as the date approached. She opened up eventually; the groom's family had demanded gold and money as dowry for the marriage. A part of me wanted to ask her to exercise caution marrying her fiancé, as he appeared to be focused on the material things his partner brought along, but another part of me questioned myself. Who was I to advise her without fully understanding her family's background or the issues they were facing? I promised we would gift her whatever gold jewellery we could afford.

Around the same time, several parts of southern India were affected by the Boxing Day Tsunami that wrought great destruction and killed thousands. My partner and I were keen to support affected communities, donating as much as we could to help restore schools. In balancing our support for the needy, we gifted our maid a piece of gold jewellery, but to our dismay, there was little excitement or happiness in her face when she received the gift. We realised she had expected something bigger and more valuable. There's enough for everyone's need, but not enough for everyone's greed.

This incident triggered several questions for me around the institution of marriage. Is it a commitment, love and respect between the partners, or a socio-legal contract between families? Can gold or wealth bring happiness to families? As partners, we have had several thought-provoking and self-realising dialogues on marriage, as well as on the expectations of society and family.

This brought me some clarity on love, and how our attachment to material things or a person can cause both happiness and sorrow. Disconnecting ourselves from attachments can give us inner peace. From that day forward, I stopped buying gold and precious jewellery, either for myself or to gift others. It was the start of my journey to lead a minimalistic life.

For Buddha, the path to happiness starts from an understanding of the root causes of suffering.

'All that we are is the result of what we have thought. It is founded on our thoughts. It is made up of our thoughts. If one speaks or acts with a pure thought, happiness follows one, like a shadow that never leaves.'

There is an ongoing tussle between our conscious and subconscious minds to follow the true inner self, but it is a beautiful journey and life is full of inspiration. Live and let others live. One doesn't have to always please others but we can be compassionate and kind to every being on this earth. Helping others doesn't have to be monetary, it includes sharing knowledge, wisdom, skills, empowering others and giving moral support.

Life and death

It was a freezing cold evening in the German winter. My son, who was in a real hurry to see this world, was born premature. A few hours after his birth, my partner had to leave the hospital for the night, and I felt vulnerable and lonely. Physically drained, I requested the duty nurse for assistance with my son, but not only was she cold, she was also quite aggressive. I later came to know she mistook me for a refugee. Not finding the energy to question her rude behaviour, I just smiled back at her. Meanwhile, my intuitions were proven true, as he started gasping for breath just a few hours after birth. He was taken away in the middle of the night and lodged in the neonatal intensive care section of another hospital.

The doctor explained the situation was dire and quite unpredictable. At that moment, there was no-one beside me to give me comfort. I missed my parents and my partner. In their absence, it was another elderly nurse, who was comforting and kind. She spoke only German, a language I wasn't fluent in at that time, however her kindness and empathy didn't need a language. Language is never a barrier when being compassionate to another human.

She encouraged me to visit my child in intensive care; my presence gave my son, who was fighting for survival, my emotional support and love. Later, together with my partner, I visited him several times daily. We could only see him from a distance; outside the glass doors of the intensive care unit. Doctors shrugged their shoulders and had a one-line response that has stayed with me ever since: 'Every day is a new day.' Life is so precious that every moment needs to be appreciated. I am eternally grateful for what I am and what I have. The struggle, pain and fear of death only comes from a fear of life.

When I looked around at the other babies in neonatal care, some were in a more serious condition, but all their parents came in with a ray of hope on their worried faces.

The duty nurse, who was rude to me earlier, was apologetic and 'nicer' to me from the next day onwards. I don't know if the change in her was brought about by my silent smile or the seriousness of my child's condition. When she told me she had earlier mistaken me for a refugee, I was able to connect the dots, helping me to relate to the struggle and discrimination refugees are faced with in many countries.

My son brought out my inner strength and helped me to reflect on who I am. I was resolved to bring up my child to enjoy a childhood full of health. The next four years were quite an experience for us all, but by the age of four he was off of all his medications. He is our mirror and teacher who helps us look at the world differently. His curious questions about life and science have helped us understand more about life.

Kahlil Gibran rightly said:

'Out of suffering have emerged the strongest souls; the most massive characters are seared with scars.'

Embrace

We have begun to embrace our body, our soul, things around us, our earth, the vast universe and the unknown. A casual dinner table conversation with my son on inclusivity inspired me to start and get involved in social impact projects.

During a recent visit to India, women from an impoverished fishing village shared their aspirations, determination and resilience to educate their kids against all odds. For those women, every day is a new day. They are used to overcoming domestic abuse, financial stress and societal taboos against women working. These *sura* (Tamil word for 'shark') ladies are my inspiration to tackle any kind of problem in life.

I also support mentally challenged women in rehabilitation shelters in India and promote their handmade products. I visit them with my family. We see pure love and innocence in their eyes. I realise now it's not them who need to be trained to live with 'mainstream' society, rather the 'mainstream' need to understand the value of an inclusive society. Recollections of their smiles bring me positivity and energy to do more.

Throughout my journey, I have seen life is full of inspiration and opportunity that we often overlook.

'Be grateful for whoever comes, because each has been sent as a guide from beyond.' – Rumi

The definition of success, achievement and happiness differs from person to person. Just seek what your inner sense loves.

'Let yourself be drawn by the stronger pull of that which you truly love.' – Rumi

My humble journey continues, inspired by Gibran's quote:

'Yesterday is but today's memory, and tomorrow is today's dream.'

Everything in the universe is within you.

ABOUT KARTHIKA

Karthika Sivarajan is an eco-conscious, kind and compassionate person.

As a mother, she has had a colourful career, playing roles as diverse as product development engineer, software professional, primary school teacher, educator, speaker, and now, an Entrepreneur who has started a social impact venture called Embrace.

Her startup Embrace is all about embracing and empowering women, particularly those from the disadvantaged sections of society.

Embrace promotes eco-friendly, sustainable products such as hand-stitched cotton, jute handbags, lunchbags and laptop bags made by mentally challenged women in rehab shelters and women others from lower socioeconomic sections areas in India.

She has seen from close quarters and experienced the way disadvantaged women are treated in developing countries (India) and the enormous difficulties they face to be financially independent in a patriarchal and abusive society.

Her resolve is to promote their products and empower them. Her vision is to expand her business to empower disadvantaged women in Australia.

A casual dinner table conversation with her family on inclusivity of differently-abled people in society served as an initial spark for an idea. Environmental consciousness, together with a deep desire to empower herself as an entrepreneur, inspired her to start this social impact venture startup.

Since childhood, she has been volunteering for community services, organising blood donation camps, free eye screening camps for senior citizens and food for the homeless. More recently, she has volunteered for education service providers, at aspect schools for autistic kids in Sydney.

Family is her strength. She has lived in India, Germany, Switzerland and currently lives in Sydney, with her partner and son. Her passion is cooking healthy, tasty food for her family and friends. She strongly believes food is the medicine and uses traditional Ayurvedic and Siddha knowledge in her cooking. During her free time, she has cooked for needy families.

She regularly speaks on SBS Tamil and Australian Tamil broadcasting radio channels on topics like women in Australian politics, education, lives of immigrant women, women's empowerment, parenting skills, and more.

She loves being with children and is passionate about learning along with them. She strongly believes that in order to develop a kind and compassionate society, children need to be nurtured in their early years with unconditional love and the freedom to question and explore things around them. Emotional, physical and mental wellbeing in their early years is an important foundation for a child to grow into a well-balanced adult.

She has a Bachelors in Instrumentation & Control Systems Engineering. She also has a Certificate in Drama Therapy for Autism. This training has helped her to be creative while engaging people in social scenarios.

She won a silver medal at the National Mathematics Olympiad, India.

She was one of the finalists at the AusMumpreneur awards in 2019 for her social impact project Embrace in the startup category.

She volunteers for the NSW Rural Fire Service for which she was awarded NSW Premier's recognition – Bushfire Emergency Citation award 2019.

www.facebook.com/embracetheworld01

MAIREAD MACKLE

'Women belong in all places where decisions are being made.'

A powerful statement from the late Justice Ruth Bader Ginsburg, a true driving force for change.

I am a great believer that if we are going to drive change, we must first be that change. I have been inspired by many great leaders of the past and hope that, in turn, my journey may serve to inspire others to be great leaders in the future.

In my chapter I want to share with you my perspective of a woman who has inspired me in life and in business.

This remarkable woman who also believed in driving change is Bertha Benz. You may not have heard of her, but she was a pioneer and inventor who transformed the motor industry (you might recognise her surname!). She was an inspiring woman who fearlessly challenged the status quo of her era and in doing so challenged the world to think a little differently.

Born in 1849 in Southern Germany to a wealthy family, Bertha went on to marry engineer Karl Benz. Once married, as the law dictated at that time, Bertha ceded control of her money to her husband. But Karl was a good man, and combining Bertha's ambition and vision with his engineering expertise, together they developed a prototype of the world's first automobile.

Initially, Karl was concerned that it wouldn't be a success. He worried about its performance and how it would be perceived, as people had already deemed the design a 'horseless carriage' – something ghostly and sinister. They needed to refine it.

Frustrated with this lack of progress, behind her husband's back, Bertha decided to take her two sons, aged thirteen and fifteen years old at the time, and set out on the sixty-six-mile journey to her parent's house in the early hours of 5 August 1888.

In this unique device – which had never been tested in such a way before, that could easily have broken down or exploded at any time – she hit the road.

For every problem she encountered, with classic female ingenuity, Bertha found a solution. When a spark plug wouldn't ignite – she used her garter to create insulation, with her hairpin she unclogged the fuel line, with failing breaks she stopped at a cobbler and applied leather, thus creating the first ever brake pad. And when low on fuel she visited a pharmacist to request ligroin solvent – establishing what would be the world's first ever fuel station.

At that time and along that journey, as you can imagine, she was laughed at and mocked, but she persevered. Her goal was clear, to prove her vision of success for her and Karl's invention. Her journey took around twelve hours and was talked about everywhere. It may seem like a small journey to us now, but it was a historic, symbolic leap for both woman and humankind.

Bertha drove more than a car that day, she drove an industry because she believed in herself. Bertha Benz is an example of a woman literally generating power, for herself and for others. She challenged to create change.

Looking back, it's incredible to think that around this same time (in the late 1800s) and only a few generations ago, women had no authority to vote, to hold their own money, to own property, or even in some cases, to have custodial control over their own children.

Our mothers, grandmothers and great-grandmothers were being controlled with unjust and unforgiving laws and traditions, that actively pushed against them getting into positions of power. It is these great women that have gone before us and stood up to the inequalities they faced, who boldly challenged the societal norms, blazing a trail of empowerment for us all.

They demonstrated fearlessness, fortitude and an inspiring willingness to act!

As we head into 2022, people might say, 'We have equality sorted, we are all equal now,' right?

But let's look at some facts …

- Of the 193 countries in the world, *only* twenty-six have women serving as head of state/government (Sept 2021). At the current rate, gender equality in the highest positions of power will not be achieved for another 130 years.
- *Only* 8% of the Fortune 500 companies have a female lead.
- *Still,* women are paid approximately 80% of what men are, for doing the same job.
- Many don't have access to the basic civil right of education – illiteracy levels are *still* needlessly high. Around three quarters of the people in the world who are illiterate are women, disallowing their chance to progress.

These are still shameful and appalling statistics. The question is, how do we, as women, get to all those places where decisions are being made? What is the next step?

I think our guiding inspiration should be Bertha Benz. Let's ask ourselves, *What would Bertha do?*

I believe it is the behaviours and cultures in society that are holding us back, so we need to challenge them, we need to change them, and we need to play our part in this movement.

The way I see it, there are two places where we can spark this change.

1. Within the home, as parents and guardians where we can inspire the minds of the next generation.

2. Within the workplace, where we can create an environment that will empower us and allow us to thrive … thus, enabling women to take their place in all the places where decisions are being made!

So, let's begin at home …

Home is where the heart is, where the foundations of our behaviours, attitudes, beliefs and values are built. It is where our characters and relationships are moulded. Home is where real, tangible change is inspired, nurtured and activated.

I grew up on a farm in Fermanagh, Northern Ireland, with parents that I can now see were forward-thinking for their time, when social attitudes were very much traditional. They treated the children equally. They were focused on education and on us all having equal opportunity. But no matter how evolved in terms of equality my parents were, I still needed to challenge change from time to time.

So, one night, many years ago, I brought my boyfriend home to meet my parents, and on that evening, a friendly neighbour (but one with very traditional views) had also called to visit. Tradition was back then that the men sat around and chatted as the women served up a steady stream of tea and biscuits … but I had other ideas. I asked my boyfriend to come and help in the kitchen, just to challenge the status quo and then I left him there while I went off and sat down next to my outraged neighbour – with my feet up for added effect. My boyfriend knew exactly what I was up to and was more than happy to play his part.

Now I'm no Bertha Benz, but from an early age, I was aware of the inequalities women faced and wanted to make a point. I wanted to challenge for change, and I most definitely did.

In hindsight, you might say it was something of a test, and fortunately, my boyfriend passed with flying colours. We've been married now for thirty-one years with seven children, aged thirty down to our six-year-old twins. We worked out that by the time our youngest has grown up we'll have been doing the school run for over forty years. Far more driving than Bertha Benz would ever have imagined.

With our own children, we continue to challenge those traditional ways and have raised them as equals who share our values. We are a team, and we hope that this sense of equality at home in our actions and our behaviours, empowers our children as they step into their own futures.

The other place where we can challenge change is in the workplace.

I have built a business with the founding principles of flexibility and freedom. I believe as a leader, you attract like-minded people into positions of trust who share your values and vision.

Just recently, I was really thrilled when one of my incredible leadership team told me that because I have created a culture within our organisation of empowering people, it has given her the opportunity for personal and career growth that she doesn't believe she could have achieved anywhere else! A delight for me.

In many organisations, however, due to the unrelenting and rigid workplace structures, it's women with children who often must make the toughest choices – go to part-time work hours, or in too many cases, leave the workplace altogether. Neither should be necessary.

How many men out there think to themselves when entering the workplace, *When I have a child will I go part time? How will I balance life being a working father?* Not many I suspect …

It is difficult to balance it all, as I'm sure my fellow mothers out there will agree with, and there is 'damned if you do and damned if you don't' pressure in society. We are criticised for working full-time, or for prioritising careers and being presumed to neglect our families ***OR*** we're given no value if we choose not to work.

Society places less value in our essential role as a mother, raising the next generation, and we end up becoming financially dependent and losing our career opportunities. It's a no-win situation.

Now think about this: the working week as we know it today. It was of course developed by a man and that man was Henry Ford. He created the forty-hour working week and introduced the concept of weekends for resting.

Whilst it was a significant improvement for people at that time, when they worked as many as one hundred hours a week, it was introduced for men working in factories – but that's **nearly one hundred years ago.**

Today, we have a much more diverse workforce with new and exciting industries and a continuously evolving professional mindset and lifestyle. However, in some cases we are still stuck in the 1920s and it's time for us to challenge this rigid routine.

Where possible, people should have the ability to mould their working day around when they're most productive and around their families, creating a more flexible working environment based on productivity and trust. Workloads should be based on required outputs, not clocking in and out.

This creates a whole new realm of possibilities, giving power back to women especially, to establish their own work week, allowing them to raise families whilst building a career, mapping out their own journey and getting into all the places where decisions are being made!

When we can change culture and behaviours within the home and within the workplace, that is when we will have real impact in the world.

The women that have gone before us have fought for the law to be on our side. It's because of the struggles and activism of our foremothers that we can now vote, have financial independence, own businesses and properties while raising our families.

Let's celebrate the strides we have made but equally appreciate that the journey is not over. For the next part of this journey, I believe it is critical that men and women join forces to drive change.

Bertha's husband, Karl Benz, recognised the value of his wife's ambition and support as critical to their collective success. In his memoir he said, '*Only one person stood by me during those times when I was heading towards the abyss. That was my wife. It was her courage that enabled me to find new hope.*'

I too, believe in the power of female leadership and I am inspired by the fact that women lead with purpose, courage and conviction.

As a female leader and entrepreneur, having run my own enterprise for over twenty-five years in a variety of different industries, I champion and support female representation at every opportunity, acutely aware of how much women contribute both to the economy and within their communities.

I'm also a mother of seven – four daughters and three sons – and I want them to be part of a world that sees them as equals. That's why the founding principle behind our not-for-profit, Evolve, is to create an 'equal world'.

Evolve is an educational platform and a community for 'empowering women to become women of power'. It's also a place where we can highlight and challenge the bias and stereotypes that we all know still exist.

In Evolve, we believe that it's only when men and women are viewed as equals, act as equals and are working together as equals in all aspects of life – fully appreciating each other's worth and contribution – is when we will have real power to change the world.

We have a responsibility to be the change we want to see in the world. Let's challenge and drive that change, as Bertha did … let her story ignite something within you, as it did me.

So, ask yourself, what is the *one* thing that *you* can do each day, be that in your home or in your workplace, to make sure that women are in all the places where decisions are being made? Because believe me, no matter how small a step you feel it is, when we are moving forward with conviction, embracing a future driven by passion and led with kindness – there are no limits to what we can achieve … we can and ***WILL*** create an equal world.

ABOUT MAIREAD

Founder and CEO, Tarasis Enterprises.

Mairead is a values-based, multi-award-winning entrepreneur who owns and operates Tarasis Enterprises – a diverse suite of progressive businesses that create both community impact and innovative solutions for the future of living, employing over 1,200 people and operating across several industries including health care, housing and renewables.

Mairead's passion for using the power of her business to create a better world led to the establishment of two not-for-profits, iCare Charity focused on 'kindness without limits' and Evolve, an educational platform supporting the social and economic empowerment of women.

A loving mother to seven children, Mairead is an investor, philanthropist and TEDx speaker. She sits on the boards of several business and lobby groups. Mairead was awarded the Irish Tatler Entrepreneur of the Year 2019 and Woman of the Year at the Natwest Everywoman Awards.

www.tarasis.com

CATHY DIMARCHOS

Can one person change the world?

As I begin to share a little about me, I encourage you to pause and think about this question, and what it means.

If you were a child, it would be a simple and instant response of 'yes' because in a child's world anything is possible. But as an adult, you question the possibility by the sheer enormity of the scope. You dare not say 'yes' because it raises all sorts of questions; even if you did believe it were possible. So, to avoid having to go through that process, to clarify or justify it all, or perhaps to avoid being judged or maybe falling short, we might find it easier to say 'no' and then retreat to playing small.

But I think I might know you a little better than that because here you are reading this book. Could I be right in thinking you too have a vision, a passion and commitment to doing something bigger? In which case, I would have to argue and say your answer is 'YES'.

Before I start to share my story, I want you to know that you would not be alone. I, and many others, will support you on your journey to change the world, because you have taken the first step of thinking beyond you, and thinking big.

So, are we now in alignment? Can you join me now in saying 'YES' and in your commitment to take others on the journey with you to change the world?

I have learnt over time to recognise fear as an emotion. It forms part of how I feel at different stages of life but it will not define who I am or where I choose to go. It is not a destination, nor is it me as a person. I have become conscious of it and acknowledge it by giving it a name, 'faith', so I can separate it from who I am.

My story, in many ways, is about self-realisation, self-reflection and belief; belief in me, belief in others and my commitment to what I call 'my true purpose'.

My purpose is to share my lived experiences so they become skills and tools for others to use. I do this by showing people what I know, followed by sharing the reasons I have made the choices I have. This allows others to consider what may work for them, as they navigate through their journey forward. I love the 'aha' moments this process creates along the way.

I'm also a big believer in calling things for what they are. It is that transparency value, as I am happy to be vulnerable and it gives permission for others to be vulnerable too.

As a qualified counsellor, I have discovered over the years, that when people are driven by emotion, it prevents them from having clarity in those moments. The brain is not able to play at its strength and therefore choices are more likely to be made in a way that does not serve them best.

When I begin to work with clients, I work through a process that establishes 'second order thinking' so they become aware of possibilities, stages and consequences beyond their immediate situation. Becoming an architect of your future enables you to consider 'what else?' at multiple levels. You can then have some clarity of the choices you make, especially under stress or in crisis. You are able to consider potential risks whilst also establishing boundaries, therefore predetermining outcomes.

I raise this early on because we all, at times, have fear overcome us. By calling it for what it is, we can better manage it. Often fear surfaces because of things we don't know, and we have a tendency to think the worst. Then a navigational process I use helps to demystify any perceptions and assumptions, so we can move forward. I use the same framework to support people in breaking down strategies. By building a process map with key milestones, everyone is on the same journey. This framework applies to individuals, organisations or multi-billion-dollar businesses.

So now we are all aligned in understanding that you are here because you too have a purpose and can, and will, change the world, let's begin the road forward together.

As I reflect back on my initial question, I recognise that fear no longer has a stronghold in what I do, and I attribute that to my mission being about a global impact being so much bigger than me. As I look forward, there is one thing I know; when I wake up each day, I have a smile on my face, and I know that I love what I do because at some stage, I know it will make a difference for *someone*. I also recognise I may never know who they are or what that impact is. How magical is that? That vision drives me to keep striving forward.

It is about the contribution I can make for others. The same will apply for you when you identify the value you are bringing to those you serve through your actions or through your business. It is important for you to sit in this moment and reflect on what it is you are doing, that you recognise your abilities and your passion to provide someone with your gift.

I really would like you to acknowledge that what you do is of value to so many people, and whilst you may see it as a job or as a product or service, the reality is you have made someone happy. You have given them exactly what they needed, so you have given them a gift. You have made a positive impact on them.

I also would like to share some of my vulnerabilities, because it's important you also know that I, like everyone else, have imperfections and weaknesses as well as strengths. It is what makes us who we are. I have come to accept I do not have the answers to everything, but I am committed to seeking them out and to ask for help.

I do not fear failure, but I do fear not taking a chance and holding back from showing others how. I fear not having a voice, because at times I have kept quiet, and in doing so I recognise that it was remiss of me to stand back and not show others that they too have permission to show up, step up and do things their way.

I share these with you because I do not want anyone to create a story for you, about who I am. It is important you see the whole of me. More so, it is important I share that I try to be conscious of my actions and work on them daily – yes, daily. I make mistakes, but that is how I learn, grow and become stronger. My mistakes are not with ill intent; it is in attempting to do things differently so as to bring about change that we shape a better tomorrow.

Over the years, I have begun to recognise my quest for that end goal and can clearly see it is not about me, but about the IMPACT I CAN MAKE for others, so they live a life they deserve.

One person at a time!

A little of my upbringing

I have come from a somewhat privileged life – it is subjective, I know. I am a first-generation Australian whose parents left a war-torn country for a better life. They faced challenges here and there, but always shared their love for Australia, where I was born and raised, as it provided them with safety and a place they called home. They instilled key values in me and taught me that people always come first. They showed me no matter what is happening in our lives, we can always lift others.

I have been blessed to have travelled the world and been to places most people have not seen. I have walked and experienced other people's paths, which is why I recognise my privilege. My lived experiences have made me who I am. From playing rugby and cricket in the lanes of an inner city suburb in Sydney, to being asked to go home and change my clothes very early in my career (because I was wearing trousers), to having a suicidal client on the phone as a young banker, living with the Maasai in Tanzania, trekking with gorillas in Uganda and sharing a night sky with a shooting star whilst staying in a monastery in Nepal. Along the way I have crossed paths with amazing humans whom I now call friends.

My path has taken many roads and none have been straightforward. There have been multiple defining moments, but one of the most recent was in March 2019.

On 31 March, I knew I needed to BE MORE, and that I needed TO DO MORE. My values were being challenged and my boundaries had been crossed. I was no longer aligned with the organisation I worked for. This was a telling sign for me.

Why? Because my values matter. They reflect who I am as a person and form the basis of my life, including the way I do business. Transparency is one of my key values, together with valuing people.

As I left keys behind and said my goodbyes, I knew I was walking forward to nothing. I had nothing in the pipeline, but I knew I could not stay, as I would not compromise my values. As I stepped away, I knew I had left everything in place for others to pick up and run successfully, because over the years I had prepared everyone around me by 'showing them how and explaining why'. I call it the 'make yourself redundant' process.

In business I have learnt that knowledge is only of value when shared, so I work on the premise that if I share what I know, others can step up and walk in my shoes, allowing me to focus on what I do best; innovate, create and develop. The endless journey of learning and asking 'what else?' is what I thrive on.

Creating strategies are my passion, but I also recognise they need to be a shared journey, one that includes everyone from the outset. It provides an opportunity for everyone's voice to be heard and this is how I operate.

Business is built on trust and trust needs to be earned. I believe we need to show people we value them, so they know they belong. Transparency is integral to everything I do. So, when you engage me, it's about showing you can trust me and we can step forward to work towards the things that you want to achieve with the right foundations.

As I stepped away from my role, I left everything documented, including my thoughts, because for me, success is for everyone.

I was sure my life-long career in finance, setting up and scaling business with a counselling degree could create impact on a larger scale, but how?

At the time I was dishevelled. I had lost clarity and focus, and most importantly for the first time since I was seventeen, I had nothing planned and nowhere to go. Through the grapevine people reached out and I began my journey of helping people navigate through their lives and their business. As my business tagline 'People Advisory and Business Transformation' suggests, I was engaged across a range of businesses locally and internationally from coaching and mentoring, to business advisory and in developing leaders to speaking and presenting.

Self-discovery became a process I indulged in, and whilst at times confronting, it also afforded me the opportunity to heal, and to discover my bigger calling.

It was through the giving process to others that I found my vibration rising; a value I had been shown throughout my life, so I drew on that more and more.

Today, in a world that is forever changing, I embrace the vulnerability, the pain, and the lessons I have learnt, and continue to learn, as I invest time and money in my own personal development through further education. I am not naive to think I know it all, and am confident in me as a person to share my weaknesses, as I know I can create greater impact by playing to my strengths.

Above all, I pay close attention to my inner voice and intuition, which has been my barometer on many occasions. The noise of the outside world can often cloud our judgement, and whilst it is often showing us choices, I make a conscious effort to only allow what is uplifting to enter my mind and for everything else to fall away.

Our fast-paced landscape is often driven by making quick decisions, so we don't miss out, or so we can move onto the next thing. But I have discovered this quick processing often prevents us from pausing and looking at the bigger picture, which would allow us to make more informed decisions, consider risk and develop second order thinking to deliver a better long-term sustainable outcome.

I am on a path to lift people across the GLOBE, one person at a time, one child at a time, one leader at a time. Developing people of today to shape a better tomorrow.

IMPACT is what we make it.

CHOICES are ours to own.

MISTAKES are opportunities to learn.

A PATH is created to take others on the journey with us.

I am Cathy Dimarchos, and www.solutions2you.com.au/raise-the-baseline is my project. Whilst I help people navigate through life and business, my commitment is to impart knowledge, skills and tools to support and instil passion and commitment in others to think beyond self.

When we focus on others and make their purpose our purpose, we create ripple effects because we show people how to do the same. My purpose is to support and develop change-makers in the Western world, so they can contribute to developing and lifting others in underdeveloped countries through the Raise the Baseline project.

'Showing' is my gift, not 'telling' or 'teaching' but doing it myself, one step, one voice at a time.

When we work as a collective to create a ripple effect, the circles that create the ripple in water as we cast a stone become more frequent and stronger.

The bond between us all will strengthen across the globe and our community becomes a wider reach.

So, as I ask the question once again, 'Can one person change the world?' I know you too believe the answer is YES!

My purpose was crystallised through the pandemic. I was engaged to speak at a national summit and I was on my last fight back from Perth on 13 March 2020. On 17 March my father had a fatal fall that would leave us devastated. By 20 March my mother was rushed to a different hospital to be treated by a cardiac team, and on 21 March, we sadly lost my father.

We had gone into full lockdown and it was amidst all of this that my road forward became clearer. I needed to do more. I needed to be more.

Mum was critical and at risk, so after twenty-four hours of her blood pressure sitting at 229, I made the decision to discharge her into my care. This meant leaving her home behind and starting a new life with me and my family.

Crisis brings about clarity and determination, and yes, it has its challenges, but what a privileged position I was in again. I was surrounded by a nurturing and understanding husband and children who would be there to support me in caring for my mother twenty-four hours a day. Mum was not well and it was months of recovery before she would be able to walk and talk to anyone, or begin her healing.

This period allowed me to think beyond myself and so I began to engage online and support young leaders in Tanzania. I found myself drawn back to what felt like my other home, a place I knew I could create impact. My commitment to doing more and being more was forming, but I still had not crystallised the bigger picture. With some grit and determination and trust in the young people I had worked with over the previous seven years in Tanzania, the global impact journey would be born.

So today, as you read my story, and that of these amazing humans in this book, you are contributing to a bigger picture. You are now part of the ripple effect that is becoming stronger with each chapter you read. My world, is your world, so as I begin to shape it in the way I know best, I encourage you to shape it in the way you know best.

Gratitude is another key value

Before I share a little more about me, I want to take the opportunity to show my gratitude a little more. I have often spoken about gratitude, and in particular for the amazing humans that have crossed my path across the world as they have shaped who I am today. Being in this book is no different.

I crossed paths with Peace and Katy twice, and it was only on the second occasion that I stopped to understand who they are and what their purpose is. It would be remiss of me if I did not genuinely acknowledge their commitment to women and their ability to bring about a sense of belonging in their network, as well as for women in general. It is only fitting that the title of this book reflects who they are and the impact they will make across the world.

Competitors are your greatest collaborators

I often talk about competitors actually being collaborators, and believe I would be of service if I share this belief with you now, especially if you are starting out in life or at crossroads and questioning where to start or where to go.

THERE IS ALWAYS ENOUGH – THERE IS MORE THAN ENOUGH!

No matter who you are or what you want to do, follow your passion and your dreams. The way you do things is what makes you shine. People buy from people.

That means no matter how many people are doing what you are doing, it's okay to do it too, if you believe it's what your purpose is. When you have clarity about what you want to provide for others, and you have a smile on your face thinking about it, you know you are on the right path. Life is a long journey and you want to get up every day knowing you love what you do because it makes a difference for someone else. The how is the easy part – I call them 'small measured steps'.

Knowing where you want to be in five years', ten years', or twenty years' time and what that looks like, as well as who is with you and what you have achieved, is what you need to invite someone in at the onset.

Your ability to be vulnerable, to ask for help and to accept it from others, will enable you to surround yourself with the right people, including competitors, because they too will see the value in collaboration.

Being able to identify your strengths and work to them enhances your productivity and also opens the opportunity for someone else to share in the journey with you. Remember everyone wants to belong so we can include them, by not just asking them to join us, but by also asking them to make decisions.

Collaborations can help you grow, scale and create a bigger impact when you align with competitors who compliment your offering, but each of you does something slightly different. Remember people buy from people, so if they like what you do and the way you do it they will buy from you. If not, why not refer them to your new colleague?

Trust is earned by showing people you value them and ensuring we listen, pause and understand so they feel valued. If we engage with people, including our competitors, as if they were members of our family, we would create alignment, loyalty and a shared path forward, bringing about increased productivity, creativity and innovation.

Our potential is what will enable us to create a bigger impact, so please don't hold back.

Have courage, be prepared to try and fail, but be sure to get back up and try it a little differently next time. It is in the trying and in asking for help that we succeed.

If you would like to contribute to Raise the Baseline as an impact contributor, or if you would to be the architect of your life and your business, or help to develop leaders who will shape a better tomorrow, I would love you to reach out and have a conversation. We create programs that work for you so that you live the life you deserve.

ABOUT CATHY

Cathy Dimarchos is an award-winning business advisor, mentor, coach and keynote speaker working internationally and locally. She is an indefatigable philanthropist who believes we can all contribute to lifting the baseline of people across the world, one person at a time.

Cathy is the founder of Solutions2you, born from her passion to serve and to leave a lasting imprint by creating paths that enable people to lead the lives they deserve. As a professional advisor and motivational voice, Cathy dedicates her time to perfecting a combination of people, business and situational skills, delivering tangible business toolkits and solutions to clients from every imaginable background.

Working across international borders and cultures highlighted the importance of seeing different perspectives and embracing her professional lives holistically. Her values took centrestage and business became honest and expressive. She believes knowledge exchange leads to effective and sustainable outcomes.

Backed by thirty-five years in finance, setting up and scaling businesses and counselling qualifications, Cathy says her calling enables her to support people to realise their unspoken ambitions, stepping outside the comfort zones that regularly hold them back. Through empathy and strategic positioning, she empowers people to establish healthy professional boundaries, think limitlessly and challenge norms, while rediscovering a curiosity for knowledge.

Cathy has said her initial trip to East Africa was one of her greatest challenges, but has also proven to be the most rewarding. Her time living with the Maasai, building water tanks, teaching English and working in orphanages and baby crisis centres, enabled her to crystalise her vision of 'paying it forward'. She has made several trips with family and friends since 2014, and is committed to a project she has developed, supporting young leaders and entrepreneurs so they can shape a better tomorrow.

Her advisory services extend to corporates, boards, teams, SMEs and individuals empowering them to become 'anti-fragile' in a world that is forever changing, stretching their boundaries and enabling them to create a psychologically safe environment with a social impact.

Cathy facilitates programs for change-makers, so they can become architects of their environment and discover how to lead and succeed as well as show others how.

Through lived experiences, Cathy shows people (not tells or teaches), how they can bring about the change they want to see for themselves. There is impact in the way she approaches the art of sharing knowledge, but before she begins that road map, she pauses to listen so she can understand your journey and where you want to be.

If you have ever wanted to dream big but held back, today is the day you will want to leap forward, as working with Cathy will inspire you to think limitlessly and identify who you will bring on the journey with you.

'When we rise, it is important to also lift those around us.'
– Cathy Dimarchos

Cathy is a number one bestselling co-author as well as authoring her book, *Same People, Different Vision – Developing Leaders of Today to Shape a Better Tomorrow.*

If you ever wanted to take a chance and do something for yourself, reach out and connect with Cathy. Don't hold yourself back. Turn a dream into your lived life.

Email: info@solutions2you.com.au
Website : www.solutions2you.com.au
FB: www.facebook.com/CathyDimarchosCoachSpeaker
Instagram: www.instagram.com/solutions2you_consulting
Linkedin: www.linkedin.com/company/solutions2you-pty-ltd

TASH TREVETON & NICOLE HALTON

WE ARE CHANGING THE WORLD FOR CHILDREN

June 2003: The children shrieked as they ran across the playground, 'snow breath' puffing out of their mouths as they laughed. They spent their days playing, discovering, wondering. And we did the same right there alongside them.

In recent years, we were prompted to consider our 'elevator pitch'. We had always struggled to succinctly define what it is we do, given the diverse and ever-changing nature of our work. And yet, when we stopped and really thought about it, each and every facet of our work was underpinned by one very simple and very powerful idea: we are changing the world for children. At first, the statement seemed a little boastful – after all, who were we to be 'changing the world'? But upon further reflection, it was clear that was exactly what we are doing and what we have been doing since the day we met back in 2003 in a chilly playground of an early education and care service.

Changing the world ... with play

We talk fondly about how we met and instantly connected. Despite being very different people – almost opposites in many ways – we bonded over a shared desire to provide children with opportunities to play, to grow, to develop and to be curious about the world around them. For several years we worked together with toddlers and preschoolers, building strong relationships with them and their families, being their advocates in times of need, and providing the materials and environment for them to flourish in their play and creativity. Those children from the early days are now adults – making us feel simultaneously old and proud.

Each day we would buzz with new ideas, or be inspired by the wonder of a child. We immersed ourselves in discovering and knowing all that we could about children's play, connecting deeply to theories and understandings that would go on to shape our future work. As our knowledge grew, so too did our passion for the work we were doing with children. We did things a little differently, and without even realising it, were forward-thinking in the way we thought about play and environments.

In this time – before the prominence and instant-share nature of social media – word of mouth spread, and soon we had other educators and local training organisations knocking on the door, wanting us to share what we were doing and why we were doing it. So, share we did. We did not claim to be experts and did not hesitate in giving credit to the thinkers and theorists who inspired our work. Our hope in sharing was simple – inspire others to do the best they could for children and children's play.

Changing the world ... with inspiration

This sharing of ideas soon morphed into an opportunity to make a little extra money – money we used to continue our professional development through conferences and other opportunities.

It was at one of these conferences that the sharing of ideas became a business idea, and in July 2007 in the beautiful city of Hobart, Tasmania, we looked at each other and knew it was our opportunity to really make a difference. Like the arrival of a long-awaited child, nine months later our business was officially born and we set about putting our dreams and plans into action. We knew we could continue to share our experiences with other educators, but we also knew we wanted to do more than that; we wanted to bring other ideas, new speakers and bigger opportunities to the amazing people in our profession. We wanted them to come to a workshop or conference and leave feeling inspired to make a difference in the lives of children and families. For several years, we plodded along – working hard while juggling our roles as early childhood educators, further study and the arrival of new babies of our own. And then, something amazing happened. We planned to have our very first conference, and through some incredible fortune – or perhaps begging – we secured one of our pedagogical idols, Claire Warden, as the keynote speaker. This was a dream come true. Not only were we providing an opportunity for educators in our home town to have a high-quality education and care conference on their doorstep, but we were also sitting down for coffee with an international expert who has since become a dear friend and mentor.

That first conference was something we were incredibly proud of, and paved the way for many more, with a range of Australian and International guest speakers who inspired educators to do the best work they could for the children in their care.

Changing the world ... with action

One Saturday in 2013, we presented a workshop at a conference for family day care educators. We regaled them with stories of tree climbing, bush walking with children, and getting out and about in nature. We shared our knowledge and our love for this work. And at the end of the workshop, there were questions – lots of questions. These passionate professionals, who worked out of their own homes providing care for up to seven children each day, were eager to engage in this nature-based practice with children, and yet their management organisations – known as services – were putting on the brakes. There were too many hoops to jump through, too many challenges and not enough support. When we urged them to speak up, to push back as advocates for children's play, they urged us to start our own service. So we did.

While it wasn't quite that simple, the idea marinated for a while and before we knew it, we were filling in application forms and developing policy manuals. Inspired Family Day Care was established in 2014 in New South Wales, and now, some seven years later, it operates in four states, with approximately seventy educators – each working from home, each supported to take children into nature and each inspired to make a difference in the lives of the children and families they provide care for.

In 2020, in the midst of a global pandemic, we took on a new challenge of setting up an out-of-school hours care program at an independent school. Inspired OSHC Linuwel opened its doors in January 2021 and ensures that before and after school programs aren't a place for homework or structured activities – but a place where play is valued and children are respected.

Changing the world ... with nature

Our work has always revolved around the natural world. We both feel a strong connection to natural spaces, spending much of our time outdoors and barefoot. In 2016 we became acutely aware of the work of Angela J Hanscom and promptly set about bringing the paediatric occupational therapist and founder of TimberNook to Australia for a speaking tour. As we listened to Angela, we knew we had to be a part of this movement, of making a difference for children through nature play. TimberNook Newcastle became the very first Australian site for the program in 2018, and to date, we have welcomed hundreds of children into the program for nature kindy, playgroup and school holiday programs.

We delight in giving children the time and space to build forts, climb trees, swing on ropes and explore their world while vital physical and sensorial development occurs, benefiting them throughout their life.

These children have the same back-to-basics outdoor childhood experience we had – an experience that seems to be rapidly disappearing in our technology-centred lives.

Changing the world ... for families

Two years into our business venture, something happened – we both found out we were pregnant. Our babies were born exactly seven months apart, and given that at that time it was just the two of us in our business, we were definitely challenged by that. On her son's due date, Tash spent hours planting over two hundred native grasses in an early childhood service playground, hoping to finish the project before the birth.

In the years following, Nicole went on to have two more babies. With each baby, our team had grown a little more, and there was better support in place to allow for time off. With each baby, we solidified a culture of flexibility and family first. Nicole delivered a training session with her infant snuggled against her chest, and when we flew to Melbourne to meet with our book publisher at the time, that same infant boarded her very first plane.

Our office has become a place where children are welcome at any time. There are often babies being rocked to sleep in the arms of their mamas – or one of the 'office mamas' – or playing on a rug testing out various resources that we stock. As our own children grow, they feel a sense of belonging and ownership within our business, and love to come in during the school holidays and help out where they can.

We recognise, though, that work doesn't need to only take place in the office, between the hours of nine and five. Much of our team work remotely, and work varied hours around the needs of their children and families. When they need a break they might duck out for a bike ride with their little one, or spend time in the backyard playing. Supporting families to do the work they love, and to care for the people they love, is something we deeply value.

Changing the world ... with our team

It takes a team to change the world, and our team has grown and evolved over the years in ways we could not have imagined in the early days. With each new team member, comes new knowledge and skills, new ways of working and new personalities. But we strongly believe we manifest the right people for our team. We attract incredible people – predominantly women – who are committed to our vision and goal of changing the world for children. A strong sense of fun, support and open-heartedness see our team connected in the most meaningful ways, despite being scattered across four states of Australia. This is not luck, though – it takes work. It is not high salaries and company cars that attract the right people.

It is an ongoing commitment to supporting their wellbeing, the flexibility of working conditions, the genuine 'how are you really?', the investment in their ongoing learning and development, and the time spent understanding who they really are.

When we commit to really knowing and valuing our team, our team commits to who we are and what we do. They become advocates for our work and feel supported to do that work in a meaningful way.

We are changing the world ... for children

Everything we do, every choice we make, is underpinned by the idea of changing the world for children. When we chose more sustainable packaging to send out the orders from our online store, it was done knowing that the earth will be a better place for future generations. When we create a resource to support educators to reflect on their relationships with children, it is done knowing those stronger connections benefit the overall wellbeing and development of children. When we wrote this chapter, of this very book, we did so knowing that if just one person reads it and it changes the way they work, interact or connect with children, then it will have achieved what we hoped it would.

In his work as a neuroscience educator, Nathan Wallis shares the importance of the first one thousand days of a child's life. These early days are vital for the developing brain and can be deeply impacted by meaningful connections with key adults in the child's life, such as parents and educators. While many still view early education and care as 'babysitting', overwhelming research shows that high-quality care, interactions and play in the early years are essential for the healthy development and wellbeing of a child. That is what keeps us going. That is what motivates us to create, to question, to advocate, to take action and to inspire others to do the same.

How you can change the world for children too

You do not need to be directly involved in the care and education of young children to make a difference in their world. Perhaps you are a parent, or perhaps you are an aunty or a business owner, or a student. It doesn't matter who you are or what you do, you can change the world for children.

You can change the world for children by speaking to them as though they matter – because they do.

You can change the world for children by spending time with them – children value our time more than any material possession.

You can change the world for children by taking care of the planet –there is a proverb that says, 'We do not inherit the earth from our ancestors, we borrow it from our children.'

You can change the world for children by taking care of the people who care for children – treat them well, support them to love and nurture children.

You can change the world by taking the time to understand how important the early years are – and by supporting others to understand it too. Be a loud voice for children.

You don't have to do big things to change the world. Change can happen in every small decision, consideration and the moment when we are thoughtful and intentional in how we approach them. So just do it. Change the world for children.

ABOUT TASH & NICOLE

We are Tash Treveton and Nicole Halton and we are changing the world for children. Yeah we know – sounds like a pretty bold statement, right? But, that is our goal. We want to wake up every morning and know what we are doing is making a difference.

In 2003, we met while working in an education and care service, and instantly connected. In the many years that have passed, we have worked together to build a company which allows us to work creatively to support educators and families. That creative work has taken the form of co-authoring several books, developing resources, establishing an online learning community, and delivering high-quality training and support to educators both in Australia and internationally. We also decided to put our money where our mouths were and not just talk the talk, but walk the walk, establishing our own Family Day Care Service and OSHC service, as well as be a provider of an internationally renowned nature play program – TimberNook Newcastle.

Behind that creative work, we are two mamas who love spending time at the beach (Tash), in the bush (Nic), and with our friends and family. We love a good laugh – often at our own expense – and are open to all kinds of 'woo-woo' practices like yoga, meditation, crystals, affirmations and manifestation.

www.inspiredec.com

ANN TOMLINSON

1. Set up

It was April 2003 when I arrived at Heathrow Airport in the United Kingdom, on a flight from South Africa.

At the tender age of twenty-three my heart was filled with hopes and dreams. Though slightly naive and with my head in the clouds, it was a feeling of euphoria.

That's until you get in front of a passport control officer, growling at you for taking too long to step forward.

There's nothing more terrifying for someone who's never left the security of their home country to be confronted by a cold, heartless, and in all fairness, necessarily evil passport control officer.

Passport please! What's your intention of being in the UK? How long are your staying for? Where are you staying?

Your mind races and you want to give some smart-arse answer, but you know better because you've watched enough *Come Fly With Me* episodes to know people get locked up for less.

It was in that terrifying moment I realised I had left everything and everyone I knew back home in South Africa. No lifeline, no turning back.

It was me, my one tiny suitcase and $750 in my pocket. It was time to put on my big girl panties and giddy the fudge up.

Anyone on a two-year working visa, living and working on minimal income in London will tell you it's hard. It's also lonely and you constantly question why you left home in the first place.

Every day was a struggle, but you get up and get on with life. You meet people who will challenge your morals, who will exploit you for everything you have; landlords locking you out because they can; sleeping rough in a London street, in the snow, because you barely have enough money to feed yourself.

Living in London was like a mixed bag of lollies; full of fruit loops, sugary goodness, nightclubs, lightshows and sticky carpets in pubs that smelled staler than a fermented wine cork.

The most difficult part for me in London was the weather. Coming from sunny South Africa with beautiful weather, with barbecues every other day, it was a hard pill to swallow to go to work in the dark, and come home in the dark. In winter, the wind cuts through your bones and the rain destroys every bit of happiness you have.

Well, that's for at least forty-five weeks of the year, the rest it's a balmy eighteen degrees, the sun is out, the gardens are in bloom, people are out and about laughing and suddenly your batteries are charged for another year of rinse and repeat!

I lived in London for the best part of a year before gradually moving north and starting my career in the rail industry. A career that would later span across multiple continents.

When I applied for my first role in Rail I responded to an ad in the local newspaper; it was the usual spiel about only apply if you have the necessary skills. Despite the fact I lacked about 85% of what they asked for, I applied anyway, and to my surprise I was invited for an interview.

The interview took place at a train station and I remember walking up to the two gentlemen about to interview me, and the looks of confusion on their faces were priceless.

This was before LinkedIn! There was no way of stalking someone on social media doing the necessary research before meeting. This was an old-fashioned meet and greet, with nowhere to turn other than grin and bear it if you didn't like who you met.

The interview lasted thirty minutes and it was clear the two were conflicted. One thought I was too young and the other interviewer saw potential. It wasn't the first time someone underestimated my capabilities and it wouldn't be the last either.

I spent nearly eight years in the UK before being head-hunted to move to Australia in 2011.

2. The incident

Moving to Australia was similar to arriving at Heathrow nearly a decade before, but this time I arrived with experience, and some might say, a chip on my shoulder. I was fortunate enough to be selected to work on multiple flagship major projects in multiple states across Australia.

As a young child I always dreamed of being an engineer and in a position to change the legacy of something.

Working on these projects gave me the opportunity for a positive contribution, connecting communities, giving them access to a reliable train network.

It was a big achievement on many levels, one being a young female working in a male-dominated work environment, but also as a foreigner. Never in my wildest dreams did I expect to have the opportunity to work in Australia when I left South Africa in 2003.

I was earning a good salary. I met great people and also met my husband. I was living the Australian dream.

Until I wasn't.

Two years after crushing it as hot shot in the industry, in one single moment my dreams of winning industry awards, reaching executive roles and leaving a lasting legacy, were crushed when I was physically assaulted at work.

It was a normal day with the usual pressures of preparing for a weekend shutdown. It's common for stress levels to be elevated if you have your back against the wall, dealing with deadlines, limited resources and a race against time to get everything in place to ensure a smooth and timely handover.

In layman's terms, a possession is a mini shutdown of the rail networks. It generally starts on a Friday night and we hand over early on Monday morning. It's a very short window of opportunity and preparation is key. If I miss a beat it has the potential to jeopardise six months of planning.

On the day of the assault, I made the difficult decision to suspend part of the works due to unsafe site conditions; gusting winds of 95km/hr had the potential of causing personal injury or worse. There was a high probability that someone could have died.

As the safety manager in charge, it wasn't an easy decision to make but one that was necessary. When you work in a compliance role, you get trained on the technical stuff but nobody could possibly have prepared me for what happened next.

A conversation to work out an alternative quickly turned into a heated debate and a headbutt in the face. It happened so quickly it was hard to make sense of it.

I was dazed, confused and scared. It was later discovered the person who assaulted me had a previous history of physical violence.

He was known to police and people were aware of his previous assault cases. I am still baffled as to how reference checks were carried out considering his previous history of violence at work.

In one moment, my dreams were shattered; my life altered in less than a heartbeat and it would take years to recover from one blow to the face.

Physical bruises heal but losing trust in yourself, questioning your ability to correctly assess a situation and for not seeing it coming is something that haunts you for a long time.

The following morning, I got out of bed feeling terrified, filled with dread and self-doubt. I guess my practical brain was still trying to catch up and process what had happened.

But I also knew that if I didn't go back and face the music everything I had worked for over the last decade would be judged by one incident. I would always be known as the safety lady who got headbutted at work.

It was hard walking in. It felt like everyone stared and talked behind my back. I felt so ashamed and humiliated.

It wasn't long before the boys' club banded together. This event divided teams and destroyed friendships.

There was one group saying it never happened, another group saying I deserved it and others making a half-arsed attempt to cover up evidence. Only a handful of people stood up and said something.

It was a classic example of the boys' club banding together and a female being victimised for being attacked. I felt so ashamed of what had happened, but I felt more ashamed of my inability to recognise the signs leading up to the attack.

I could have walked away when he started shouting and hurling abuse at me. Well, that's what people said. I wish I had walked away but the reality is it happened so quickly it was hard to predict.

In my twenty years of working in high-risk industries, never in my life had I ever heard of someone being physically assaulted. Who in the twenty-first century headbutts someone at work, right?

It wasn't long before the trauma kicked in and a few weeks later I was diagnosed with PTSD; a mental health illness that robbed me of every single shred of joy, pride and love I had before the incident. It nearly cost me my relationship with my husband and those around me.

3. Challenge

I didn't return to work for about three years as I started a family in that time. Still recovering from PTSD, I was diagnosed with postnatal depression within a few weeks of being new mum.

I refused to believe it though. It took about six months for me to accept how much my mental health had deteriorated. My mind wasn't my own. I was going through the daily motion of living and breathing but felt like an empty carcass. It was debilitating and I often wondered if I would make it out alive. As C.S Lewis said, 'Denial is the shock absorber for the soul, it protects us until we are equipped to cope with reality.'

My husband, medical team and the love for our daughter helped me get back on track.

You never really fully recover; you mend the broken pieces but the cracks are always there.

As part of the healing process I knew I needed something else. I needed a project. Most people go on a holiday, take up painting or go on a road trip.

I started a business.

I knew it was the only way to reconnect with my creativity, my identity and to honour the entrepreneur that was fighting to get out in the open.

It sounds crazy, I know, but despite all the challenges, it was one of the best decisions of my life.

4. Change

Living in a small town called Welkom, South Africa, in 1986 during apartheid had its challenges but they are my fondest memories of when my entrepreneurial journey started.

These days, some would consider door-knocking selling mangoes a crime, but for me it was a way of life.

My dad worked in the mines and my mum started a side hustle selling mangoes to make ends meet. Every Saturday we would get up early, pack our car full of mangoes and off we went.

These weren't ordinary mangoes from the local fruit shop though.

These sweet juicy, slightly soft, yellow and red mangoes were imported all the way from Durban, about 780km from where we lived. They were 'imported' interstate and therefore exotic! Probably the most exciting thing to happen to a lot of people in those days.

We lived in a mining community where all the houses looked the same; same front lawns, all the dogs were called Sheeba, and having three or more children was considered the norm. For the life of me, I still don't know why a Nissan Skyline 1986 was the car to have!

Nothing overly exciting happened there, until after 3pm.

My mum, clearly an entrepreneur at heart, ran a shebeen; an illegal operation selling alcohol from a residential house, and as Google says, it was 'slightly disreputable'. The shebeen was an exclusive event, for a select few by invitation only, and never more than eight people were allowed at any given time.

The whole operation was managed under the watchful eye of Miriam, a strong, kind and wise woman.

Miriam raised us as children. She cooked, she cleaned, loved us as her own and we loved her. I can still remember her wrinkles and how her face lit up when we took her to see the sea one year.

The thing with an illegal drinking establishment is that most of our exclusive visitors smoked. They believed in organically growing their own though, and soon the seeds of the finest Orange Free State marijuana would find its way into my veggie patch, located a few feet away from where our guests would sit.

Like my mum, I wanted to sell something of my own. I decided to grow spinach. Business was booming.

As a six-year-old, I made a ton of money. More money than I should have because people, including my teachers, became very curious. It always baffled me why my spinach was so popular.

It took a long time to realise that I was, in fact, selling marijuana plants and not spinach to our local community.

Funny thing is, most of the money I raised from my veggie patch, including my spinach, was donated to local charities because I believed in doing good in the world.

Fast forward to today, that entrepreneurial spirit is as strong as ever, coupled with a mission to bring innovation to an industry in desperate need of change.

Despite the assault, I still love working in the rail industry. I consider myself part of the family and will do whatever is within my power to leave a positive legacy for others to follow.

In one of his book, Viktor E. Frankl says that, as people, at our core we yearn to serve, to help, to contribute and to be part of the something bigger than ourselves. While I didn't know this as a young child, it was inherently part of my DNA.

Earlier this year we signed up to join the United Nations Global Goals and made a fundamental decision to use our Business for Good through B1G1.

Using your business for good is more than a pretty slogan. It takes commitment and constant evaluation of you as a person. You have to be in 100% alignment of the principle of paying it forward and using a systematic approach.

So why did I decide to go down this path? Because I consider myself lucky that despite my lack of experience, industry knowledge, being too young or completely underqualified for a role, someone gave me an opportunity.

Throughout my life there were people who backed me and believed in me even though I couldn't see my own worth at the time. They made a decision to look at me as a human on equal footing with no strings attached.

Because of someone else's compassion and giving, I have built a successful career and now a successful business designed to help others. I acknowledge there were adverse events that nearly crippled me, but I got up again and now it's my turn to pay it forward.

The way I see it, I am in a position to help others and it is my humanitarian duty to do so.

I think of it as being the taller person in the grocery store, getting something from the top shelf for someone who might be struggling to reach because they're not as tall as me.

'I believe business can and must be a force for good in the world, and that this is also good for business' – Richard Branson

5. Outcomes

When I started Alium Works I wanted our business to stand for something. I didn't want to be another company driven by high profit margins where people were treated as faceless numbers.

We introduced systems designed to provide actual human support, sometimes to our detriment. We soon fell into a trap of 'too much giving' and barely earning enough to cover our operating costs. The thing about giving too much is you think you're doing good but you are actually lowering your perceived value and we lost customers as a result.

While giving is an inherent part of my DNA, financial donation was more of a philosophical notion. For years I was reluctant to support charities because all too often I'd read the horror stories of fraud, high administration costs and misuse of funds. It seems you never truly know if the funds are allocated to the people you think you are supporting.

That was until I was introduced to B1G1 in late 2020. Ironically though, I was introduced to the program when we hit our all-time low. We were trying to make ends meet after losing 75% of our revenue due to COVID-19.

B1G1 started in 2007 with a simple but genius idea. What if a business can do good by doing what they do every day, whether it is selling a product, servicing a client or getting feedback through a survey?

By doing the due diligence and creating awareness of thousands of worthy projects around the world, B1G1 provides a gateway for others to support projects that resonate with their mission, vision and values.

If I said, *Let's sponsor a village in Ghana with fresh drinking water for a day, a week or a month,* you would be forgiven if you thought it would cost thousands of dollars.

When I heard about the program, I knew it was important to bring the team onboard. Not for me to lead it from the top down, but for the team to be part of the solution.

The team was in charge of choosing their projects. They chose several projects to align with each of our product lines, i.e. a student enrolment into our diploma course equals one year high school education for a student in need. Through supporting the projects the team could see quantifiable and tangible outcomes of the work they put in. As a direct result, we have a team that actively promotes giving; they push a bit harder to meet B1G1 targets and as a result business is great once again. When everyone believes and supports the same ecosystem there is no need for sticks and carrots. It becomes the driving force and the purpose for getting out of bed in the morning.

Since introducing the program in May 2021, and thanks to our students, corporate clients and sponsors, nearly fifty children are in full-time education, more than nine hundred days of fresh water has been provided to communities, and we have funded fifty-two days of young children now able to access early childhood education.

The way we see it, our work has only just begun and with the help of our team, we've set ambitious targets to provide 100,000 days of fresh water to schools and villages, as well as start the journey for one thousand early learners and secure full-time education for one thousand high school students in the next twelve months.

We are only a small cog in the wheel but we believe in doing better and using our business for good.

To Wynand Zaayman

There are no words to explain the gratitude and respect I have for you. Through troubled waters and international borders you always reminded me to hold myself to a higher standard. Rest softly knowing you ignited a burning desire for me to do more good in the word.

ABOUT ANN

As the founder and director of Alium Works, Ann Tomlinson works with jobseekers and employers in the rail and construction industries to deliver more productive, rewarding and safer workplaces. She has over twenty years experience working in the traditionally male-dominated rail industry including senior roles leading multimillion-dollar projects in Australia and internationally.

Ann has been recognised both personally and professionally for her commitment to innovation and creating pathways with an AusMumpreneur Women Will Change the World Award in 2020, a Digital Transformation Award in 2020 and a Diversity Award in 2019 for her career-building Pathway Program. Her focus is on providing opportunities and pathways for career growth to a broad range of jobseekers, while she uses ground-breaking technology to help leading employers to acquire, grow and retain the right talent.

www.aliumworks.com.au

VANESSA FIDUCIA

The starting point

My business journey probably began like a lot of mums in business.

I was affected by a situation and wanted to make a change and a difference in the world.

I'm going to take you through my journey, from where it all began.

I grew up in a beautiful family where my parents, and both sets of grandparents, worked around the clock owning businesses, working themselves into the ground. I thought this was how life worked. I knew no different.

At the young age of sixteen, I met my high school sweetheart, now my husband. We went through our teenage years as normal people do; fun, parties and studying.

At seventeen, I was diagnosed with lupus, an autoimmune disease.

It took me a while to get my head around that diagnosis and its implications. I was a little unsure what I wanted to do once I left school, with my high school years coming to end, but I had an interest in law and accounting.

A good family friend offered me a traineeship as a bookkeeper with her small bookkeeping and personal organising business. I took the opportunity and was excited to see where it could lead. I got to continue with my studies and earn an income at the same time, as MD and I decided to build our first house and get ahead.

At eighteen I found out I was pregnant with my first child. This was a whoopsie, fresh out of school and starting my new career. A short six weeks later, I miscarried. At my doctor's appointment I was told it would be unlikely for me to have a successful pregnancy due to my health issues. I will always remember how I felt that day – I was devastated.

This is where my journey started. I realised I desperately wanted to be a mother, but I also wanted a career. You can have your cake and eat it too, right?

The incident

I like to look on the bright side of life. I believe whenever there are storms there are rainbows. MD and I agreed we wanted to try and have children and we were not giving up!

Later that year we got engaged, and just a short six months later, we got married; a surprise wedding at our engagement party. While a big wedding would have been lovely, we wanted to save money as we had just signed contracts to build our first family home.

During this time, we saw multiple specialists in our attempt to have a child, and unfortunately in the process suffered through five miscarriages. This caused us both some serious mental and physical pain.

BUT …

… One day we received news of a breakthrough. They found what might be causing my miscarriages and how they may be able to stop them. Amazingly, I fell pregnant with our now eight-year-old son – our miracle boy.

This was the miracle we'd been hoping for, however, I had taken a significant amount of time off work during all my testing and miscarriages, and when I told my employer I was pregnant *again*, I was made redundant.

I was beside myself. Twelve weeks pregnant, medical bills piling up, being unwell due to pregnancy, and now unemployed.

From the age of thirteen I had been working in a fish and chip shop washing dishes and I had never in my life been left without work. I was totally deflated.

I needed to do something, and I needed to do it fast.

The challenge

I had many choices; apply for jobs, go through an agency, sit at home and wallow. None of these were truly what I wanted.

After speaking with my family who had all ran businesses for most of their lives, I started to consider running my own business. I knew I could do it, and I had MD's backing.

I still had doubts though, as I had seen everyone in my life with a business struggle working long hours while trying to manage their work-life balance and cashflow. I took a leap of faith, decided to register an ABN (Australian business number) and start contracting. I began by contacting friends who had businesses. I rang local accounting firms, and started to hustle.

I was worried too that no-one would want to hire me when they found out I was pregnant.

I finally got hold of one firm, 'TAH', and spoke with their director, EI. They were not hiring but she asked me in for an interview anyway.

When I got there, I told her my story and what I could do to help her and her clients. When she realised I was pregnant, she cleared some space and gave me a desk. I started work the very next day.

I worked right up until thirty-seven weeks of my pregnancy with the support of the 'TAH' team. While contracting there I was also able to build a small bookkeeping business, Mornington Peninsula Bookkeeping Services.

I contracted with 'TAH' over the next four years, and fell pregnant again, with our beautiful daughter, who is now six years old.

I also had multiple bookkeeping clients of my own, and worked at a couple of schools doing their accounts, while being mummy to both my babies.

I was working around the clock and never seeing the two kids I wanted so badly. I had seen this my whole life, right – you have to work hard to make a living.

One morning, I went to work on my usual Tuesday to do the accounts at the school, and it was the week of Mother's Day. My son was in kindergarten and I was invited to my very first Mother's Day breakfast. I was so excited as I had missed so many of his first moments while I was building my business. I was told though that I couldn't have time off as I was needed to prepare for the annual audit. The penny dropped. I missed the Mother's Day breakfast and MD could tell I was heartbroken. I couldn't do it anymore.

Earlier that year MD had back surgery, so I was the only income earner in the house. In my eyes, giving up that income was not an option, as we needed every dollar. But at what cost? Family is number one in my eyes, and this was not aligning with me internally.

During this time, I had a meeting with EI at 'TAH' and was informed the business had been sold. I was shocked. I really hadn't seen it coming.

However, a few months on the sale of the business fell through.

I saw an opportunity that would help us both out of a pickle. I could leave the schools and build a business that truly reflected who I am and what I believe a business should be and EI could recoup some of the losses she incurred from the lost sale of her business.

Yes, again I had a brainwave moment. It was the entrepreneur coming out in me.

I went to her with my idea.

'I'll give up my other jobs at the schools and we can combine our two small businesses to create one.'

We were both ALL-IN …

The very next day I handed in my resignation letter to the schools and our merger began.

We hired a business coach to hit the ground running. Just a week later we went to an accounting tech seminar to discover the latest upcoming technology in our industry. Our minds were totally blown.

The change

It was a few months into our new business venture that I got very sick. I ended up in the ICU for a couple of weeks and EI attended our business coaches' live intensive workshop on her own.

When I got out of hospital and back to the office (which at this point was at the front of my house) she told me about something that really stood out to her that I must investigate.

The Profit First methodology!

From there we rebranded and we knew our purpose! Profit first accounting.

We needed to teach, live and breathe this methodology with all our clients.

The penny dropped.

We were working around the clock and paying ourselves $250 a week! This $250 a week to not see my family didn't seem like much of a lifestyle choice at that point.

We needed to work smarter not harder.

We set out to become a certified Profit First accounting business; which we did. From there we looked at our pricing and our packages. Once we got the model right, we began onboarding clients.

We let go of the old: SALES – EXPENSES = PROFIT

We started paying ourselves what we were worth.

We began making profit on each sale, *cash profit.*

We had no tax debt.

We ran our business on a leaner model.

We started to grow quickly.

We began living and breathing Profit First and its flipped formula of: SALES – PROFIT = EXPENSES

How were all businesses not doing this already, or more to the point, still surviving without it?

I had found my calling: to get this methodology taught and implemented to as many businesses as I could reach.

It wasn't long before we outgrew my little home office and needed a bigger space. We sublet an office and hired our first employee.

As with most people in business, the first time for anything new is a learning experience. This first hire was a major learning experience, one in which we learned our mission, vision and values.

Our values being P = passion, F = flexibility and A = accountability

These values were so important, and I wanted them ingrained in our business culture and team.

Growth didn't stop there. It was more than just profits; it was mindset and personal growth.

With the onboarding of more team members, we quickly outgrew the sublet office and had to upsize again into a space of our own. This was an exciting moment; our very own place to call home.

During such a growth phase both personally and professionally, and after identifying our values, EI and I came to realise we were on different paths and were no longer aligned in our vision for PFA (Profit First accounting).This was impacting the business and our relationship.

We decided to part ways. EI went back to her previous business 'TAH' and I continued with PFA and the vision that was in place.

While this was a big decision, it was best for us both and best for the business. It's important to recognise that with growth comes hard decisions.

Since then, we have worked internally to focus on the culture of our business and what we stand for.

We have a team of eight, some who are mums and dads, and this was important to me because of my personal journey.

We have implemented a four-day work week with every Friday off. We call this Family/Flexible Friday.

I have an open-door policy and find it so important for the team to feel they can come to me whenever they need to and that we feel like a family.

I never had this in a workplace and it's what I wanted to create.

The outcome

Through my journey as a woman and a mum in business, I have learnt much about what I thought a business should and shouldn't look like, and every day is a learning process.

These are some of my biggest lessons so far:

1. Never give up

Even when the odds are stacked up against you and you feel the weight of the world on your shoulders, never give up. After a storm there is always a rainbow. If I had given up every time I thought things were getting hard or I was told something I didn't want to hear, I wouldn't have two amazing healthy children. I also wouldn't have the business I have now which is helping other businesses grow and make cash profit they never imagined before.

2. Create a business that works for you, not you working for it

There is no point running yourself into the ground and working around the clock if it's not why you got into business in the first place.

Work smarter not harder. Just because this is how we have seen it done for years, doesn't mean this is the only way and it is never too late to go against the gain and change it up to do what you believe in. Someone might look at what you're doing and what you are implementing and be inspired to do the same. Before you know it, the world is changing for the better.

3. Implement a cashflow system that works for you, PROFIT FIRST

If you have a business or you are starting a business, this is one of the most important parts. Your finances are the backbone for your decision-making. Having clarity around your numbers will push you in the right direction and steer your business forward. You can make decisions without looking in the rear-view mirror. I'm proud to be certified to teach this methodology and implement it for our clients, as it's a total game-changer for all businesses around the world.

4. Mission, vision and values

Without having a clear mission, vision and values in place, what type of culture are you creating? Is your business a true reflection of what you want it to be? Is it somewhere your team wants to be or a place your clients want to engage? Once we established our values everything was much clearer, and they continue to help with all our decision-making. 'Is this choice aligned with our business mission, vision and values?' 'Will this goal push us closer, without steering us away from the bigger picture?'

5. Be a leader not a boss

Let your team take ownership of their role. Let them have a voice. Lead them and show the way rather then be the 'boss'. Through doing this you gain more respect and the culture you create will shift. You will have long-lasting and loyal employees.

Business is such an exciting journey so don't let someone else's experiences or the what-ifs stop you.

Create your own story.

ABOUT VANESSA

I started my business journey because, like most of us, I wanted to create a balance between work and spending quality time with my family; a business that was financially stable and worked for me.

When I first started my business journey in 2013, at the age of twenty-one, I mostly focused on bookkeeping services. I soon realised there was a gap in the market and that many businesses, myself included, had cashflow issues. I wanted to help businesses overcome this significant issue holding them back.

In 2018 I became certified in the Profit First methodology which helps businesses manage their cashflow, pay themselves (the business owner) first and teach them how to manage their expenses while making a profit, instead of leaving it to chance or hoping it happens by the end of the year.

It hasn't happened overnight but there has been a lot of personal growth along the way.

My qualifications include Certificate IV in Financial Services, BAS Agent Registration, Tax Agent Registration, IPA Fellow, ICB Member in

Practice, Profit First Certification, Xero Partner, Fix This Next Fixologist and Pure Bookkeeping Licensee.

Looking back over the years, I find myself pausing to appreciate all I have achieved. As the CEO/director of Profit First Accounting, I now have a work-life balance. I am able to be there for my kids special moments and help with homework after school. It has taken a great deal of leadership and trust in my team, but we can now all work a four-day work week and enjoy our Fridays off, having a three-day weekend every week. This is something we are super proud of. It provides everyone in our workplace with a work-life balance.

Some of my recent achievements include being nominated for a number of business awards. In 2021 I have been nominated for ROAR Awards, AusMumpreneur awards and Telstra Business Awards.

In 2020 I came runner-up in the AusMumpreneur award for Service Business and Business Excellence.

In 2020, I was extremely honoured to co-author the book *Back Yourself.*

While every day in business is a learning journey, I feel we are always growing and evolving. I am creating a business I am proud of and one that works, not only for me and my family, but for my team.

I can now call my dream a reality. I want you to know that no matter what, you too can build a business that works for you, whatever that looks like. Your dream can be your reality.

www.profitfirstaccounting.com.au

PETINA TIEMAN

Using your past to generate your future!

Now let me ask you a question … do you want to start a business (or have you already) because you:

- Want to work for yourself?
- Want to work your own hours?
- Want to earn a lot of money to afford nice things?
- Felt it was necessary because of not fitting in or being bullied?
- Just thought you could because you have been working in the same role?
- Have a driving urge to do what you love without anybody putting restrictions on you?

Most of you will have answered to a few of the above, but out of the hundreds of people I mentor every year, 80% of them are women, the last option is rarely their answer.

Have you been, or are you becoming, an introvert, a recluse, withdrawing from the world because you have 'stuff' going on in your home environment that is bringing you down? Or have you stuff in your past that is regularly triggered in your mind?

People come to me for 'business mentoring' but in most instances they have 'personal stuff' they haven't dealt with properly, so they allow it to keep holding them back from achieving success. Often we don't want to share this 'stuff' going on in our mind with our friends and family for fear of being judged, or fear they will react negatively and make us feel worse! Instead, we tend to internalise our thoughts and without realising it, it brings us down further.

Many women believe they are putting up a strong facade – seemingly happy, positive, fun, 'normal' to those that know them, thinking they are a 'tower of strength' to their family and friends. However, most of those connections are likely to be thinking, *Something is off with my friend and I'm not sure how to help her.*

Does this sound familiar?

Have you seen the changes across social media in the past twelve months of COVID-19? There are so many depressing posts, people posting affirmations and aphorisms, silently reaching out across a public forum that they are in a rut and in need of help. They don't know who to turn to, and can't afford, or don't feel they need, counselling or psychs.

My unique method, combining my skills in spiritual healing, counselling, life coaching, training and business mentoring results in women rediscovering their true selves, usually a new and improved version. I enable them to move forward in leaps and bounds, not afraid to reach for the stars and manifest their goals and dreams.

What drove me to become who I am today ...

I was raised by the school of hard knocks and abandonment ... it all started when my father died in a car accident aged twenty-one; my mother was just four months pregnant with me. My mother is a hard woman with a heart of stone due to her life of suffering from abusive relationships. My sufferings being treated as a sex object, or a physical and verbal punching bag, as if it were 'normal', subsequently impacted my life, and that of my younger sister.

My childhood was one of adversity, abuse (both physical and sexual by stepfathers, stepbrother and bosses), and constant transition moving from state to state, school to school. With the break-up of every marriage my mother had, my sister and I were told, 'You're going to meet your new daddy so you have to forget about everyone else,' – 'everyone else' being our previous stepfather, extended family and school friends. This created a life of fearing emotional attachment and not allowing people to get close to me because I would soon have to move away and cut ties. Mum is on her fifth marriage now to a gorgeous-hearted man. It's a shame he didn't come into our lives before my thirties!

So the school of hard knocks and my emotionally detached mother taught me to be the best at everything I applied myself to, and out of everything I've been through in my life, that is the one lesson I thank my mother for. Without her hard ways, I would not have had the resilience or strength to be able to face the obstacles, challenges, fear and adversity to become the person I am today.

I am the queen of manifestation. I have studied, worked close with and adopted the learnings of some of the true masters of the world – Deepak Chopra, Anthony Robbins, Allan Pease and Rhonda Byrne, from which I have achieved many successes and rewards!

Who is Petina Tieman now?

I live my life every day through my passion; my mantra of 'lives changed, people empowered!' I get to do what I want, how I want, with who I want, as long as I stay true to myself, my values, my integrity and my professionalism. More than 45% of my work (in excess of $150,000 annually) is provided pro bono to disadvantaged people in poverty, of poor mental health or our First Nation's people in remote communities … and there's nobody to tell me I can't!

Every year, in addition to the pro bono work I provide, I donate over $10,000 in cash, vouchers or prizes to local charities, not-for-profit groups or to the homeless and people in poverty … because I can!

Further, every year, much to my husband's dismay, I provide opportunity to people through employment, even when they don't have skills that align to the roles we need to fill.

You see, I suffer from 'rescue sydrome' … I *have* to help others, because nobody was there to help me! I know what it's like to suffer in shame, suffer in silence, and feel you have no choice but to do horrible things far beneath you just to survive! Don't get me wrong, I still have many challenges I face every day, but I face them head-on, deal with them, allowing my mind space and emotions to move forward!

Femeconomy refer to me as an Indigenous serial entrepreneur … which is true! I currently own and operate seven businesses and am soon to launch another two – some of them are dormant or inactive, while others are powering along despite the impacts of COVID-19. I am hands-on operationally with all of them.

Throughout my career, and especially over the past three years, I have been recognised with numerous local, state and national awards, media articles and accolades. I hold fourteen qualifications and currently hold fifteen contracts across all three tiers of government to provide services.

My career past and present has included projects that won international acclaim, government board appointments, advocacy work, leadership round tables with government and key stakeholders, founding and or serving on many NGO boards and networking groups, and being a keynote on many occasions across audiences of thousands.

I am currently married to my biggest and best challenge, which is also the hardest choice I've ever made, as he suffers chronic depression, PTSD, narcissism and is a Gemini … what a mixed basket, hey? But through it all, he loves and accepts me for all of my past, present and future. My husband is not just my business partner, and partner in life, but my soulmate … my uniquely different, happy ever after!

My proudest achievement in life is my one beautiful daughter (now twenty-six), who has given me three grandchildren already. She has been my rock, keeping me grounded and surrounded by the best kind of love everyone is meant to experience in life. I raised her as a single mum, as my past just wouldn't allow me to have a man in my life whilst raising her. I feared my daughter would end up being exposed to the disgusting things I suffered in my life.

Raising my daughter as a single mum had numerous challenges, mostly around money, as her father detached from any involvement, including financial. Back then, Centrelink didn't pay the costs of living in Sydney.

Throughout my career, I have had to endure depression, financial ruin, loss of loved ones, four miscarriages, major spinal surgery, an autoimmune disease of the thyroid and gaining 30kg. The biggest challenge throughout has been fighting my way to the top of male-dominated industries, and being the subject of the consequences of success … I'm often the brunt of gossip and tall poppy syndrome, being considered a threat by competitors even when I try to collaborate with them!

When did the entrepreneurial talent kick in …

Take a step back to 1995 when I was pregnant with my daughter and we were living in Coffs Harbour, New South Wales. Although I was married to her father, all our finances were separate so I had to figure out how I could work and stay at home to raise my child. I taught myself 'desktop publishing' with word and publisher. Remember, back in the nineties these programs were not as advanced as they are today.

I rang a Xerox centre to get pricing for printing, and the owner offered me a job. The offer was too low, so he accepted a counter offer. I paid him $100 per week to use all of his design software and equipment, and his database of clients. I would simply earn the money selling my design services to his clients. What a joke!

Within the first few weeks, I had lost all of his clients as my skills weren't good enough to be called 'entry-level' graphic design. I had no alternate employment option and a child to raise who had extreme health problems, so I taught myself how to use the commercial graphic design programs.

In just six months, I had not only regained all of his previous clients and others, but I had outgrown the Xerox centre, brought in another staff member, and equipped and established a new graphic design house on the main street in Coffs Harbour. This was opened by the mayor, because it was the first and only graphic design house between Newcastle and Brisbane. Aged twenty-five, this was my first real career accomplishment. The next was at the same age; I co-founded my first women's networking group in Coffs Harbour, called WISEAM!

One of my biggest career successes was that I single-handedly conceptualised, developed and launched the legacy of the 2000 Sydney Olympic Games which won international acclaim.

I realised I could do anything I wanted to, if only I applied myself. I become a sponge for knowledge, learning anything and everything, and set my goals and intentions for what it is *I truly want* ... not what others think I should do. But it takes hard work, self-reflection, regular goal setting, constant openness to learning, reaching out for help and asking others!

My diverse career .... I am known as the rainmaker! Building business, empowering people!

One of the first jobs I ever applied for in Cairns, when I first relocated back here early 2015, was as a manager for an Indigenous Corporation. I will never forget the day the CEO rang to advise that, although I was the best out of the two candidates interviewed, he was NOT going to give me the job because I am a RAINMAKER! When I asked him what that meant, he said to 'look it up', learn and do something with it! He didn't want to cap or restrict me in an employment role.

A rainmaker is someone who builds something out of nothing! Yep, that's me!

Every single business I have owned has been started without savings, no access to finance, no investors … just pure determination! I have boot strapped every step of the way, and I'm proud of it because then I know it's because I have worked for it. I earn whatever rewards I generate, and if it fails (oh, and trust me there have been some huge failures) I can own those too and learn from them!

Many people walk into my current 800sqm state-of-the art business hub in Cairns and assume it's been funded. They are shocked when we share we started operating with no internal walls and no electricity. I was running workshops with coloured crepe ribbon taped to the carpet floor and long extension leads from the neighbouring premises to put a fan on for airflow.

Over the next twelve months, we would work hard, earn some money, buy another desk, work harder, earn some more money, buy another computer, and build a wall. Little by little, piece by piece, we completed the premises to be what it is today!

Every client I work with, I mentor on how to build their business out of nothing, without dependency on funding or investors … and it is possible with every single business across any industry if you just have an open mind or reach out and ask for help from those who might know!

Over thirty-five years of my career I have usually worked two jobs at a time, and never been satisfied working for someone else. My childhood and adolescent past has instilled a drive and ambition to always work hard, learn to be the best, and when you're the best, you can still achieve more, either by learning new things or moving onto new challenges.

My employment roles have never lasted long as I am too motivated, too driven and want more! More important is the realisation that I hate being told to conform. I hate feeling trapped and restricted. When I work for someone else, they not only tell me what to do, but they restrict me from being the best I can be. Either they are not ready for the growth of their business, don't have the resources to manage the influx of new business, or they just don't want to pay me for growing their business.

I would rather work for myself, but that's REALLY HARD WORK! If you don't earn money, it's because you haven't worked hard enough or smart enough or haven't planned enough!

During the past thirty-five years, I have founded, owned and operated numerous businesses across several industries. Although some businesses seem mainstream, none of them were! Every business I own and/or operate, I change to have more genuine purpose … every business has an outcome to genuinely help people. I am not someone who thinks about getting financially rich! I live a comfortable life, I still want more, but I have bills to pay, COVID-19 impacts to struggle through, and to be honest, I prefer to help the needy and the disadvantaged because that makes me feel great! It also helps me to heal from my past.

Someone called me humble the other day as I withdrew from two awards I was nominated for because past clients were also nominated in the same category. I want to enable them a stronger chance to shine! You see, for me, I have already been recognised with more than twenty state and national awards across community, training, business, leadership and Indigenous affairs.

My turning point …

I will never forget the turning point in my life! I was thirty-six years old and in the midst of building the legacy of the Sydney Olympic Games, but my life as a single mum was struggling due to the work hours, the logistics in the big city, the high living costs and day care. It just didn't fit in with the single mum requirements or budget.

So at a total loss, I rang a psychic 1300 number from the newspaper and got someone in America. The woman told me I would be standing at the front of classrooms training people and regularly speaking onstage to hundreds, if not thousands, of people. I laughed so hard I cried! What was this woman on about? I'm a nobody who's been raised in a traumatic upbringing … who would listen to anything I had to say? How could I have anything worthy of sharing and get paid for it?

However, I rang this psychic for a reason … I wanted guidance and direction and she just gave it to me! Totally left of field, yes, but I had nobody else offering me advice, and I just paid her, so shouldn't I take notice of what she said?

First, I had to deal with my 'stuff' … so I began the very long journey of spiritual healing. I studied, I attended courses and workshops, I participated in some 'weird' stuff like crystal healing, reiki, past life regression and I loved it that much, I became a spiritual healer, reiki master, qualified coach and counsellor myself! This further led me to the world of mentoring and training.

Now it's your turn …

Now I'm not suggesting you go and ring a psychic 1300 number, however …

Turning back to the questions I asked you at the start about why you wanted to, or have already, started a business … what is your answer?

Many women come to me and don't know what they want to do or fear they wouldn't be good enough to make a sustainable livelihood from it.

Never let your past hold you back. Instead find a POSITIVE out of every experience you endure in life and use that to drive your wants, dreams, goals and future to whatever you want it to be.

If, like me, you were told you were not good enough, laughed at and ridiculed, hold onto that and use it to fuel your drive to prove others wrong!

Reach out and ask for help from those who can be impartial, neutral and objective! Those who have been there and done that!

And lastly, write this as a Post-it note on your computer or bathroom mirror … *I will NOT be a SNIOP!* (SNIOP stands for … subject to the negative influence of other people!

I'm hoping through this chapter some content may resonate with what you're experiencing, and you will find hope and strength in knowing that anything is possible if you just hold yourself accountable to take the actions required to achieve it!

ABOUT PETINA

Petina Tieman, managing director of Complete Business Solutions (QLD), founder and director of iiHub (soon to be rebranded as Cairns Business Hub) and five other businesses has been recognised with multiple state and national awards and accolades for the outcomes achieved for clients. Petina is a serial entrepreneur who is dedicated to helping startups, micros, SMEs and Indigenous businesses to thrive.

Mentoring business owners nationally for twenty-five years, she deeply understands the business ecosystem, and what drives business success without dependency on investment or funding. She lives her life through her passion, using a holistic approach to help disadvantaged business owners, in particular remote community Aboriginal and Torres Strait Islanders become independent businesses.

The fundamental values across all her businesses are: to build skills, capability and capacity in others through education, empowerment, collaboration and connectivity!

www.completebs.com.au

YEMI PENN

So why and how am I a woman changing the world?

Firstly, it's important for me to explain why I define myself as a woman, and that has become important being that we now have different pronouns. I definitely came into a world where there wasn't a choice. You were either a man or a woman, and that theory was basic biology.

Biology gave the impression you were either one or the other. However, as a woman of science and engineering, I now see evidence that says you can be neither, although I don't know the details. It's important I make it clear that I do identify as a woman, however, I do not identify or subscribe to the limitations that have been placed on women since the beginning of recorded time, and I'm probably in a stage of my life whereby I'm thinking, *What the fuck? How is it that women chose to accept the role of being the 'amazing helper' who has always been behind a successful man?*

Defining myself further, I am not a woman and then black; I am a black woman. The limitations the world has placed on me are of a greater magnitude than many other races, but this isn't a competition. I say in my TED Talk that my trauma really is no bigger than others, but I'm also aware that some people's plights run deeper, over years of cultural oppression.

I have a burning desire that sometimes keeps me up at night, to try to undo the work that has been done for centuries; work that gives the impression that women, people of colour and other marginalised groups are not worthy to be on the same plane as others.

I have to admit, I was hesitant when asked to contribute to this book because throughout history, whenever there's been a women's movement, it's been predominantly white women. Though it's good t

o see we are now taking a different route; we are challenging the narrative and empowering women to step up, highlighting the inequalities that still prevail. Even Hollywood is better representing people of my skin tone, but we have a lot of catching up to do.

So, I guess that answers my WHY – why I am dedicated to working with women and people of colour.

I'm not quite forty yet, but I think forty is the stage of life where you start to ask, 'Am I really living on purpose?' In the past decade, it's become apparent to me how unjust the world is.

It's also become apparent that using your mind, changing your perspective and how you think, and having the audacity to dream big and take action can really change the course of your life. But I also acknowledge that even with all those fearless steps, you can still face significant gender and race barriers. And that's why I am dedicated to working with women and people of colour because I believe within my bones and my being that I simply can't have the audacity to sit back and look pretty and just enjoy life on a singular plane. What I mean by that is we have been taught the idea of separation to a ridiculous degree. We've been taught to focus on ourselves, our job, our partner's job and our kids – and that is it. But what about humanity? What about caring for others?

If I had decided to focus purely on myself, I would probably have about ten properties right now, and would definitely be driving the latest car. I'd be travelling business and first class every time. But my being is not comfortable with that.

I'm not trying to make anybody else feel guilty for whatever life they are living, but I can't live like that. I had my first loss in 2018 when my father passed away, and I realised then just how short, fragile and potentially insignificant our life can be. Because if you haven't lived a life on purpose, there's every possibility you leave your body in this realm, this plane, this life and literally be forgotten.

Now I'm not suggesting we all need to be the Oprahs or Nelson Mandelas of the world, but I'd like my life to be what my dad had. People came to me after he died and told me how he had paid for their education. That's why I'm a doctor today. I really want to leave a big footprint, similar to the dinosaurs. Now that might be a little bit to do with ego, but more than ego, I want the words of the Nelson Mandelas, the Rosa Parks, the Malcolm Xs, the Martin Luther Kings of the world, and the people still with us today, Oprah Winfrey and Tererai Trent to continue to be heard into the future. Like Beyonce's lyrics, these amazing people are encouraging us all to remember who we really are.

I want to do that because I believe I'm in a race called life. I believe it is an Olympic relay, with billions of people, which is why it's so fucking exhausting doing the race. I don't think I could live with myself if I just decided to say, 'You know what, I'm out,' and the person who was meant to pass me the baton finds nothing but a 'gap' and they've got to start again because I'm not there.

My WHY is to continue the race; to get to a place of equilibrium, a place of balance. Sometimes I get in my feelings and worry I'm not going to be around to see the fruits of my labour and my love, but that's okay because if it's not my children, I will have impacted somebody else's life. So my WHY is because I have immense love for the human race and immense love for our environment. I have immense love for life on this plane and I'm so interested in what other lives there are.

I want to put my best foot forward. In all the different businesses and life experiences I've been through, the one thing I feel I know is this: to unlock some of the pain and suffering we experience in the world, we must face our trauma head-on. Now, I'm not suggesting it's the epitome of what life is. This isn't about trauma porn. This is about talking about a taboo subject, but in a safe container that allows us to look at it. Here's an analogy to best describe it – let's say you've been in a nasty car crash and you have a gaping wound in your thigh. When the paramedics come, they say, 'Don't look at it, we're just going to cover it up and it will heal.'

And I think society has done that with trauma – just cover it up and don't look at it. The world has been built to just churn, churn, churn, and make, make, make but really it's reduced our productivity. I believe it's time we start to learn when we have 'enough'. Why do we have so much more than we need? There are many people who live to excess, but don't give back to those who need it. When I see that I think, *What are you going to do with all that money?* but people do find a way to spend it. I really do believe in contributing to society, and there are many ways to do that, but I would never suggest we trade in our mental and physical health for this excess productivity.

So going back to the wound and the cover-up – I'm saying we need to look at it. There's a way we can look at our trauma wounds, heal them and actually come back more productive. Not by being a workhorse, not by being a slave, but by being efficient. We can operate from a place of love, by using energy as currency, as opposed to money. I truly believe that unhealed trauma is a big part of the world's suffering. And scarily, it's prominent in our world leaders and our governments. These leaders are having UN conversations, putting rules and mandatory laws into our homes where we are raising our children to become the next generation.

Now I'm still very young in my work, especially around the documentary area, but I want to get to a point where we can tell the story of the perpetrator, the person who inflicts pain on someone else, therefore causing trauma, and thereby giving everyone an invitation to look at their own trauma.

So, how am I changing the world? I wanted to say 'by being fearless', but I am a bit scared. There is definitely fear ahead, but I'm learning to take it for a dance. I'm changing the world by feeling the fear and doing it anyway. I'm changing the world by using my voice to tell my story. I'm changing the world by eliminating the shame that has been attached to my story. I'm changing the world by creating numerous platforms; for people to be heard, for people to listen and for people to speak. I'm changing the world by talking about trauma in safe containers so people can operate better in their life, without feeling like their wounds have been opened up without the opportunity of them being sutured back together. I'm changing the world by being a voice of compassion, a voice of courage, a voice of change.

I'm making a change in the world by triggering a global revolution.

ABOUT YEMI

Yemi Penn is a fearless businesswoman and thought leader on creating your own memo, meaning *she* gets to write the script of her life and encourages others to do the same.

She is a serial entrepreneur with a common thread of transformation across her businesses, whether it be transforming Sydney's rail network as an engineer, transforming physical health in her F45 gym or shifting the perspective of our minds as she supports people in creating a life that they not only want but deserve.

More recently, Yemi has added documentary producer to her repertoire as she shifts her core life's purpose to raising the vibration of acknowledging and healing our individual and therefore collective trauma.

Simply put? She engineers powerful people.

www.yemipenn.com

RACHELLE HARVEY

Kindness always wins

I have always been inspired by Dolly Parton; a true philanthropist in every sense, with a love for humankind and making an impact on children's lives globally. I realised early on I wanted to do the same. However, I was held back by crippling self-doubt, and unlike Dolly, I didn't have a lot of money, so how was I going to make anyone's life better? I simply had no idea!

But I have been able to achieve my dream, despite my doubts, with my journey a true example that kindness is all that is needed to make a real difference. My journey began in my final years of high school. I knew I wanted to graduate and do something meaningful to help others, but I wasn't sure how to get there. I chose subjects to ensure I would graduate with my HSC, nothing more. I didn't leave school knowing what my passion was, but I had faith my calling would come to me throughout my journey and would present as an opportunity at some point.

After a few jobs in cafes and promotions, I thought I had figured out my dream career: a massage therapist aboard a cruise ship. I could travel, make people feel good through the modality of massage, and make money to somehow make a difference in the world. After a year of study, I commenced work as a massage and spa therapist onboard the Royal Caribbean Cruise Line, sailing between Miami and the Caribbean.

However, it turned out that massage therapy and cruise ship life wasn't my dream after all, and I couldn't have hated it more! Massaging for fourteen hours a day, selling overpriced spa products to guests who weren't interested and living in a shoebox for nine months at a time was certainly not the glamorous career I envisioned. I felt like a failure as I walked off the cruise ship in Miami, questioning my self-worth. When would I find my true calling and be able to help people in the way my heart ached so badly to do?

Arriving back in Australia I took a job at an RSL, working on the front desk. I loved all the elderly people who came in each day, sharing their stories with me, and I made lifelong friendships. I had pretty much decided it was the job for me, without any further thoughts of a career moving forward.

It wasn't until I met Josephine, an amazing, successful businesswoman, that I truly experienced the sheer power of kindness. Jo would bring her dad to the club, and we would talk. I learned she ran a business school for women and did amazing things in the community. Jo would ask about my life's dreams and goals and very quickly she could sense I had given up on myself. She reminded me I was worthy of a career I loved and it was important to not forget my heart's desires and goals just because of a few failed jobs. Jo kindly became my mentor, with her advice invaluable.

She gave me workbooks and activities to spark ideas on what I could do to enhance my life through entrepreneurship. I slowly began to believe, that maybe, I could start my own business. If it wasn't for Jo's kindness, I believe I would not have taken the leap to start my own business; I just didn't have the self-worth or confidence in myself to do so. It was then I realised you only need one person in your life to truly believe in you. Jo didn't know me, yet took the time to mentor me, seeing the potential

I did not see in myself. A truly wonderful, kind, inspiring woman; an earth angel!

It took me some time to figure out what kind of business I could start. I thought about what I was passionate about at the time, and only one thing came to mind; eBay. How could I start a business around eBay? It had been a joke amongst my friends for many years that I was the eBay queen, always buying and reselling with great results. People were always asking me if I could help them sell on eBay. Then I began getting approached by small business owners who were starting out and wanting to know how to sell correctly on ebay to be successful. They needed someone to assist them and I felt that eBay consulting would be a good fit for me. Maybe my true calling was mentoring people? So, I went for it and started my own business as an eBay consultant. I wasn't sure if it would be my end goal, but I enjoyed (and still VERY much enjoy) coaching people to run successful eBay businesses. I was good at what I did and for the first time in my life, I had a strong sense of worth.

eBay consulting filled my years, and my business grew from strength to strength, solely through word of mouth. I was able to build my business with three virtual assistants working full-time, and clients spanning Australia, the UK and the US. I was proud of building this tech-based, niched, one-on-one consulting business from the ground up. However, even though I was making a difference in people's lives, mentoring them to use the eBay platform successfully, it wasn't fulfilling my desire to make a true difference to people or the planet. Many times, I had clients who were not able to pay for my services, but desperately needed another stream of income coming in. Also, not-for-profit charities needed assistance, so I would mentor them for free. It felt amazing to be able to give back, but it wasn't quite enough. I needed more. My soul needed more.

When my first son Koa was born my focus shifted. I had this adorable little boy who I wanted to dress up and show off to the world. I wanted to dress him in funky cool clothes, not baby blue outfits with ducks;

something I would wear but mini, like leather jackets and acid-wash tees. But no matter how hard I looked I couldn't find anything in stores or online. Seeing the gap in the market, and without any fashion or design experience, I launched my own children's label.

Having my successful eBay consulting business, I now knew the work involved in starting a new business and had the confidence and self-belief to dive in, headfirst. I chose Koa's name because it had a strong meaning; a brave and fearless warrior. It seemed fitting that I named the label after him: Brave & Fearless – for the Rad Little Lad. I found a local seamstress and with a roll of fabric from the thrift store, I made my first lot of samples. I popped them up on Instagram and another boy mama snatched them up instantly. It was an amazing feeling, inspiring me to keep creating.

I started with a free website for creatives on Big Cartel, and combined with Instagram, I was selling pieces daily. The feeling was incredible, and I wanted more! I had a newborn, the label and was still consulting, so sleep was minimal. I just swapped the tea for coffee and powered on!

The label really gained some traction when I was accepted to sell at the local Gold Coast boutique fashion market; The Village Markets. Stockists would find us there and want to stock the label in their boutiques, and journalists would contact me after visiting the markets and write articles about the label. We even had a front-page spread in a local magazine which was a real highlight! I loved these markets, as I would meet the most amazing, stylish mamas and papas who would buy every piece I created and tell all their friends about the label too. Seeing tiny humans dressed in my threads was so fun and rewarding!

I soon realised if I wanted to grow, I was going to have to take some of my manufacturing offshore. So, when Koa was one, we took a trip to Bali. It was here I formed a wonderful business relationship with a supplier who understood my vision and helped me create my first acid wash shirt, the Rad Little Lad Tee. After releasing it on the site it sold out within minutes, with many wholesale inquiries. It is and always will be our flagship piece in our store. I was amazed to see such success considering my lack of fashion industry and design experience. I was learning so many things: lookbooks, children's sizing, line sheets, grading patterns, international manufacturing policies, customs, duties, taxes, etc.

There were many challenges, but lots of highs as well. The label went from strength to strength, with over one hundred stockists in five countries including Donavan Frankenreiter's store: The Barn 808 in Hawaii. I started branching out and designing other things like cushions and jewellery and even produced an organic hair wax in collaboration with a local sustainable bee farmer in Queensland. Our wax became one of our bestsellers.

When Koa was two, we decided as a family, to move to Bali. Our life was incredibly hectic, and we needed some quality time together. Being able to stay on top of manufacturing by living in Bali was a huge bonus. I found a beautiful staff member, Gab, who kept everything running in Australia. A mama herself, Gab was a complete all-rounder and did everything from posting orders to running markets.

She had also studied fashion design so brought a wealth of industry knowledge. The label wouldn't still be around if it wasn't for Gab's strong work ethic and true love for my label, and I will always be grateful for her kindness and contribution. Another earth angel came into my life.

I began thinking of ways to make Brave & Fearless a purpose-led business. I realised this could be my chance to make a real change in people's lives and I had the perfect platform to do it. I built our Instagram following up to 24,000 followers, with a solid database following too. In Bali, I was witnessing firsthand the devastating effects of plastic on the planet. The wet season meant beaches were covered in plastic toothbrushes, straws and various other single-use plastics. Inspired, I created our zero waste range to help encourage plastic-free parenting. I launched a range of bamboo cutlery, straws and coconut bowls, sourcing sustainable products made in fairtrade working conditions, providing jobs for local Balinese people. The concept was well supported, and it was amazing to make a difference to the local economy and the planet. But I still didn't feel I was doing enough!

It was Koa who provided my next inspiration after telling me at Christmas he wanted to provide happiness to local children through gifts.

Balinese don't traditionally celebrate Christmas due to Hindu and Muslim faiths, nevertheless, children always love gifts! So, we created our 'kindness bags' working with an amazing and reputable Yayasan (Balinese charity) called Solemen. The charity, led by founder Robert and co-worker Sarah were helping over two thousand disadvantaged and 'diffabled' (their endearing term) people on the island. They like to refer to them as Sole Buddies, distributing medicine, mental health assistance and food packages to people all over Bali, including into the villages where help is very limited. Sarah and Robert are the true definition of earth angels.

Through the generous donations from our Brave & Fearless followers via social media, we were able to make fifty kindness bags filled with Indonesian lollies, books, pencils and toys. Koa proudly packaged each one himself and was also able to hand out the gifts to each of the children. As a mama, it was one of the proudest and most special moments I've had as a parent. Having a heart-led business and being able to teach my son the power of kindness filled my cup immensely. I realised I was finally able to use a platform I had created to spread kindness to others, with the smile of each Sole Buddy (child) reaffirming this was my life's true purpose. Solemen kindly awarded Koa with a Sole Buddy Kindness award, which he cherishes dearly.

Our kindness didn't end there, and with the assistance of our loyal followers, we continued to help Solemen. We raised money for Luh; a little girl who sat in a box all day in desperate need of a wheelchair. With donations from our followers, we were able to make this purchase. We also raised money for baby Kadek, helping fund vital heart surgery in Jakarta.

Koa enjoyed the second year of kindness bags, and by using our social media highlighting our work, we received another influx of generous donations. Koa and I rode around on our scooter collecting the goodies to make the bags, with businesses like the local toyshop also providing generous discounts, knowing the products were for charity.

Koa's school also became involved, with students helping to make the kindness bags, which was truly a dream come true. We were able to distribute five hundred bags – ten times the amount from the previous year! Koa took along school friends to help distribute the bags and to see them all engaging and smiling together with the local children was beyond beautiful.

The third year of kindness bags was our absolute best yet. With lots of donations, we were able to distribute to not only our favourite Yayasan Solemen Charity but also to other charities in Bali; Bali Mother & Baby House, YKPA Tabanan Panti Asuhan Orphanage, YKPA Bali Orphanage Street Kids Project, and Metta Mama & Maggha Foundation, through the Bali Family Foundation, a school in Pesinggahan and two villages. By the time the donations stopped, we were able to distribute 1,800 kindness bags!!

We also had an increase in community participation in the project, with people all over Bali volunteering to help make and distribute the bags. It was so amazing to see how far kindness had been spread throughout Bali that year. Through donations from our Brave & Fearless customers and an idea from my own earth angel son Koa, I had finally created a purpose-led business.

Due to COVID-19 and the risks associated with the pandemic, we were unable to distribute the kindness bags in 2020, but we hope to continue bringing smiles to Balinese children this year, at a time when they need it most.

Bali has changed the person I once was, and my heart and home will always be there. Considering this, I decided I needed to continue giving to Indonesia while based back in Australia temporarily, so I partnered with B1G1, a phenomenal platform assisting businesses in giving.

B1G1 is automated through our website, with each customer purchase supporting a cause such as planting a tree in Borneo for an orangutan, providing two days of education to students in Nusa Penida, and helping build classrooms in Bali from plastic waste. These impacts, however small, can collectively make a big difference in the world. So, while we can't physically be in Indonesia on the ground, we can still be giving.

I am by no means Dolly Parton, but like Dolly, I am helping to spread and teach kindness, which can make a huge difference in people's lives. My message to others is to believe in yourself. You don't need to be highly successful or have the wealth of a celebrity to make a true difference in the world. No act of kindness, no matter how small, is ever wasted. Earth angels are everywhere and bring humility and kindness to the world, you never know when you will meet one and they will change your life.

As Brave & Fearless continues to thrive I will continue to use my platform to spread kindness across the world. I'm currently working on an exciting project that helps children alleviate anxiety, empowers them to talk about their feelings and promotes positive mental health. Stay tuned for the launch of the Brave & Fear.Less Superfriends, it is our next big passion project.

ABOUT RACHELLE

As the owner of two incredibly different businesses, which are special to me and I love both for varying reasons, they do keep me very busy. My first business and love is my eBay consultancy business where I work directly with small businesses, helping to establish their business on the eBay platform and mentor them through the startup phase and beyond for ultimate business success. After the birth of my first son, Koa, a creative side within me emerged and I was driven towards the unfamiliar. This spark led me, without any prior fashion design experience, to launch my second business, a children's clothing label named Brave & Fearless. Edgy on-trend clothing for the Rad Little Lad & Hip Little Chick being featured in *Vogue, Elle* and *Mama Magazine* and showcased on the catwalk at fashion week, the label has gone from strength to strength.

www.braveandfearless.com

SALLY ANDREW

Introduction – lift the 'barre'

The safest option is not the one for me. Wherever I'm going and no matter what I'm doing, I am listening for the call to find the higher path; the tiny whisper that can't be heard over the din of the TV or the sound of fighting kids. I really need to lean in and listen. It is ever so faint, but it's there … the call to lift the 'barre' on the way I am doing life.

It would be so easy for me to want to sit down in my comfy chair, pull out my phone, scroll through my feed, and while away the minutes, days and years just making do. But I do not want to just survive these years. I want to look back and know my actions made a difference, that my life was lived on purpose, and I licked the bowl clean.

In every area of my life, I want to live my biggest, boldest and most authentic existence. With my marriage and family life, I am not content to be a wife and mother by name only, I want to bring my A game to my loved ones – day in and day out. I want to truly laugh while swimming in the pool; I want to play Monopoly to win; I want to wrestle with my kids in the mornings until they fall off the bed laughing; I want the people in my life to know they are absolutely loved.

When I'm working, I am driven with intensity, excellence and grit. My business has grown exponentially and is thriving in our community. The work I have in my hands, I will do with integrity, strength and wholeheartedness. As a businesswoman, I have won innumerable awards, but this is not my resting place. It is simply a springboard. I can do better, achieve more, reach higher and unearth the unique position that is mine in the marketplace. I will never 'make it' to my destination but will veraciously pursue the call to excellence in the business world.

I want to give you a glimpse into the core pillars I believe help me to get a leg-up in the world. These simple ideas have helped me build an exciting, full and rewarding life for myself and my people. Although these principles are not new or unique to me, when pulled altogether into one existence, they have the ability to make a profound impact on your life.

What is on your private beach?

We can use whatever it is we have in our hands to change our world. If we take our unique gifts, our passions and experiences (good and bad) and apply them with diligence and expertise, our world can become more expansive. Each of us is uniquely endowed with capacities, tendencies and preferences that make up an exceptional and matchless avatar. And each of us has walked through peculiar situations, developed relationships and created distinctive narratives that tell the story of who we are, what we can do and where we are going. If we combine our particular avatar and weave our evocative narrative around it, we will have everything we need for our next big adventure.

From my earliest childhood, the extracurricular activities I pursued, the experiences I lived and my family of origin have helped to shape me with distinct characteristics. These random and seemingly haphazard jumble of puzzle pieces are precisely the fragments needed to create my full and robust life. Down to the tiniest flaw or most insignificant moment, nothing has been wasted on the journey to fashion a passionate and significant life.

Looking around you, what can you see that is sincerely yours? Scour the beach for the driftwood of life, search for the parts of you that have washed up on the shore, discover the things that have gone missing for a time and start to piece them together. If we pile up an impressive totem of talents, passions, experiences, failures and connections, we are left with something as unique as our fingerprint. When combined skilfully and artistically this wealth of resources can create an impressive masterpiece from the ordinary and mundane.

Excellence is achievable!

In Australia, where average is celebrated and the tall poppy decimated, I think it's time we start to believe that excellence is achievable. There is a huge difference between a glamorous Instagram influencer and a 'real' person of excellence. Sometimes it's hard to spot the dissimilarities at a glance, but the person of excellence is progressing and developing in and out of the public eye. Their strength of character is not for effect and applause but motivated by a deep sense of valuing quality. Hunger is often seen as a negative quality. However, an appetite to live a life of true distinction should be something we crave.

For me, in my home, relationships, business enterprises, finances, study and all areas of my life I have some control over, I am relentless with my pursuit of excellence. I am not content to be a victim of circumstance, I am constantly hustling for improvement. With clarity of thought, and the ability to see the big picture, I am plotting, planning and developing a strategy for growth and improvement.

This precept can be translated into any situation you discover yourself facing. No matter what your vocation, socioeconomic state or family condition, there is always something for you to nurture, change or perfect. In a world where all our desires can be instantly satiated, it is okay to feel the unfulfilled hunger for a life of excellence. Remember, this moment is not binding; change is more than possible and the future is your own creation.

The power of five minutes

We have no ability to change the past or recover the time. The irreplaceable but fleeting moments we have are only given the value we assign to them. If we are constantly wasting, whiling, killing and marking time, the worth of that instance is gone without it assuming any significance. The sheer volume of uncultivated time in most people's diaries is confounding. While there is obviously a case for squandering time on and with the ones you love, the value given to those relationships would qualify the waste no longer waste, but treasure instead.

I am so passionate about the power of five minutes because I am a wife, a mother of three busy children, a business owner who routinely works forty to sixty hours per week, a student studying part-time, a budding author, a volunteer at a local organisation, a slack gardener and an aquarium enthusiast. I love making my moments count. I value family dinnertime enormously. We make the most of these moments to sit down together, device-free, and connect with each other every single day. Although I admit to spending too much time on my phone, as a rule, I am ringing every drop of value from my day. Even those in-between moments are used gratefully – driving in the car, doing my hair and make-up, getting ready for work – in these moments, I am listening to podcasts or mentoring webinars.

I want to challenge the notion that we are all 'too busy'; this is such a cliché. What are you too busy for? If something is not getting done, make a plan to change that issue; don't let it sit unresolved in the 'too busy' basket. Everyone has enough time for the things they value in their life. If it is important enough to you, you will find a way!

Kindness instead of Karen

Everyone is jesting about the latest phenomenon of becoming a Karen. Women who display rudeness, bullying and public displays of aggression are now labelled a 'Karen'. I do admit feeling sadness for all the delightful Karens in the world, however, it is a spotlight on the issue that these behaviours have increasingly crept out from behind online trolling, and are now openly spotted in everyday activities.

I love the Ikea experiment #SayNoToBullying Bully A Plant, as it tangibly shows the power of words. In my life, kindness is one of my core pillars of behaviour. I will treat people with kindness and respect no matter what. But why is it that because I value kindness others seem to assume I have been suddenly transported into a world of perfection? This lofty notion is admirable but unrealistic. But the more we practice the art of kindness the more proficient we will become.

Lifelong learning

There are infinite mysteries hidden in the world of nature, art, people and business, and the opportunities for learning and advancement are limitless. The quest to search out the answers is a posture to be held for life. And the thirst for discovery will be rewarded with wisdom and direction.

Since I purchased my business, I have been studying nonstop. Although I have not tackled difficult subjects like nuclear physics or aeronautics, the study I have done has grown my ability and opportunities. I have been fortunate to position myself to learn from incredible mentors. I won a package from our local chamber of commerce and received mentoring for a year from a local multimillionaire business entrepreneur. This brilliant man expanded my mindset and fortified my desire to make it a practice to absorb wisdom from others. I then went on to seek out further mentoring opportunities and have been equipped by some of Australia's most revered business minds. To this day, I make it my practice to listen well, position myself below incredible people, and soak up all intelligence that flows my way.

No matter your education level, there are always possibilities for discovery and opportunity. If you stay hungry for knowledge and possess a quality of humility and teachability, you are ready to absorb the sagacity you require.

Wield the white-knuckles

The world is a scary place filled with difficult decisions, daunting situations and intimidating opportunities. The possibility of making incorrect moves, embarrassing ourselves and failing, can cause paralysing fear. To add to the struggle, our mental health and peer pressure can exacerbate those feelings of alarm. In these moments, we subconsciously or consciously decide to shrink or grow our world. Through self-talk and grit (or lack thereof), we resolve to either retreat or face our fear!

Imagine the make-believe world of Mr Awkward. At first, he discovers he is afraid of big crowds and large malls. He rationalises that he will not do anything to make him feel upset or uncomfortable. He shrinks his world to accommodate his fear and begins to live in a downsized version of his town. Further down the track, the fear grows to small crowds and local shops. He changes his habits to exclude those things and limit anything that would press those buttons. Unfortunately, Mr Awkward's fear keeps growing because whatever we feed grows! Soon the fear hits anytime he leaves the yard. He decides to limit any and every event that would cause him to feel afraid and make him leave the yard. His world shrinks again. Finally, his fear begins to set in when he is opening the front door. With each setback, Mr Awkward is making concessions and reducing the size of his world. Each time he gives in to the fear, his world shrinks. So what happens if we turn Mr Awkward around? At the very outset of his journey with fear, what if he decides not to be pushed around by his feelings? What if he decides to face his fear of the mall and the people despite how he feels? What if he goes to the mall afraid? Mr Awkward's life is now bigger and brighter for having faced his fears. He is now ready to face the next challenge and go to an amusement park and get amongst large crowds and colourful people. Each test Mr Awkward faces is leading him to a wide-open world or a closed-in house. He has the power to choose the scary option with unknown outcomes but unlimited possibilities, or the closed-in house with less fear, clear outcomes and extremely limited adventure.

I understand this is a silly and childlike analogy, however, I know many people who have shrunk their world due to feeling fearful, awkward or lazy. Each decision we make is leading us upwards to a wide-open adventure-filled world or downwards into a closed-in safe house. Most people don't have the insight to articulate why they are taking the easy or safe option. I don't think they even consciously choose. But if we could wrap thought and language around our inability to take even tiny risks, we could free ourselves from the fear and apprehension around these risks. So many people have brilliant ideas, great intentions and incredible intellect but lack the fortitude to just leave the house.

So much of my adult life, I have white-knuckled and done it afraid. Every challenge, opportunity and adventure I have been on has caused me to hesitate and assess whether I really want to step into the next undertaking. But each time I do, my world grows ever so slightly. On the back of each win, my confidence, excitement and perseverance grow. This upwards progression produces a spiral of advancement that motivates and inspires even more. The upward momentum doesn't need to be big. Tiny wins produce the same euphoric feeling that big ones do. And each time your world grows, so do the opportunities.

Conclusion

It's exciting that we can all be instruments of change in our world. If we can find the strength, valour and grit, we can turn our life and the lives of those around us, upside down. It is easy to rationalise that we have not been given the same opportunities to grow, expand and succeed as others, but I challenge you to stop making excuses and playing the victim. Wherever you are sitting, there is an opportunity to change something in your existence – even if it is only an attitude. Can you hear the gentle whisper? Can you hear the call to the higher road? Although this isn't the easiest road, the view is unbelievable as we journey along the windy path, and we lift the 'barre' of mediocrity in our lives!

ABOUT SALLY

My name is Sally Andrew and I am a wife, mother and business owner in regional Queensland. From a very young age, I studied dance seriously and devotedly. During these times I had some incredible teachers including Beth Baudistel, Harold Collins, Jacqueline Pascoe and Shane Weatherby to mention just a few. These incredible artists inspired my journey as a dancer and as a teacher.

As a teenager I accidentally fell into the teaching of dance by mistake and discovered a supplementary passion. After completing my schooling, I combined part-time dance and part-time work and continued to pursue the arts. I travelled to Melbourne from our regional area to complete my Vaganova teacher training at the Australian Conservatoire of Ballet. After some time flipping between working in public health, the private sector, helping with my husband's business and having a family, I returned to my first love of ballet and renewed my teaching. From there it was quick progression from being an employee to purchasing a dance studio and rebranding as Radiance Academy Toowoomba.

Since 2015 when I acquired the business, I have grown the client base 731%. The original studio has now grown to three award-winning businesses wrapped neatly into one. These include multiple dance studios, a retail outlet and vocational training centre, all of which would rival the big city locations. We host classes for toddlers, school children, elite dancers, trainee teachers, adults, seniors, and our Dance for Parkinson's community class. With approximately one hundred classes per week and a clientele from eighteen months to eighty-one years, there really is a class to suit everyone.

Using my love of dance, my business experience and my hindsight as a mummy consumer, I run the dance studio from a different angle than most. With a heavy emphasis on inclusivity, kindness and excellence, our business is attempting to stand out from the rest for all the right reasons. My dance destination has been recognised locally, nationally and internationally for our contribution to the arts and I am excited to continue to grow and develop the business.

To ensure that my teaching is of the highest calibre, I embarked upon a journey to gain additional credentials. I have continued to grow professionally and now have three more nationally recognised qualifications in dance and teaching, accreditation to teach four different dance syllabuses and certification in another niche dance style. I have also taken a serious approach to mentoring and have sought incredible corporate coaches throughout my years in business.

During the last six years I have been busy juggling the plates of family life, multiple businesses, study, friendship and other additional responsibilities that all adults face. I have, however, discovered the power of five minutes. This concept has unlocked for me the beauty of using every second to its fullest advantage. With my incredible husband I have discovered that when we both bring our A game, the cogs of family life all turn much more smoothly.

I have faced many obstacles as a business owner over the years and have confronted all of these with courage and resolve. In fact, a lot of the challenges we have faced have turned out to be our greatest opportunities. With Richard Branson's words always on my mind, I have said yes to so many opportunities that have been outside of my comfort zone and I have grown into in time. The staff I have hired are incredible and talented individuals who are thriving in their professional endeavours. With their unbelievable ability and my business model, Radiance Academy has ripened into an established and mature enterprise.

www.radianceacademytoowoomba.com

Giving Back

Proceeds from the sale of this book go to providing women with scholarships to enable them to receive support, mentoring and education through The Women's Business School.

We believe that investing in women is the most powerful way to change the world and these scholarships provide opportunities for deserving women to receive the support they need to succeed.

Ingram Content Group UK Ltd.
Milton Keynes UK
UKHW012230080323
418239UK00004B/307

9 780645 16698